The Burden of Guilt

S.S. troops at Nuremberg Rally

The Burden of Guilt

A SHORT HISTORY OF GERMANY, 1914-1945

Hannah Vogt

translated by Herbert Strauss
with an Introduction by Gordon A. Craig

NEW YORK OXFORD UNIVERSITY PRESS

Printed in the United States of America

Preface

An eighteen-year-old boy, studying for his high school diploma in a German night school, heard recordings of Hitler's and Goebbels's speeches in his history class. With the impression of these speeches still fresh in his mind, he wrote to an older acquaintance: "I cannot understand it. If somebody had told me earlier that my father's generation tortured human beings to death merely because they were Jews, I would have slapped his face. I almost cried tonight because I am a German. . . . We needn't wonder that foreigners often don't want to have anything to do with us. . . . How can it be that there are still people today who approve of the crimes of that period?"

This letter, though written by a young man shaken by his first encounter with Germany's most recent past, answers our questions succinctly. Nobody can seriously claim that today's youth should be held responsible for the events of German history and politics from 1914 to 1945. But what happened then concerns the younger generation today, if merely because they have inherited a divided fatherland, and must understand the unchecked power politics which caused this division. The past also concerns young German people because no nation on earth can live isolated and on its own. We cannot be indifferent to what others think about us as a people, and it does no good to close our eyes to the disagreeable facts of this past. This will not erase the horror from the memory of other nations. Above all else, today's German youth must concern itself with the past in order to avoid repeating the crimes of what now lies definitely behind us. From this, three conclusions are to be drawn.

We need more, and more reliable, information about this recent past. What a young person learns accidentally here or there is often full of contradictions. He sees films about General Rommel, about Admiral Canaris, about the assassination attempt of July 20, 1944, or about Hitler's life. He reads memoirs in which people who were themselves involved, describe their own small or large participation in the events of the Third *Reich,* and not infrequently try to justify themselves or their activities. Newspapers and weeklies give reports on trials of former concentration camp guards, physicians, or *Kommandants,* which are still being conducted, even at this late date, because some of them have until now managed to evade the hands of justice. On the other hand, there are also people who lived through the Hitler period at a responsible age, and say things like: "We earned good money then. Under Hitler even the common laborer could take pleasure trips to Madeira with the help of the National Socialist Strength through Joy organization. Hitler had finally put things in order, and put an end to those thirty odd parties of the Weimar Republic. And he did away with unemployment too. We never heard of the extermination camp at Auschwitz until the war was over. But it's obvious today that Hitler sized up Bolshevism right from the very beginning! And if it hadn't been for treason and sabotage, we Germans would certainly have won the war too!"

Well, what was it really like? How can we understand how millions of Germans could cheer a man capable of ordering the cold-blooded murder of millions of innocent Jews? How can we understand how he found enough people to execute his orders? Was there only *one* guilty person, namely, Hitler himself? Or, must we assume that the German nation is more prone to brutality and cruelty than other nations? Or was it in the last analysis those other nations who were guilty of the errors and the misfortunes of the German people because they failed to understand us, as was illustrated, for example, in the immoderate demands made in the Versailles Treaty?

The answers to these questions can only be found through a more thorough study of recent history. And while this is being done let nobody be deceived by people who try to evade their own responsibility with arguments like the following: "Why not let the grass finally grow over the past! Why do we keep soiling ourselves by talking continually about those persecutions of Jews, concentration camps, mass gassings, and other atrocities? And is it not unwise to beat our breasts before the whole world? The other nations and their leaders are guilty of a few misdeeds too!"

To sit in judgment on the history of one's own nation is neither dishonorable nor injurious to national dignity. We cannot avoid the responsibility for examining ourselves by pointing out that other people have reason to do likewise. The responsibility for dropping the first atomic bomb on Hiroshima has been discussed critically before the American public often enough and nobody criticized the disastrous English invasion of Suez more strongly than the leader of Her Majesty's Opposition, Hugh Gaitskell. It is good that democratic states do scrutinize their own policies.

Aside from this, self-examination and a repudiation of false political principles are the only means we have of winning new trust among those peoples who were forced to suffer fearful things under Hitler's brutal policy of force. Our technical and economic efficiency will win us no friends as long as other peoples fear that this efficiency may once again be abused by a criminal. Only if we draw the right conclusions from the mistakes of the past and apply them to our thought and action can we win new trust.

When one builds a new house, he should not put it on shaky foundations. He must know which parts of the old house he will be able to use, and which he will have to discard because they are rotten or worm-eaten. Then, too, the discussion of the past ultimately serves the future, which must not be determined by those who excuse or approve crimes committed in the name of Germany.

Anyone who makes an effort to understand recent political history will learn that in politics not every means is just, that law and the dignity of man are not empty phrases, that force merely produces counter-force, and that he who sows the wind will reap the whirlwind. As early as 1923, Albert Schweitzer made this statement, which applies even more directly to the world today:

> Our world cannot make a really new start unless we first become new men, even under the old conditions, and, as a morally re-dedicated society, overcome conflicts between nations in such a manner that culture can rise again. Anything else is more or less lost labor for then the seed does not fall on spiritual, but merely on material soil.

Contents

IV The Second World War

Introduction

No question, probably, is raised more frequently in American discussions of German affairs than that of the attitudes of contemporary Germans toward their own past. Is it not true, speakers are likely to be asked, that Germany's recovery from the ravages of the war was too speedy for its own good and that the very success of the "economic miracle" prevented the German people from subjecting themselves to the kind of sober self-examination they sorely needed? Is it not true that, in their preoccupation with material things, they have succeeded in shutting the Nazi period out of their minds so completely that they no longer recognize any responsibility for the dreadful things that were done in their name between 1933 and 1945? And does not this convenient amnesia represent the gravest danger to any hope of establishing a viable democracy in Germany in our own time?

It is difficult to answer these questions to the satisfaction of those who pose them, for a very simple reason. Germans vary in attitude and opinion just as much as Americans do. It is true that there are many people in the *Bundesrepublik* today—probably more than is good for the political health of the country—who have never reflected seriously on the fateful course taken by their nation after 1933, or who have succeeded in persuading themselves that it was unavoidable; there are countless others who, for various reasons, resist any discussion of things that happened in Hitler's time and would be happy if the whole Nazi period could be swept under a rug and forgotten. But the number of these people is certainly matched and probably exceeded by those who, despite the comfortable distractions of economic prosperity, go on struggling with the problems of German history, seeking to understand how their people could have tolerated the crimes committed before 1945 by their political leaders, and insisting that only the most circumstantial revelation of the brutal facts of the past will make such understanding possible.

It is no exaggeration to say that one can hardly attend a church service or enter a theater lobby or go into a bookstore, or even buy a magazine, in Western Germany today without being made aware of this preoccupation with the past. From pulpits that were once pillars of the established order, the Dibeliuses and the Gollwitzers, and many lesser pastors as well, invoke the Nazi era in order to remind their flocks of the terrible things that can result from political indifference or unquestioning acquiescence in any decree handed down by a government. In the theaters, writers like Max Frisch and Rolf Hochhuth present dramatic elaborations of the same theme, with specific reference to the moral capitulation of the German people during the Hitler period. The motion-picture theaters, in addition to showing the current productions of American and European studios, regularly advertise re-runs of features like *Die Brücke,* the resistance film *Canaris,* and the Swedish documentary *Mein Kampf;* and, as these lines are being written, all three of these films are playing in little theaters in the Lichterfelde, Steglitz, and Charlottenburg districts of West Berlin. The display windows of bookstores are filled, not only with well-established works like Karl Bracher *et al., The National Socialist Seizure of Power,* and the Hitler biographies of Walter Görlitz and Alan Bullock (the latter in a new paperback edition), but also with a remarkable number of new books about Nazi Germany—J. C. Fest's *The Face of the Third Reich,* Gunter Schubert's *The Beginnings of National Socialist Foreign Policy,* and Hans Berd Gisevius's *Adolf Hitler: An Attempt at an Interpretation,* to mention only the most important. Simultaneously, the most widely read newsmagazine in Germany, *Der Spiegel,* having touched off a lively controversy in its letter columns by serializing the Göttingen historian Percy Schramm's introduction to the new edition of *Hitler's Table Talk,* has now widened the field of discussion by printing those chapters of Barbara Tuchmann's *The Guns of August* which deal with the war-guilt question in 1914. In doing this, the magazine's editor, Rudolf Augstein, has made it clear that, as far as it lies within his power, he will prevent those who would like the past to be forgotten from having their way. "I consider it a sacred duty," he has written, "for us to keep before our eyes what fearful things we Germans have inflicted on our neighbors over the past fifty years, as a result of our excessive self-satisfaction, our military-technical perfectionism, and our distorted sense of values."

This evident willingness to view the past with a critical spirit may perhaps give some measure of reassurance to those who suffer recurring doubts about the prospects of German democracy. Yet it is questionable whether this kind of artistic and journalistic activity can by itself have much positive effect upon the future political behavior of the German people. Of much greater significance in that regard will be the nature of historical instruction in the elementary and secondary schools.

How good a job are the German schools doing today in presenting a fair picture of the "fearful things the Germans have inflicted on their neighbors" in the recent past? On more than one occasion, Herr Augstein has not only expressed doubts about the quality of their performance but has intimated that there is in the country active and strong resistance to attempts on the part of the schools to do better. He is not alone in holding this view. In a speech given two years ago in the Paulskirche in Frankfurt am Main, Hans Graf von Lehndorff said, "I keep hearing the opinion that we shouldn't burden the younger generation with the so-called guilt question. Youth, it is said, should have the privilege of being able to think and act without prejudice, and we should not deprive them of that. Life is hard enough, and we shouldn't make it harder for the young. And whenever I hear that sort of thing, I always ask myself: In whose interest is this really being said? Do the young really resist this burden? Or is it not really we older people who would like to hide behind the young in order not to have to admit our own mistakes?"

In the first years after the war, there is no doubt that the attitude described by Count von Lehndorff was effective in delaying and, in some parts of Germany, blocking not only much needed changes in school curricula but also the vitally important task of revising old history texts and finding new ones that would meet the requirements of the new German democracy. Despite the fact that the national teachers' organization had noted the inadequacy of available teaching materials as early as 1947, the correction of this situation was slow and uneven for over a decade. It was not, indeed, until 1959 that reform of history instruction was taken up in earnest, and that was because a sudden outburst of antisemitic incidents in Cologne and other parts of the country shocked people into realizing that failure to deal adequately with Germany's past in the schools was already having a deleterious effect. It was leaving young people dangerously susceptible to the myths of neo-Nazism and the rationalizations of those who had an interest in blaming Germany's present plight upon anyone but the real culprits. The sobering experience of seeing swastikas smeared on synagogue walls again put an end to attempts to prevent history instruction in the schools from going beyond the end of the nineteenth century. In February 1960 the Federal Conference of Ministers of Education declared that instruction in the history of Germany in the modern period should be made part of the curriculum of all elementary and secondary schools; and in the subsequent period those *Länderregierungen* which had not already done so began to take the necessary steps to implement that declaration.

One of the first effects of this was an accelerated effort to provide the schools with readable and objective textbooks dealing with the Weimar and National Socialist periods. The progress that has been made in this respect was described last year by Grace Richards Conant in an excellent brief report published in *The Saturday Review*. Mrs. Conant pointed out that, not only have new books been provided quickly, but, in a country that had been notorious for the extreme nationalism of its historical scholarship, publishers of school books have fallen into the habit of submitting manuscripts to the International School Book Institute at Braunschweig for analysis and correction of bias and error, while state governments have demonstrated their willingness to withdraw books from use which failed to meet the standards of that organization. The results of this revolutionary procedure have been heartening. After examining ten of the most widely adopted history texts, Mrs. Conant found them free of the kind of distortion that marred German school books in the interwar period and noted that, without exception, they "contained drastic judgments of German national policy" after 1933 and provided detailed accounts of the brutalities practiced by the Nazi government against fellow Germans before 1939 and of the horrors of the Final Solution pursued during the war years.

Hannah Vogt's *Schuld oder Verhängnis?* here published under the title *The Burden of Guilt,* is representative of this new type of German school text and is not only one of the most widely used books of its kind but one of the most interesting in its method. Its author is not a professional historian, but rather a civil servant who has specialized in problems of civic education. For six years a town councillor in the city of Göttingen, Miss Vogt has been connected since 1954 with the *Landeszentrale für politische Bildung* in the state of Hessen, and during these years she has traveled all over Western Germany, as well as a good part of the United States, visiting elementary and secondary schools, holding seminars with young people and talking to adult education classes, and constantly seeking new methods of stimulating discussion of contemporary and recent history and making it contribute to the political education of future citizens. Her previous books include an introduction to legal history and education, a *Handbook for the Citizen,* and an anthology of selections from the writings of Friedrich Naumann, one of the founders in 1919 of the Democratic Party and a man who sought, throughout his life, to alleviate class conflict and awaken political responsibility in his country.

The Burden of Guilt was in a real sense the result of the antisemitic outrages of 1959. Those incidents not only gave Miss Vogt the idea of writing a book of this kind but also prompted the Diesterweg Press to ask her to write it, after the press in its turn had been stimulated by parliamentary demands for a speedy reexamination of historical instruction in the Hessen school system. The book was written with commendable dispatch, was published in 1961, and was an immediate success, 400,000 copies being sold in the first two years. The Minister of Education in Hessen made it prescribed reading in all final classes in the *Volksschulen;* it was put on the approved lists of ten other Ministries of Education and of the *Senat* of West Berlin; and it enjoyed a respectable sale in the commercial market, thousands of copies being bought by ordinary adult readers.

The book's success is to be explained in part by the clarity and directness of Miss Vogt's style—qualities uncommon in German academic writing—and by the happy wedding of text and illustration. But even more important in this respect is the way in which Miss Vogt approaches her material. She is less intent upon writing a detailed narrative history of the past half-century than she is upon dealing with the problems which she has heard most frequently raised in discussion groups, with the questions students ask (or would like to ask) their parents and teachers, and with the rationalizations and half-truths that one hears in private conversation and in the speeches of the less responsible politicians. How many times a day, for example, is it not said somewhere in Germany that the country's present misfortunes really stem from the First World War, a conflict forced upon Germany by envious powers, who wished to encircle her, and which she would nevertheless have won if her armies had not been betrayed by subversive forces on the home front? Miss Vogt asks her readers whether there is any support for these beliefs and proceeds to demonstrate that there is not, by an analysis of the pre-war policies of Germany and her neighbors and by an examination of the war situation in 1918. How many times a day does not someone say that Hitler was doubtless a very bad man but that he would never have come to power in Germany if it had not been for the iniquitous Versailles Treaty? Miss Vogt asks her readers to consider this theory in the light of the Weimar period and to ask themselves whether there were not many other factors as important in bringing support to Hitler as the Versailles Treaty, and whether the most important were not "lack of judgment and inadequate willingness to assume responsibility on the part of specific groups of Germans themselves." How many Germans still believe (and are willing to say so in public-opinion polls) that the Nazi period was the most comfortable, prosperous, and presumably happy period of their lives?

To the children of parents who feel this way, Miss Vogt points out, in the section called "Life in the Third *Reich*," what a questionable judgment that is, at whose cost the comforts of the average German were purchased, and what frightful political consequences followed from his enjoyment of them.

As a work of historical analysis, this volume is not free of faults. Specialists in German history will note that Miss Vogt has a tendency to see things in black and white and that, in her desire to reveal Hitler for what he was, she has been somewhat uncritical of some of his predecessors, notably Stresemann and Brüning. But even the specialists—and this is not a book for them anyway!—will admire the thoroughness with which the author has gone about demolishing the kinds of myths that have distorted German historical instruction in the past: the stab-in-the-back legend, the myth of the legality of Hitler's assumption of power, the theory, now being propagated by certain people in our own country, that the Fuehrer was a sincere lover of peace and that war came against his will and as a result of the blunders or the schemes of certain foreign statesmen, and the thesis that Germany would really have won the Second World War if only this or that had, or had not, intervened. Nor will they deny the skill with which she has avoided the mistake of presenting a purely negative picture of the past, and the persuasiveness with which she has demonstrated, in her treatment of the Weimar Republic and her chapter on the German resistance to Hitler, that among the dark pages of their history there are others upon which today's generation can find examples of courage and steadfastness and of the kind of values that must be cultivated if Germany's new democracy is to survive.

During their serialization of Schramm's introduction to *Hitler's Table Talk,* the editors of *Der Spiegel* received some letters from readers who seemed fearful lest too much writing about Hitler serve merely to advertise neo-Nazism, and one letter from a reader who asked querulously, "Why don't you leave the dead in peace?" Other writers, however, and younger ones thanked them for having thrown more light upon the troubled past, and one girl wrote firmly, "It is a bitter necessity for us to go on working away at the Hitler phenomenon, because, inseparable from it, is the phenomenon of the German people." It was for these last correspondents and all their contemporaries who are trying to come to terms with their country's past that Miss Vogt's book was written. By Americans, *The Burden of Guilt* can be read simply as a good brief account of German history from Wilhelm II to Hitler. It will assume greater interest, however, if it is seen for what it really is—a document of our times, a weapon in the continuing struggle for German democracy.

Stanford, California   GORDON A. CRAIG
and Berlin-Dahlem
April 1964

The Burden of Guilt

Kaiser Wilhelm II (1859-1941)

I
The First World War

1: Was Germany Responsible for World War I?

In the Versailles Treaty which concluded the First World War, the victorious powers claimed that Germany and her allies bore the sole responsibility for the recently extinguished conflagration. This claim corresponded in no way with historical truth and has long since been refuted by scholars. Many German historians of the post-war period made it their special task to study the origins of the First World War, and historians in other countries as well made efforts to ascertain the facts. The diplomatic archives were opened; documents and correspondence, treaties and diplomatic notes were published. The result was best summarized by the former British Prime Minister David Lloyd George. Himself one of the *dramatis personae,* he said later that no European statesman of that time had wanted war: "The nations slithered over the brink into the boiling cauldron of war without any trace of apprehension."

How the First World War originated cannot be explained in a few sentences; and we Germans must certainly avoid turning the argument against the British by saying, perhaps, that it was they who were guilty of secretly causing the war to rid themselves of German economic competition. Assertions of this kind distort reality. Instead, we must realize that many stupidities, wrong decisions, and disastrous errors combined to bring the nations of Europe to the point of believing, in 1914, that only war could resolve their difficulties.

People outside Germany believed that Kaiser Wilhelm II was hell-bent on war, and they attributed a great deal of the blame to him. For this reason the Versailles Treaty stipulated that he be surrendered to the Allies and arraigned before a special tribunal "for a supreme offense against international morality and the sanctity of treaties." Was this belief correct?

It cannot be denied that the pre-war German Constitution placed considerable political responsibility upon the Kaiser. He not only had to serve as a symbol and representative of the *Reich* for the foreigner, he was not merely the embodiment of the national image and the state as a whole (like the English monarch), but he was also the chief executive of the state. He alone had the right to appoint the Chancellor and the cabinet, and through the persons he chose, he also determined to a considerable degree the direction of policy.

There is hardly a figure in recent history who can be judged by his contemporaries and by posterity in such contradictory ways as the last Kaiser. Some see him as the scion of a decadent dynasty, facing tasks above his capabilities, suffering from near-pathological delusions of grandeur. Others admire his astonishing intellectual flexibility, his honesty, his catholic interests. Contradictions of this sort, arising from the opinions of unprejudiced contemporaries and scholars, cannot be resolved in a universally accepted judgment.

The speeches the Kaiser was prepared to deliver frequently and at the least provocation, gave him the reputation of being war-like and bloodthirsty. He lacked tact, people believed, an opinion borne out by the comments he wrote in the margins of his ambassadors' reports; and in his speeches this failing led to the worst kind of *faux pas,* which became known the world over. One example was the so-called "Speech on the Huns."

In 1900, a rebellion, led by the secret Boxer Society, broke out in China. It was directed against foreign supremacy, and, in the course of the rebellion, the German ambassador in Peking was assassinated. The great powers intervened; and Germany, too, sent troops to quell the Boxer Rebellion. The Kaiser sent off his soldiers from Bremerhaven, and addressed them in the following words:

> Give no pardon! Take no prisoners! Those you capture are your property! A thousand years ago the Huns under their King Attila acquired a reputation which still, in song and story, makes them appear terrible. So may the name *German* be fixed for a thousand years in China in such manner that never again will a Chinese dare even to cast a disparaging glance at a German!

When Allied propaganda in the First World War called German troops "huns," they were merely taking up a phrase the Kaiser himself had applied to his own soldiers.

The year 1908 witnessed a scandal which had far-reaching consequences and unleashed a storm of criticism and indignation in the *Reichstag* and in the German press. It was caused by an interview the Kaiser had given to the London *Daily Telegraph*. Even the Kaiser himself was thoroughly shaken by the effect of his words. Unfortunately, people failed to use the general indignation to force through a constitutional revision which would have made the German cabinet responsible to parliament, as was the case in England and France. Such a reform might have limited or ended the political influence of the Kaiser. Instead, the disastrous "personal regime" of Wilhelm II continued, affecting, above all, important appointments, and making few friends for Germany in the world. Max Weber, an outstanding political thinker of the period, wrote in 1906: "We are being 'isolated' because this man governs us in this fashion, and we tolerate and excuse it . . ."

Still, it would be wrong to conclude from the Kaiser's speeches that he wanted war; his deeds were far more moderate. He wanted no risks, no revolution, no wars. Someone at court once said in regard to future domestic problems in Germany: "Let him talk as tough as he pleases, when the trouble really starts and he must order his soldiers to shoot at Social Democrats, he will draw back." The same was true of foreign affairs. Although he talked of "shining armor" and of "keeping the powder dry," he did not want war. And when finally the peoples of Europe tottered over the brink into war, the Kaiser was shocked and shaken and knew no

Europe before the First World War

more than his Chancellor Bethmann-Hollweg just how this could have happened.

At the outbreak of the First World War, Germany and her ally Austria-Hungary stood practically alone. How did Germany get into this situation? Had it been necessary? Was it caused by the "policy of encirclement" pursued by the other European powers, by British "economic jealousy," as German nationalist literature never tired of repeating? Or was it due to a series of political miscalculations which the German government could have avoided?

Bismarck had founded the German Empire in the wake of a war against France. Since then, German policies had to reckon with France's using the first occasion to undo defeat. France had managed, in an astonishingly short time, to pay the indemnity of 5 billion francs imposed on her to defray the costs of the war, but she would never forget Alsace-Lorraine. A statue symbolizing the lost province was erected in Paris, and it remained draped in black until 1918. Under these circumstances, the policy of each country was determined by its need to feel secure against the other.

Bismarck had sought to guarantee Germany's security through an alliance with Austria-Hungary (the Dual Alliance of 1879), and a secret neutrality treaty with Russia (the so-called Re-Insurance Treaty). The possibility that, one day, Russia might come to an understanding with France over the head of Germany was a constant preoccupation of his, for he knew that this would mean that, in the case of armed conflict, the German Empire would be threatened with a "two-front war," in the east and the west. Yet, barely two years after Bismarck's dismissal, Russia and France concluded a military agreement, after specialists in the Berlin Foreign Office had advised the Kaiser against renewing the Re-Insurance Treaty. Although Bismarck had succeeded in adding Italy to the Dual Alliance, and thus expanding it to a Triple Alliance, Germany felt isolated, and even more so since she doubted that Italy would keep faith with it.

In these circumstances, there arose the opportunity of linking the German Empire more closely with England. Since the demise of the Napoleonic Empire, Britain had not entered into alliances with continental European governments. Throughout the nineteenth century, she was most concerned with preserving a balance of power on the continent: no continental nation was to gain hegemony over the others. But her global colonial policies had caused friction with France in North and Central Africa and conflicts of interest with Russia in East Asia. Any of these crises might have led to war, in which case England would need strong support on the continent of Europe. Thus around the turn of the century, English statesmen decided to reverse their previous policy of isolation and to seek *rapprochement* with Germany.

In March 1898, Joseph Chamberlain, then British Colonial

The British General Henry Wilson in pre-war discussions with
Marshal Foch and Col. Haguet of the French army

Secretary, approached the German ambassador in London with
some apposite proposals. But the German Foreign Office did not
understand the urgency of the British requests and feared complications. German public opinion had no love for England at the time
either; for Germany had taken the Boers' side in the Boer War with
great fervor. The English renewed their first proposals three years
later in spite of the cool reception they had previously received.
This time, however, they hinted that they would seek terms with
France and Russia if they were turned down again. Privy Councillor von Holstein, the influential expert in the Foreign Office, considered this hint "an absolute bluff." He was of the opinion that the
whale (England) and the bear (Russia) could never unite. Thus,
once again, just as in the case of the lapse of the Re-Insurance
Treaty, the issue was decided by a man who never faced the

limelight of parliamentary responsibility, but operated behind the scenes. Here again we see a flaw in the German system of government: civil servants functioned almost completely without supervision by parliament. Before very long, events were to prove Holstein's lack of foresight.

During the second round, the negotiations with the English had gone into greater detail. Germany had insisted that England openly join the Triple Alliance. England, on its side, wished for a less formal understanding which would serve to neutralize conflicts of interest, and to defend common concerns. From the very beginning, however, England did not want to get involved in Austrian ambitions in the Balkans. Bismarck once had said: "The Germans always make the mistake of aiming at all or nothing, and of rigidly embracing one single method." It was this mistake which wrecked the negotiations of 1901. England now quickly turned to the very policy she had threatened and which German statesmen had considered an impossibility. England concluded a treaty with Japan, ended existing frictions with France in North Africa, and came to terms with Russia over conflicts in Persia, Afghanistan, and Tibet (1907). State visits by Edward VII to Paris and St. Petersburg further cemented the new, so-called Triple Entente (England, Russia, France)—although no written agreement backed up these very real understandings.

Thus the isolation of Germany grew to the threatening proportions which were to determine the nation's fate in the First World War. Too late, Privy Councillor von Holstein realized (as he was to admit in a letter) that his government had "let slip the opportunity to be friends, both with England and Russia."

The English offer to negotiate a treaty with Germany gives the clear lie to the legend that the powers wished to encircle Germany. It was true that certain economic groups in England favored a weakening of their German competitors, yet British foreign policy before the war was not determined by interests of this type.

After the treaty negotiations failed, Germany pushed forward its naval building program with great fanfare; as a consequence, Anglo-German relations deteriorated quickly. English and German diplomats repeatedly tried to agree on a limitation of naval strength, but could not overcome the resistance of Admiral von

Tirpitz, who refused to give up his naval construction program for which he had the prime responsibility.

Living as we do today, we find the years before 1914 so peaceful and serene that we tend to believe that people in that era must have enjoyed a sense of security, and must have been stunned by the outbreak of the First World War as by an earthquake. In this we are wrong. The world drifted into war because both the statesmen and the people got used to the idea of considering war inevitable. Once people believe in an inevitable fate, reason and patience which could stem the tide retreat, and passion and panic take over.

This mood was encouraged by a series of crises, in which war was repeatedly avoided by a hair's breadth. Many people finally came to feel that the tensions had to be discharged in some violent storm, and they hoped that this would clear the air. Hopes were certainly high that future conflicts could be controlled, but even so fear spread that they might ultimately engulf the world. Under such pressures, all Europe increased its armaments, lengthened terms of military service, and brought armies up to combat strength.

Morocco, Turkey, and the Balkans were the critical areas before the war. The Turks had controlled the southeastern part of the Balkans for centuries. Since the middle of the nineteenth century, the peoples of the Balkans had been engaged in revolutions and wars for independence, and finally they had succeeded in ousting the Turks. This created a series of independent states, including the kingdom of Serbia, bordering upon Austria.

As a multi-national state, the Austro-Hungarian dual monarchy was committed to oppose the national aspirations of the Balkan peoples. Russia, with her desire for an outlet to the Mediterranean through the Dardanelles, also had a vital stake in Balkan problems, which further increased tensions. On top of this, Slavic Russia wished to act as protector to the small Slavic nations in the Balkans. For all these reasons the Balkans were considered the "powder-keg" or the "fiery wheel" upon which Europe was chained. Any change in status of the Balkans could well precipitate a European war.

One especially grave event on the road to war was the annexation of Bosnia by Austria-Hungary in 1908. Since the population of this area was ethnically related to the Serbs, Serbia also laid claim to it, but it was persuaded by the great powers to renounce its claims. Thus the hatred of the Serbian nationalists against the Danubian monarchy was fanned to white heat.

As early as 1912 and 1913, wars had erupted in the Balkans, rent as they were by national tensions, but on both occasions it was still possible to contain the flames. A year later, however, playing with fire led to the long-feared explosion.

In June 1914, Archduke Franz Ferdinand, heir to the Austro-Hungarian throne and Inspector General of the Army, visited Austrian troops in Bosnia. Although Austrian officials knew that secret societies in Bosnia were striving for unification with Serbia at all costs, and even though they had been warned of the danger to the Archduke's life if he stepped on Bosnian soil, no special security measures were taken. Thus, when the Archduke visited the Bosnian capital of Sarajevo, a young Bosnian conspirator managed to jump on the running board of his car, and shot him and his wife dead.

Archduke Franz Ferdinand with his wife leaving Sarajevo Town Hall.
28 June 1914

The assassination was political provocation and was regarded in Vienna as an attack on the Danubian monarchy. Deeper examination would have shown that it was a problem of domestic politics; the murderer was a subject of the Austrian Emperor not a Serbian national. Nevertheless, Vienna decided, from the outset, to use the murder for a squaring of accounts with Serbia. It is unclear to this day—in spite of a good deal of research—whether the Serbian government was really privy to the conspiracy, but certainly at that time no one had any definite proof of its complicity.

Before the Austro-Hungarian foreign minister carried his plans any further, he inquired in Berlin whether he could count on the backing of the Kaiser. Wilhelm II answered that "His Majesty will stand faithfully at Austria-Hungary's side," although he added his expressed desire that the Austro-Serbian quarrel should be kept from developing into an international conflict. But with foolhardy neglect, the conditions under which Germany was to fulfill her treaty obligations were not clarified. Thus Vienna felt no need for restraint. Wilhelm II had acted without asking his diplomatic advisers, thus creating a situation well described by a later German historian:

> Every German recruit, every German regular, would have to march, every German family would have to part with its most precious members, if Vienna decided that Austria-Hungary's prestige required that the torch be put to Europe.[1]

Since Berlin had given the diplomats in Vienna a free hand, they could now recklessly pursue the alleged interests of the Danubian monarchy. It goes without saying that they had no intention of unleashing a world war. They allowed themselves rather to be deluded by the thought that this time—as in the Balkan crisis of 1908-09—Russia would stand still. Under these assumptions, the Austro-Hungarian government took its next steps: on July 23, an ultimatum was handed to Serbia bearing a time limit of 48 hours. Its demands were so exaggerated that diplomats all over the world considered them unacceptable. It became apparent that Vienna did not expect Serbia to accept them, but wanted merely to provoke a rejection, and thus have an excuse for military action. To everybody's surprise, however, the Serbs "displayed brilliant diplomatic skill" and accepted the Austrian demands with certain reservations. The Serbian government circularized copies of its note to Austria to all other European governments, and thereby won their sympathies. Vienna took two days to comment on the answer, and to declare its content "unsatisfactory." This was followed by the mobilization of the Austro-Hungarian army, and, on July 28, by a declaration of war on Serbia.

Austria-Hungary had consulted her German ally neither in the drafting of the ultimatum nor the declaration of war. Wilhelm II, after reading the cleverly worded Serbian reply to the ultimatum, exclaimed with relief: "Now there can be no object in going to war." And even after Austria had declared war on Serbia, England and Germany worked especially hard to localize the conflict. During the night of July 29, Chancellor Bethmann-Hollweg cabled to Vienna: "We are ready to fulfill our treaty obligations, but we refuse to be drawn into a world conflagration by a frivolous Vienna which fails to consider our advice."

By then, however, it was too late; the avalanche had gained momentum. Russia had told Serbia that it could count on Russian support. The empire of the Czars valued "pan-slavism" more than the solidarity of the monarchs whose inviolability was threatened by the murder in Sarajevo. Russia ordered a partial mobilization directed against Austria-Hungary, after she had declared war on Serbia (July 29). The next day the Czar decreed general mobilization, thus threatening Germany as well.

Even at this late hour, Bethmann-Hollweg sought to compromise, but by then purely military considerations began to overshadow political policy. Moltke, the German Chief of Staff, feared that any delay would worsen Germany's military situation. He therefore intervened in the course of events and, without informing either Kaiser or Chancellor, urged Austrian mobilization against Russia (in a cable to the Austrian General Staff, dated July 30) and promised German mobilization at the same time.

On July 31, Russia's ally, France, mobilized, too. Germany, threatened with a two-front war, demanded in an ultimatum that Russia suspend all military measures against Germany and Austria within twelve hours. The same day, Germany asked France

Joyful response to mobilization in Berlin, 1914   *Ullstein*

for assurances of neutrality in case of war. When neither of these
assurances were forthcoming, Germany declared war on Russia
(August 1) and on France (August 3).

At the same time, German soldiers invaded Belgium after that
government—as expected—had refused them permission to march
through its territory. German action against Belgium was based
on the military plans drawn up in 1905 by Field Marshal Alfred
Count Schlieffen, then Chief of the General Staff. Although
Schlieffen had allowed for a war on two fronts, he wished to
maintain a defensive position in the east and obtain a quick result
through a concentrated attack in the west. This plan, from its inception, took exaggerated military risks, and it could only be executed
by disregarding Belgian neutrality. Militarily everything depended
on the quick success of the Schlieffen Plan; but its execution inevitably made Germany's political situation deteriorate.

The violation of Belgian neutrality triggered England's declaration of war. England would have taken this step in any event in

order to fulfill her obligations toward France incurred through the Entente Cordiale. But the violation of Belgian neutrality had a decisive effect on the movement of public opinion in England. Now Bethmann-Hollweg—who had been especially active in seeking an understanding with England during the preceding period— saw all his efforts destroyed. "For a scrap of paper you destroy my whole, my only work," he said in anguish to the British ambassador as the latter took his leave. This phrase—the "scrap of paper" which referred to England's guarantee of Belgian neutrality—was to gain notoriety around the world and do much damage as an anti-German propaganda slogan. Yet Bethmann's statement was not intended to question the validity of the old legal principle that "treaties must be kept." Only with Hitler did scruples and morality go completely by the board; for him, indeed, all treaties were mere "scraps of paper."

The British declaration of war completed the line-up of the European powers. The nations of Europe, step by step, had "stumbled into war." Few people of that generation had even the vaguest idea of the full consequences of that event.

2: Did the First World War End Through a "Stab in the Back"?

In August 1919, the *Nationalversammlung,* the first parliament of the German Republic, appointed a Commission of Inquiry. Its task was to determine whether war could have been avoided, and, especially, whether it could not have been ended sooner. This commission, meeting in public session, was told by a former Secretary of State, Helfferich, that Russian money had financed the German Revolution of November 1918, and that its instigators had, as it were, attacked the German army from the rear. Soon afterwards, Field Marshal von Hindenburg testified before the same body. He was asked some questions but disregarded them; instead, he read a prepared statement along the lines that the army and the military chiefs had always done their best. The German people and the political parties, however, had deserted the men fighting at the front, and, in the words of a British general, "stabbed the army in the back."

Thus was born the notorious stab-in-the-back legend. It was

Battlefield in northern France

accepted eagerly, for many Germans drew comfort from the idea that the German army had remained "unvanquished in battle." The stab-in-the-back legend afforded them a rationale for their hatred of democracy, of the Republic, of anything new. Later on, it was grist for the Nazi mill and thus it turned into one of the most pernicious political myths of the recent past. But how did Germany really lose the war?

Memoirs, newspapers, and pictures reflect the strange intoxication which overwhelmed the whole of Germany when war broke out. Men marched to defend their threatened fatherland, recalling the glorious campaigns of 1814 and 1870. Soldiers going to the front hoped to be "back with mother" within six weeks. Women and young girls pressed flowers and presents on the troops en route. Volunteers who lined up at recruiting stations were worried that the war would be over before they arrived at the front.

But very soon it became obvious that a quick military decision could not be reached. In the west, the battle of the Marne had to be broken off. This finished the Schlieffen Plan, which had been the basis for German strategy. A second offensive (October 1914) bounced off the iron defenses of the French Army, led by General Foch. Despite the courageous sacrifice of many young volunteers in the battle of Langemarck all exertions were in vain. The western front solidified into a war of position, corroding nerves and consuming material. Attempts made over many months to exhaust French manpower by attacking the fortifications of Verdun also failed. The Germans paid with 280,000 dead, wounded, and prisoners for the attack, while the defending French lost 300,000 men. And the commander of the Verdun fortress, General Pétain, became "the hero of Verdun."

Over the top—British troops at the Somme, 1916   *Bettmann Archive*

In the east, meanwhile, generals Hindenburg and Ludendorff had won important battles. But these victories failed to force Russia to her knees, and were thus indecisive. As the war spread to additional theaters, extending the battle lines to Italy and Turkey in 1915, Germany and her allies found themselves in a situation which was deteriorating.

Well aware that it would be almost impossible to win the war by military means alone, the German Chief of Staff, General von Falkenhayn, urged the Chancellor to seek a compromise peace. But nobody listened.

During the first few days of the war, the German industrialist, Walther Rathenau, 47 years of age and thus too old for the army, reported to the German Ministry of War and offered his services. He pointed out that manufacturers needed to be assured that they could continue to receive supplies of raw materials, and that central controls would have to be imposed. Thereupon he was entrusted with the control of German raw material procurement, and succeeded in organizing it with dedication, persistent effort, and intelligence. It was mainly due to his initiative that industry quickly made use of an invention of the German scientist Fritz Haber, by which ammonia was synthesized directly by combining hydrogen and nitrogen. Only by this means was the German production of ammunition assured.

The food situation was even less favorable than industrial production. As early as 1915, the sealing off of the North Sea by the British navy began to have a serious effect on Germany. It countered this breach of maritime law with submarine warfare, but this failed to improve its food supply or to force the English to their knees.

Since there was no way out of scarcity, the limited supplies had to be rationed. Food rationing, however, immediately produced a black market. The peasants resented enforced delivery quotas. The workers, especially in the big cities, were underfed, and were embittered because higher income groups escaped the general misery by buying under the counter.

Germany resembled a beleaguered fortress at the time. People living in these conditions will only put up with great suffering if they can reasonably expect relief or supplies from the outside.

Theobald von Bethmann-Hollweg   *Ullstein*

Failing this, they must capitulate in time, or heroically accept annihilation. Since the latter alternative is obviously impossible for 60 million people, the economic necessities should have persuaded the political leaders to sue for peace within a short time.

Constitutionally, the Kaiser was Commander in Chief of the Armed Forces as well as head of the government. During the war, however, he remained much in the background. Bethmann-Hollweg, the Chancellor, was a prudent and honest man, but he lacked creative imagination, and was unable to anticipate events or devise long-range plans. His foreign policy was half-hearted throughout, and he failed to carry out domestic reforms which would have given parliament greater responsibility.

At the beginning of the war, members of the German *Reichstag,* who represented twelve parties, had concluded a political truce. They included 110 Social Democrats, 88 representatives of political Catholicism (Center Party), 86 middle-class liberals, and 45 right-wing Conservatives. By this agreement, or *Burgfrieden,* they suppressed all differences of opinion on domestic issues in

19

an attempt to secure a common front in foreign affairs. The large Social Democratic representation had also voted with the other parties for the first war credits. The Socialist deputy Haase spoke for millions of Socialist workers (4.2 million in 1912, a third of all votes cast) when he made his well-known declaration in the *Reichstag* on August 4, 1914:

> We are now faced with the brutal fact of war and the threat of enemy invasion. We must take sides today not for or against war, but rather on the means needed for the defense of the country. . . . We shall stand by what we have always emphasized, we shall not abandon the fatherland in its hour of danger.

Wilhelm II voiced the mood of the *Burgfrieden* in his speech from the throne: "I no longer know of any parties; I know only Germans."

After the *Reichstag* had voted for war credits, it adjourned for an indefinite period. This clearly revealed that parliament did not wish to assume political leadership at that time. The prevalent opinion was that the guns had to speak first. Yet Karl von Clausewitz, the most intelligent among German military authorities, had demanded the opposite course just a hundred years earlier:

> War is merely a continuation of political relations with different means. . . . War can never be divorced from the political give and take. If any theoretician proposes such a separation at any time, he, as it were, breaks all connecting threads of the relationship and creates a senseless and purposeless thing.

Yet this is precisely what happened during the First World War, thanks to the weakness of political leadership in Germany.

In August 1916, the Kaiser appointed Field Marshal von Hindenburg as Chief of General Staff, and General Ludendorff Quartermaster General.

Both had earned high praise for their achievements on the eastern front. For purely military purposes the Kaiser could not have chosen better men. In fact, however, it was a fateful choice, for Ludendorff in particular chose to use his authority to overstep his military office and trespass upon politics. Why was this bound to head German politics for catastrophe? The reason can be found in the different principles upon which political and military thinking are based.

> Political and military thinking are basically different. Political thought and action grow out of an awareness of political relationships that is based on historical experience. The statesman looks to the future. He aims at permanent solutions, and, in the last analysis, never works for the immediate present. A soldier's mind works in a radically different manner; where does the enemy stand? What is the present situation? These are his first questions. How he answers them will determine his plan of action, so that a new and better situation will come about in the shortest possible time. He aims to defeat the enemy so that an opportunity will be created whereby the art of politics can conclude a favorable peace as soon as possible. War never is an end in itself. Political considerations determine its beginning and its end.[2]

Yet, Hindenburg's and Ludendorff's interference in political affairs turned warfare into an end in itself. Bethmann-Hollweg's carefully considered judgment was that "these men of genius aim purposefully at militarizing every aspect of the state." The abdication of the political way of thinking in the interest of the military is precisely what is called "militarism."

The military mind triumphed openly over political considerations in January 1917, when Hindenburg and Ludendorff pressed for unlimited submarine warfare to achieve the purely military objective of increasing the security and efficiency of the submarines. They were backed by navy experts, who claimed that if German submarines could operate without restrictions they could manage to sink on an average 600,000 tons of English shipping a month. This would so cripple England's food supply and industrial production that within six months the English government would be forced to capitulate.

In vain did Bethmann-Hollweg point out that unrestricted submarine warfare which would also affect neutral shipping in enemy waters would thus do irreparable damage to relations with the neutrals, especially the United States. The generals appealed to the Kaiser, who allowed himself to be persuaded by their arguments. Thus, unrestricted submarine warfare was unleashed on February

Hindenburg, Wilhelm II, and Ludendorff at Headquarters, early 1917

1, 1917, and had the immediate effect of bringing the USA into the war. But even the hoped-for military effects failed to materialize, in spite of heroic efforts by German submarine crews, and in spite of the experts' calculations, which incidentally had been based on inadequate statistics. The six months passed during which these tactics were supposed to defeat England, but England showed no sign of yielding.

In the spring of 1917, Bethmann-Hollweg persuaded the Kaiser to release an Easter message promising political reforms to his people, and hinting at the abolition of the limited (three-class) suffrage in Prussia. Hindenburg and Ludendorff thereupon intervened openly in domestic politics by demanding the dismissal of Bethmann-Hollweg. The manner in which the two generals engineered the fall of the Chancellor defied all military tradition. They sent word to the Kaiser that they would resign, since they were unable to work with Bethmann-Hollweg. It was usurpation of authority, blackmail, and insubordination, all in one. If supreme commanders were allowed to desert their commands in this way, surely private Tom, Dick, or Harry should also have been permitted to leave his trench if he disliked the war aims.[3]

If he had acted correctly, the Kaiser should have had General Ludendorff court-martialled for mutiny then and there; but, instead, he backed down and accepted Bethmann-Hollweg's resignation. He then asked Hindenburg his wishes as to the new Chancellor! The choice fell on the Under-Secretary of State, Michaelis, a conscientious official, but one totally unseasoned in politics. Hindenburg, however, considered him an "upright, God-fearing man," so the Kaiser appointed him Chancellor. After Rathenau had met the new Imperial Chancellor, he wrote to a friend: "Everything he utters is totally naïve." In France and England, meanwhile, the helm had been taken by Clemenceau and Lloyd George, both dynamic men who had acquired substantial political experience during years of parliamentary activities.

The German military chiefs gave conclusive proof of their political ineptitude by being unable to produce even one rational plan for terminating the war. Nothing characterizes this better than Ludendorff's question to a conservative representative (November 1916): "Is there any way at all to end this war?" He should have been racking his brains day and night over this very political question, but his military mind grasped only the concepts "victory or defeat." He was unable to realize that victories can have value only if they lead to an enduring peace, and that it is possible to kill oneself with victories, allowing the enemy to win the last and decisive battle. Ludendorff identified defeat with "destruction," which made it sound somber and hollow, and neglected the fact that 60 million people could survive even a defeat.

There actually were some clear-thinking, farsighted men in Germany, who, even during the first intoxication brought on by the victories of 1914, had pondered ways of bringing about a peace. Bismarck once said, in relation to a possible war of revenge, started by the French, that the French should be offered peace after the first victorious battle, with no strings attached, since it was not in the German interest to weaken France any further. In a similar vein, Walter Rathenau wrote to Bethmann-Hollweg on September 7, 1914, that Bismarck's conciliatory policy ought to be heeded and a voluntary peace obtained from France. He called it a mistake to expect England to sue for peace at an early date, or to be forced into capitulating by economic necessities, as some sections of German public opinion then believed. The error arose because "we more often read a map than look at a globe." An understanding with France had to be reached. Soon afterwards, Rathenau wrote to a friend:

> Let us never forget that no nation stands isolated in this world; in war, prepare for peace, and make the peace a true one. In introducing peace, we must see to it, above all else, that mutual hatreds will diminish on every side. . . . The more conciliatory the future peace is, the more enduring it is likely to be.

Among his peers, among industrialists, hardly anybody shared Rathenau's view. Workers, however, and their political leaders, the Social Democratic Party, generally urged a moderate and conciliatory policy. Even while he had voted for the war credits, *Reichstag* deputy Haase had condemned all wars of conquest:

> We demand that the war be ended as soon as we are secure, and the enemy is willing to make peace, and through a peace which will allow us to live in friendship with the neighbor states.

But these moderates had no influence on the public. Opinion was determined by the so-called "Pan-German League," which was a hodgepodge of hot-headed nationalists. The league wanted "global prestige" and colonies for Germany; they held that in politics no holds were barred, that might makes for right, and that Germany had to wage an aggressive "struggle for existence." Mixed with these goals were a hatred of socialists, antisemitism, and a rejection of the democratic way of life. The Pan-Germans further increased their influence because censorship, instituted at the outbreak of the war, impeded public discussions. As a result, matters were continually presented in a rosy light. The government wished to create a mood of optimism, and prop up state authority. They suppressed unfavorable facts, and failed to explain the truth about doubtful "conquests." Instead, loudmouthed show-

Matthias Erzberger   *Ullstein*

offs took the lead, and spread the illusion that Germany would obtain "peace with victory" and dictate its demands.

Two memoranda of 1915 illustrate the war goals of the annexationists. In one of these, the six most powerful German business associations called for the complete annexation of Belgium, a strip of the French coast reaching to the Somme, the iron ore of Longwy and Briey, and coal mines in some French departments. To balance this gain in industrial power, "an equivalent agricultural area to be acquired in the east" was considered necessary.

The second memorandum, nearly topping the first in its demands, was signed by German university professors and civil servants. They advised making maximum demands. France was to be ruthlessly subjugated politically and economically, and forced without mercy to pay the highest war indemnities. Belgium's annexation was demanded "by the most immaculate concept of honor." No demand for reparations could be high enough for England, that "nation of shopkeepers." Russia was to cede land expropriated from previous owners. Quite a few other phantasies adorned this memorandum. Typically, its authors feared that the "pen of the diplomats would lose what the victorious sword had won." In reality the opposite danger existed, that victories would be in vain because politicians failed to use them with moderation.

Thus a carefully planned initiative launched by the Center Party leader Erzberger also proved unsuccessful. The unrestricted submarine warfare and subsequent United States intervention into the war had ended the exchange of views, initiated by President Wilson, on conditions for a peace. The German military had played its last card. Erzberger saw this clearly, and found the courage to suggest a compromise peace. He heatedly rejected the Pan-German argument that a peace offer would amount to an admission of defeat. Only if it could be proved to the Allies that most Germans were moderate and loved peace could the Chancellor negotiate in good faith.

The *Reichstag* accepted Erzberger's initiative, and, in July 1917, 240 of its 397 members voted for a resolution, the principal clauses of which were:

> The *Reichstag* strives for a peace of understanding and lasting reconciliation of nations. Such a peace is not in keeping with enforced annexations of territory, or forcible political, economic, or financial impositions. The *Reichstag* also rejects all plans which would lead to economic isolation, and hostility among the nations after the war. . . .

At the time this resolution was passed, the generals had already overthrown Bethmann-Hollweg. Michaelis, the new Chancellor, sympathized with the Pan-Germans and was not inclined to make proper use of the resolution. Thus, the Supreme Command retained power, and continued its "go for broke" policy until the end of the war.

In the spring of 1917, strikes and riots erupted in Petrograd. Soldiers joined the revolutionaries, and the Czar was forced to abdicate. The provisional government, backed by Liberals and moderate Socialists, tried to continue the war. Vladimir Ilich Lenin, the leader of the extreme Left, was living in Switzerland as an emigrant. Ludendorff sped him and some other Bolshevik leaders back to Russia by allowing them to travel through Germany to Sweden in a sealed train. Ludendorff was correct in ex-

Lenin addressing the crowds in St. Petersburg, 1917

pecting that these radical revolutionaries would induce Russia to make peace, and thus relieve the pressure on Germany. Nobody, of course, anticipated the world-shaking effects of these measures.

Lenin immediately called for decisive changes: nationalization of all land, redistribution of the land to the land-starved peasants, an end to war, and "all power to the workers' and soldiers' councils [Soviets]." Supported by regiments of radical sailors, he managed to drive the moderate parties out of the All-Russian Congress of Soviets on November 7. From then on, the Bolsheviks extended their revolution to the whole country. The Reds and the Whites began their long and bloody struggle.

Already on November 8, Lenin had issued a Peace Program, calling for an armistice and the conclusion of peace treaties among all belligerents. On December 15, an armistice was concluded with Germany. Negotiations for a peace treaty followed. They were broken off a number of times, but the combination of a threat of a renewed German advance and Lenin's insistence induced the Russian delegation to accept the unfavorable German conditions. Latvia, Lithuania, and Poland remained under German military occupation. This peace of Brest-Litovsk was to create a bad precedent when the Entente in turn came to dictate conditions to the German Empire.

The breathing spell in the east persuaded the German Supreme Command to make one more attempt to take the initiative in the west. They planned to launch another attack with 200 divisions (3.5 million men), which gave them a slight numerical superiority over the French and English. The plan was to drive a wedge between the English and the French, to pin the English on the Channel, and to beat the French in a vast encirclement battle of the type that had been envisioned in 1914 but had failed then. There was hope that the Americans would get out of the war, once the planned operation had succeeded. Such a foolish hope, of course, cast doubt on the whole scheme. How could a great power be expected to fail its allies so miserably! England, moreover, was supported by a whole empire.

In all probability, then, final military victory had eluded Germany. At that moment, it would have been much better to offer peace in line with the *Reichstag* resolution. The enemy powers would certainly have thought twice before they dismissed an offer backed up by the threat of 200 divisions.

German politics, however, were decided by military leaders, and thus the great offensive in the west began on March 21, 1918. It was a well-planned military operation, for as a soldier Ludendorff knew his job. One must admire him if merely for his ability to turn the war of position once more into a war of movement in a narrow segment of space where 7 million soldiers had been massed. Equally astonishing was the spirit of the soldiers, who after three years of exhausting trench warfare, made a last supreme effort.

Five times decisive attacks were launched during this last German offensive. Each time these attacks achieved some tactical success, but decisive victory still eluded the German forces. Each month the number of Americans in the European theater grew; there were 300,000 men in March, but already 1.2 million by July. After the fifth attack had spent itself in July 1918, the enemies, led by Marshal Foch, began counter-attacks. Superior in troops and material, they scored quick triumphs, especially since the German army had nothing to match a new British weapon—the tank. With the tank the British succeeded in slashing a deep gap into the German front lines on August 8. Ludendorff called the day the "black day of the German Army." From that day on at least, he must have known the war was lost militarily.

It was hardly astonishing, then, that a mood of despair seized the troops after the immense efforts and setbacks of that spring and summer. But even if the spirit of the front line had been better, and people had not been starving at home, no general in the world could have defeated the superior forces at hand. It speaks well for the spirit of the German army in the west that they managed to hold a shortened front line against all Allied attacks until November. Until the last moment, German troops were disciplined and did their duty. But it would be false to conclude from this that the German soldiers were "unvanquished in battle," since the defeat of the leaders is also the defeat of the soldiers.

In September 1918, the Balkan fronts collapsed. Thereupon Hindenburg and Ludendorff, facing up to facts, demanded that armistice negotiations be undertaken immediately. They knew full well that only a new government would be able to undertake such negotiations. Ludendorff passed word to the party leaders in the German *Reichstag*. Political reforms, blocked so long by the Supreme Command, were now ordered in the very face of defeat.

The *Reichstag* accepted Prince Max von Baden, a liberal, as Chancellor. Prince Max energetically opposed issuing a precipitate appeal for an armistice, since, in his opinion, such a step was bound to decrease the influence his new government hoped to exert on the peace. He made it clear that he would go ahead only

British tanks advancing, 1917   *Ullstein*

if he received a written request from the Supreme Command. Thereupon, Hindenburg, in a letter of October 3, unequivocally established that the Supreme Command was responsible for the termination of the war in form as well as in substance:

> The Supreme Command continues to insist on its demands of Sunday, September 29, of this year that an appeal for an Armistice should be issued forthwith. As a result of the collapse of the Macedonian front and the consequent weakening of our reserves on the Western front, we cannot make good the severe losses which we have suffered in battle during the last few days. We cannot force a peace any longer on our enemies, as far as it is humanly possible to judge. The enemy, on his side, keeps throwing new and fresh reserves into the battle. The German army still holds up solidly, and repels all attacks victoriously. With each passing day, conditions deteriorate, and the Supreme Command may be forced to make extremely grave decisions. Under such circumstances, the fighting must be broken off in order to spare the German people and its allies needless sacrifices. Each day that is lost costs the lives of thousands of brave soldiers.

This left Prince Max no choice. With a heavy heart he addressed a note to President Wilson on October 4, asking him to act as mediator in the arrangement of an armistice.

If one compares Hindenburg's attitude with Hitler's in the Second World War, one is led to agree fully with the historian's verdict: "The men of the Supreme Command acted at the time from most honorable motives, based on an intrinsically correct estimate of the military situation."[4] They ought also to have known that fighting could not be renewed, once they had admitted that all military means had been exhausted. Hindenburg's call for "a battle to the last man," ostensibly to keep the enemy from imposing overly harsh conditions, may have served as a psychological crutch, allowing him to take this responsible step; it bore no relation, however, to political realities. A nation cannot be forced to go on shedding the blood of its sons for a cause that is lost.

Hindenburg's letter needs to be read with great care. It includes not a word about a failure on the part of the people, or about a revolution, or even a revolutionary mood that made necessary a termination of hostilities. This makes it even harder to understand

To the last man—German cemetery in the Vosges

how, little more than a year later, the writer of this letter dared to deny his own responsibilities, and to blame the loss of the war on the German nation and the revolution.

In view of this legend, it must be stated with utmost clarity that, from the very beginning, a total German victory was hardly possible, and that each passing year made it even less likely. Total defeat perhaps could have been avoided if the political leaders had been determined to use military successes at the proper time, and had sought a moderate peace of understanding. The German nation also bears responsibility in so far as it surrendered to authoritarian leadership all too willingly, and failed to demand more energetically its right to a share in the making of decisions. The revolution of November 1918 was an effect not a cause of the defeat.

Gustav Stresemann (1878-1929)

II
The Weimar Republic

3: Was It All the Fault of the Versailles Treaty?

The Treaty of Versailles is often blamed for the failure of the Weimar Republic and for Hitler's rise to power. Partisans of this view find some support in the fact that those who dictated this Treaty to the German people have since come to see it as a political mistake. It was in fact not negotiated, like a treaty among equal partners, but was "dictated" by the victors to the vanquished. But we must ask ourselves whether the truly extraordinary financial and moral burdens which the Versailles Treaty imposed upon Germany really left the nation no choice but headlong flight into Hitler's dictatorship. To clarify matters we must ask: How did the Treaty originate, and what were its consequences?

As long as General Ludendorff continued to believe in military victory, he himself made all political decisions. He had forced these decisions through by insisting on his "responsibility" and by threatening to resign whenever he "could not assume responsibility" for this or that measure.

When he finally recognized that victory could no longer be won, he quickly pushed the responsibility on to others. He demanded that a new government be formed, and that this government, as its first official act, issue an appeal for an armistice. That the generals failed to comprehend fully the consequences of their actions was demonstrated when President Wilson sent his answer on October 23. He made it quite clear that the Allied Powers would accept the Armistice only on such conditions as would render any renewal of hostilities impossible. The generals, in their bungling way, once more attempted to intervene in political affairs by issuing an army bulletin which denounced Wilson's note as unacceptable. As a result, the Chancellor, Max von Baden, had Ludendorff removed from office, while Hindenburg stayed on.

The generals had obviously lost touch with the emergency situation at home, otherwise they would not have expected (as did Ludendorff) that fiery words would rekindle resistance. As early as the spring of 1917, the living conditions of the German people during the notorious "winter of turnips" had triggered off massive strikes in the large industrial centers. The workers had protested against the inadequate food supply, but had raised practically no political demands. Since then, the situation had deteriorated, and the people's mood had fallen correspondingly. But people were still willing to suffer deprivations. Extreme left-wing Spartacist* calls to emulate the Russian Revolution found few supporters. Only when the armistice appeal revealed how hopeless the situation had become did people lose the will to continue the struggle. The general agreement was: "End the war, and end the needless sacrifices!"

Then the Russian example sparked action. Unrest, street riots, and mutinies began to develop. When the German naval command decided, late in October 1918, to strike a blow against England (which, seen from a strictly military point of view, they had a right to do), the sailors disobeyed, since defeat had become inevitable. The operation was broken off, and 600 sailors were thrown into prison. As a result, however, 100,000 sailors joined the civilian revolutionaries, occupied the city of Kiel, and formed "soldiers' and workers' councils." The movement spread quickly from Kiel and Hamburg as military discipline broke down.

Although the sailors had raised almost no political demands, and did not wish to overthrow the government or to overturn the

---

* The *Spartakusbund,* a radical pacifist and revolutionary group led by Rosa Luxemburg, Karl Liebknecht, and Leo Jogiches, had splintered off the left wing of the Social Democratic Party during the war. It formed the nucleus of the subsequent German Communist Party. *Trl.*

The Kaiser in exile at Doorn, Holland, 1919

monarchy, the latter fell as the first victim to the universal discontent.

It is true that Wilson's answer of October 23 had not stated formally that the Allies would not negotiate with Wilhelm II, but this demand could be read between the lines of the note. In the new government and in the *Reichstag,* the opinion gained ground that Wilhelm ought to abdicate to assure the German Empire of a better basis for the coming negotiations. When the Kaiser was appraised of this view, he wanted to march on Berlin at the head of his active army and "establish order"! In the end, however, he yielded to the promptings of the Chancellor, and to Hindenburg's counsel, and announced that he and the Crown Prince were abdicating the throne. Developments, however, had already passed beyond his control. Induced by the pressure of Berlin's working masses, and by his correct appraisal of the mood prevailing among the other social classes, the Social Democratic deputy Scheidemann had proclaimed the Republic from a balcony of the German *Reichstag* building. This was on November 9, 1918.

In the German states, too, the monarchies toppled one after the other. Neither the rank and file of the army, who had sworn a military oath, nor the people rose in their defense. Without fanfare or ceremony, the monarchs stepped off the stage of history. Their time was up. The idea of the monarchy, however, continued to play a role in Germany.

We have become accustomed to calling the events of November 1918 a revolution. Since the German people has had little liking for revolutions, nationalistic and reactionary groups wanted to bully them into believing that the republican and democratic forms of government had been forced upon them. The same considerations decided Hitler to coin his slogan of the "November criminals." It hides one of the most evil demagogic frauds concocted by poisonous Nazi propaganda.

The German events resembled other revolutions in that the government and the constitution were replaced, and that some isolated bloody incidents occurred. Sailors and soldiers patrolled the streets with loaded guns. But in Munich, for example, every-

Crowds watching funeral procession of sailors
killed on 9 November, 1918 *Ullstein*

thing passed so quietly that one acute political commentator stated in his memoirs that he had slept through the revolution. Upon entering his office one morning, he had found on his desk a proclamation of the new government, admonishing everybody to maintain calm. The revolution, he continued, succeeded because nobody opposed it: "It was fortunate that the defenders of the old order did not want to fight."[5] These revolutionaries felt, above all, no urge to revolutionize the whole social structure. In this respect, nothing changed: the nobles kept their estates, the officials retained their positions, and the industrialists their factories. Although the Social Democratic Party had for decades sworn to uphold a "revolutionary program," the majority of its members merely wanted a share in a parliamentary government as determined by democratic elections. The Independent Social Democratic party (USPD), which was more leftist, worked for a government by councils (Soviets) on the Russian model, but lacked enough influence and the kind of ruthless determination to adopt dictatorial measures which Lenin possessed.

Typical of November 9, 1918, was the style in which the Social Democratic deputies, Ebert and Scheidemann, were received in the Imperial Chancellory by Prince Max, in an atmosphere of dignity and calm to be invested with the burdens of their new offices. Otto Braun, a future Prussian Prime Minister, described the mood of the moment well:

> Strange thoughts came to me; I was filled with grave anxieties. Was it true that the centuries-old Empire of the Hohenzollern, so powerful, had disintegrated so completely and miserably? Who was to inherit it? It was an awesome legacy: two million dead, millions of widows, orphans, and wounded; the economy prostrate after four years of war— underfed children lying in paper shirts in their beds, metal turned into ammunition down to the last church bell, the last door knob—a people bled white through hunger and undernourishment, now joined by millions of more or less brutalized soldiers, flooding in from the front lines, asking for food and work. And, in the bargain, a government in debt beyond its assets and with its currency failing. The men who were to pick up the reins of government dropped by the previous rulers faced a tremendous, thankless task.

This was indeed true. The previous rulers disappeared without offering any resistance, and the Social Democrats were left to fill the void: to re-establish order and to prevent a Communist revolution. This, then, was the first great task facing the new government which had called itself, at first, the "Council of People's Representatives." It consisted of three members each of the Social Democratic and the Independent Social Democratic parties.

The "Spartacists" who constituted themselves as the Communist Party of Germany at the beginning of 1919 threatened to overthrow the government by violence. "Spartacists" in Berlin, the Ruhr area, and Central Germany continued to advocate a "Soviet Germany" patterned after Soviet Russia, while the Independent Social Democrats continued to accept majority rule by the Social Democratic majority. In January 1919 the Spartacist leaders Rosa Luxemburg and Karl Liebknecht were assassinated in Berlin.

If street fighting was to be stopped, the troops stationed in Berlin would have to be placed under a governor. Ebert offered the job to a fellow Social Democrat, Gustav Noske, who accepted with these words: "Someone must become the bloodhound; I am not afraid of the responsibility." This man, who in Churchill's words, "amid universal confusion acted without fear in a public cause," received no thanks for his courage. Communist propaganda taunted the Social Democrats with Bloodhound Noske for 14 years. Even less grateful were those whom his decisive measures

Spartacists in the streets of Berlin

Ullstein

Friedrich Ebert

Historisches Bildarchiv Handke

had saved from Communist terror. They came forward again as soon as the tide of left-wing radicalism had receded, and began to heap abuse on those who had done the dirty work for them.

With the appointment of Ebert as *Reich* Chancellor on November 9, 1918, the Armistice Commission entrained for negotiations with Marshal Foch. Wilson had announced the Allies' willingness to conclude peace on the basis of his Fourteen Points. The terms of the Armistice were designed to make any future counter-attacks by Germany impossible. German troops were required to evacuate occupied territory within 15 days, and great quantities of war material and transportation equipment were to be surrendered. In addition, all submarines, fighter planes, and bombers were to be handed over. Hindenburg sent the German Commission a telegram ordering them to sign even if the terms could not be modified, and thus the Armistice was signed in Compiègne on November 11.

With the conclusion of the Armistice the Allies began preparations for the Peace Treaty. The German people pinned their hopes on President Wilson and the Fourteen Points laid down in January 1918 as guidelines for the future peace. In the Fourteen Points, Wilson proposed that Belgium be restored, Alsace-Lorraine ceded to France, international guarantees be given to the Balkan states, an independent Poland be established, the frontiers be redrawn along lines of national self-determination, and, finally, that a "general association of nations" be established. Wilson had set forth his ideas with great conviction, and, since he represented a powerful nation, German hopes seemed well justified. They were all the more disappointed, therefore, when Wilson failed to assert himself against the English and the French, mainly because he had failed to rally American public opinion. Then, too, the USA never joined the League of Nations, which Wilson himself had proposed. Wilson, the idealist, deprived of backing in his own country, had to see his principles applied only where they favored the Allies, but disregarded when they would have benefited the German people. Thus, for example, the Bohemian (Sudeten) Germans were denied the right to national self-determination, and the Austrians, who wanted an *Anschluss* at the time, forbidden to join Germany.

The idea of national self-determination was to have a bright future in spite of its bad start. Under this banner subjugated colonials, too, fought for their liberty. No less significant for our day was the founding of the League of Nations, since it paved the way for the United Nations.

French views prevailed increasingly as the negotiations dragged on. They were represented by the tough and bitter "Tiger" Clemenceau, who had propagated the "idea of revenge" since 1870-71. He knew only one goal: Security for France! Realizing that there were 20 million more Germans than Frenchmen, he believed that security could only be won at the price of completely weakening the German economy. Thus, among other things, he demanded that the territory west of the Rhine be ceded to France. The English, however, were determined to reject this, since they did not wish to create "another Alsace-Lorraine," and had no interest in strengthening France too much at Germany's expense. In general, the English took a more moderate stand, especially when it came to supplying Germany with food. Lloyd George insisted

The Big Four at Versailles:
Lloyd George, Orlando, Clemenceau, and Wilson

that the German population be provided with grain and meat. But even this statesman, unfortunately, was under pressure from the passions still rankling the English public, and to secure his re-election, yet against his better judgment, he agreed to the imposition of heavy reparations against Germany.

What finally emerged was the evil result of hatred and fear. In a double sense, Schiller's phrase of "the evil deed which consistently bears more evil on its future course" was to come true. The Treaty of Versailles born of four years of hapless, mutual destruction became, in its turn, one of the causes of future misery.

But if one compares the harsh terms of the Treaty of Versailles with the demands of wartime annexationists in Germany, one is tempted to believe that the Allies had copied them. In any event, these German groups have least reason to complain that the spirits they had called up were now unleashed against Germany.

The victors were not satisfied with exploiting their new powers to the utmost, with the aid of the Treaty of Versailles. They also sought to justify the injustices created by this Treaty. French Premier Poincaré expressed this in typical fashion when he welcomed the delegates to the Peace Conference in Paris. Ten times the word "justice" was mentioned in his speech. There were references to a ridiculous program of world domination held by the German General Staff, to misdeeds never to be forgotten, to treacherous conspiracies, etc. Speaking to the Allies, Poincaré said:

> What endows you with any conceivable power to establish a just peace is that none of the nations that sent you here had a share in injustice. Humanity will trust you because you are not among those who violated the rights of humanity.

Out of such cant was born Article 231 of the Treaty, which sought to pin the guilt for the war exclusively on Germany, and more than any other clause poisoned this peace. One may concede to the victors that, at the time, not all details of the preliminaries to the World War were known yet. But what was maintained here in foolish haste, smacked much too clearly of their need for self-justification and of malicious slander of the defeated foe. If the Germans had been asked to pay because they had lost the war, and not for such "moral" reasons, reparations would have been much more acceptable.

These are some of the key terms of the Versailles Treaty:

> a. Territorial clauses: Alsace-Lorraine was to be returned to France. Substantial portions of the provinces Posen (Poznan), West Prussia, and Pomerania were restored to Poland, which had been reconstituted 124 years after it had last been divided up. The city of Memel and its surrounding district were occupied by French troops, and, later on, annexed by Lithuania. Danzig became a free city under the supervision of the League of Nations. The German colonies, too, were placed under the League of Nations and parcelled out as mandates, mostly to France and England. Plebiscites were arranged in some German frontier areas (such as Upper Silesia and Schleswig). The Saar Basin was to be administered by the League of Nations for 15 years, after which time its people would be permitted to decide its ultimate political status in a plebiscite.

b. Recognition of those European states created by the Treaty; of particular significance, the prohibition to annex German Austria to Germany (*Anschluss*).

c. Disarmament: Germany was not permitted universal military service, its professional army limited to 100,000 men. There was to be no air force. Nearly all available war material had to be surrendered. The left bank of the Rhine was to become a demilitarized zone, to be occupied by Allied troops for 5, 10, or 15 years, in order to guarantee compliance with the Treaty of Versailles.

d. Germany was to surrender so-called "war criminals." The former Kaiser also was indicted. (This part of the Treaty never took effect, because Germany refused to co-operate.)

e. Restitution (Reparations): Germany was to make good all the damages suffered by the Allies during the war. A Reparations Commission was to determine the amount.

Besides the catastrophic war guilt clause, the absurd demands for reparations contained in the Treaty also played a most disastrous role in the years to come. Germany might very well have contributed its fair share to the reconstruction of Belgium and France. It was ready and willing to do so. But it was an economic absurdity to believe that Europe could be torn apart into a "paying and a paid part," and that the damage suffered by the victors could be undone by heaping them manifold upon the defeated. It was still not realized that nobody can profit from another's impoverishment in the modern world, where all countries are economically interdependent.

The victorious powers (including Italy, which had thrown in its lot with the Entente in 1915) negotiated in Versailles for three months. Then the draft treaty was handed over to the German delegation. The chief German delegate rejected the war guilt clause, but, for the rest, acknowledged Germany's willingness to make up for the injustices done, especially to Belgium. He underlined the danger of the German economy collapsing under an exaggerated burden of restitution obligations, with unpredictable consequences also for the victors.

After the draft was made known, the Social Democratic Chancellor Scheidemann called the delegates of the National Assembly

Europe after the First World War

to Berlin. When its contents were revealed, there was naturally great dismay. Scheidemann on his side delivered a blazing speech, asking for the rejection of the draft treaty:

> This book must not become a code for the future. . . !
> What honest man—I do not even say, which German—what
> honest man, faithful to a contract, can accept such condi-
> tions? What hand will not wither that binds itself and us
> with such irons? In the opinion of the *Reich* government,
> this treaty is unacceptable. . . . If it is really to be signed,
> it will not be Germany's corpse alone which will lie on the

battlefield of Versailles. . . . Such a Treaty of Versailles would result in an unprecedented brutalization of all ethical and moral standards; it would usher in a period in which again . . . every man would be an enemy to every man.

One may ask today whether it would not really have been right to reject the Treaty. If one side no longer wished to fight, then it could have passively allowed the victors to occupy Germany completely, and then the Allies would have had to take full responsibility for the occupied country—as was the case after the Second World War in 1945. In 1919, too, they would have been forced to set up a government sooner or later, and would probably have realized much quicker that the economy of a nation, the foundation of its existence, cannot be destroyed with impunity. But, above all, the German Nationalists would have been prevented from ever attempting to identify Republic and democracy with self-abasement and dishonor. The acceptance of the Treaty was to serve them as an excellent pretext for this form of propaganda.

But it is always easier to be wiser after the event than at the moment of decision. The Germans of 1919 had no means of foretelling what would befall them if they rejected the draft treaty. They feared, above all, the catastrophic possibility of renewed bloodshed. They feared, too, that the blockade would be reinstituted, a move which would certainly have led to serious unrest and possibly a Bolshevik victory. They feared also that the already active "separatists" would succeed in tearing parts of the Rhineland from Germany, and that France and Poland would annex German territory in east and west.

How much the German government acted under duress was pointed out by Erzberger who was Finance Minister: "Who among us would refuse to sign if he were bound hand and foot, a gun pointed at his heart, and then be asked to sign a promise that he would fly to the moon within 48 hours? Duress knows no dishonesty."

The German National Assembly, by 237 to 138, accepted the draft as a dictated peace, not as a treaty, on June 23, 1919. On this occasion the right-wing party used tactics which were later to become familiar. Having ascertained that there was in the *Reichstag* a sufficient majority in favor of the Treaty (to which they

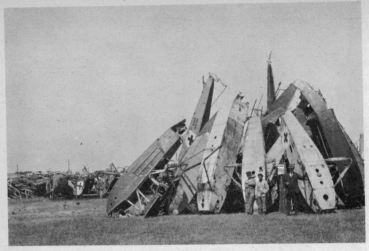

German planes scrapped under the terms of the Versailles Treaty

themselves saw no alternative), they declared themselves unanimously against it, thus establishing their innocence in the eyes of the nation. This use of cheap and shameless demagoguery was to prove sadly successful.

Once the Treaty was accepted, reasonable German statesmen could only try, on the one hand, to carry out their obligations and thus demonstrate their good will, and, on the other, to work for its piecemeal revision with dogged patience.

This first aim was frustrated from the very beginning when the crews of the German navy, interned at Scapa Flow, scuttled the fleet rather than surrender it, as the Treaty demanded. It is easy to understand that military and patriotic pride suggested this course —but politically it was hardly a wise move. More serious yet was the fact that the Germans, with their doubts and reservations about the Treaty, tended to regard all those who were obliged to implement the clauses therein as degraded political opportunists (*Erfüllungspolitiker*).*

* *Erfüllungspolitik* means literally a policy of fulfillment, i.e. compliance with the provisions of the Treaty of Versailles. *Trl.*

46

Hopes for gradual revision of the Treaty were by no means unfounded. Very soon critical voices were raised in the English-speaking countries. The Congress of the United States refused to ratify the Treaty. The United States, therefore, did not join the League of Nations. In England, John Maynard Keynes, professor of economics, published a polemical treatise against the Treaty which could be considered a model of that political self-criticism which has always flourished in England. (In contrast to Germany, where certain people, to this very day, denounce self-criticism as a form of mud-slinging.) Keynes stressed especially the need to reduce the demands for reparations, since they were economic nonsense.

Thus there was reason to believe that, one day, better judgment would prevail. In politics problems are resolved with passion as well as patience.[6] The gradual revision of the Versailles Treaty was a task for the politicians. The German people suffered because they were too passionate and lacked patience. This was true not only of its leaders but also of the common man, always more affected by the cries of passion than the voice of reason.

As the Treaty had shown, the right-wing parties, and above all the German Nationalists, had from the very beginning decided to leave the responsibilities and unpleasant obligations to other parties; they meanwhile inveighed against the "infamous treaty" and represented themselves to the German people as the only true patriots.

In this, the art of drawing political advantages from the "struggle against Versailles," the German Nationalists were soon to find an effective competitor. In 1924, Adolf Hitler, from his Landsberg prison, thus characterized the Versailles Treaty in *Mein Kampf*:

> When the peace treaty was imposed upon the German nation in 1919, one had reasonable hopes that this tool of boundless oppression would give a powerful boost to the German cry for liberty. . . . What could have been made of this Versailles Treaty! How a willing government might have used this instrument of outrageous blackmail and infamous oppression to heat the national passions to the boiling point!! How ingenious propaganda might have exploited these sadistic cruelties and turned the indifference

of the nation into indignation, and the indignation into the hottest fury! How one might have burned every single clause into the brains and the emotions of this people until the common shame and the common hatred would have turned into a raging ocean of fire, in sixty million men and women, until a will of steel would have risen from the flames and a cry would have been heard: We want weapons! Yes, this purpose the peace treaty could have served!

After his release from prison, Hitler began to follow his convictions. To repudiate the so-called "infamous treaty" was not an end but merely a means of gaining power.

4: Why Did the Weimar Republic Fail?

The first attempt made by the German people to adopt democratic self-government failed and ended in Hitler's dictatorship fourteen years later. It is extremely important for us to see why this happened. We have already established that it merely oversimplifies matters to say the Treaty of Versailles is responsible for the course of events. Nor can the economic crisis of 1929 and its severe effects be blamed for the failure of the Weimar Republic; the United States, and the other European nations, also suffered from the depression, yet they did not resort to dictatorships. Many factors had to coincide to drive so many Germans into Hitler's arms: foreign policy problems, the belated understanding of Germany's difficult situation on the part of the victors, the blindness and lack of willingness to assume responsibilities among some sections of the German nation—these were the strands of which the history of these years was woven.

The German Republic had been proclaimed on November 9, 1918. On January 19, 1919, elections were held for the German National Assembly which was to give Germany a new constitution. It was convened in Weimar, the city of Goethe and Schiller. Because the Republic received its constitution there, we call it the "Weimar Republic."

In the Weimar National Assembly, the Social Democrats controlled 163 votes, the Catholic Center Party 91, and the newly

The National Theater, Weimar, where the Assembly first met in 1919

founded Democratic Party 75. This gave the parties of the center and the moderate left 329 of 421 delegates, and enabled them to realize their common goal of giving Germany a democratic and parliamentary constitution.

Hugo Preuss, a professor of constitutional law, had been commissioned to draft the constitution. He patterned it after the constitutions of the United States, England, France, and Switzerland, and tried to combine the strong points of each. As in England and France of the time, the government was to originate in parliament (the *Reichstag*) and to be dependent on its confidence. For this reason, the system is called "parliamentary." (In contrast, the presidential system of the United States has the government, i.e. the President, elected by the people, and he cannot be voted out of office by parliament; whereas, according to the English consti-

49

tution and the traditional French constitution, the will of the people can be expressed only in parliament.) Hugo Preuss followed the Swiss model in providing for a direct referendum (the so-called *Volksentscheid*). The President of the *Reich* could initiate this process on his own authority, or it could be initiated through petitions signed by one tenth of the voters (*Volksbegehren*). This constitutional provision, which had proved its worth for four million people living in a small and compact area, was grafted onto the totally different conditions of the much larger German nation.

As in France, a president replaced the monarch as chief of state. But whereas in France the president was elected by delegates of local communal committees, Preuss suggested that in Germany he should be elected by the nation, as in the United States. There was another significant difference: in the American presidency, the roles of chief of state and chief executive are combined.

This mixture of alleged strong points taken from various constitutions was later to prove less than fortunate. Discussions of the draft in committee showed already that German politicians still thought in terms of a monarchy, and had barely grasped the meaning of a "parliamentary system," a method which only functions satisfactorily if the members of the government provide effective support for the ministers they have selected. As in the Kaiser's day, however, German parliamentarians still considered themselves as checks upon the government nominated by the Kaiser. They failed to grasp the fact that the government was now blood of their blood, and flesh of their flesh. Often they let themselves be guided by one overweening aim: to tie down the government and keep it from acting. This naturally weakened the young democracy.[7]

Thus, at its very beginning a major shortcoming was revealed in the Weimar Republic: the fact that its political knowledge lagged behind its constitution. The constitution was designed for a democratic people. It presupposed an extremely high confidence in the people, and frequently left the final decision to them. In reality, however, many Germans still hankered after the previous state authority, and were neither ready nor willing to justify the confidence placed in them.

It proved especially disastrous for the future that Article 22 of the Constitution had been based on an old Social Democratic demand whose far-reaching consequences had never been examined. The previous *Reichstag* had been elected by single-constituency voting (with run-off elections, if necessary); now the new Weimar Republic committed itself to proportional representation. The small electoral precincts were abolished and replaced by large election districts. After 1920, the latter lost all meaning. At that time "automatic procedure" was introduced, under which any 60,000 votes elected a representative, no matter where the votes had been cast. If the voters had concentrated their votes on two or three large parties, and if they really had accepted the idea of political parties and their functions, this electoral procedure might have proved adequate for want of a better. As it was, however, the system merely splintered the middle parties, and strengthened the extreme left and right wings.

If the old system of single-member constituencies had been retained, and if the long-awaited reform had been confined to the reorganization of electoral districts, the Social Democratic Party would probably have won a true majority. This would have shown clearly where power and responsibilities lay. As it was, the Social Democratic Party itself let the auspicious moment pass. Political paralysis soon ensued. However frequently the German people voted, and whomever they voted for, political majorities never changed drastically. The party leaders were assured of seats in every successive parliament, and they were certain to retain the reins of power. Thus in forming a new government each parliament (*Reichstag*) was basically faced with the same difficulties as its predecessor.[8] An electoral system which denies the voter the chance to change the fundamental distribution of political forces will either drive him to political apathy, or into the arms of those extremists who lure him with promises of radical reform in "this useless chatter shop."

On August 11, 1919, Friedrich Ebert, the German President elected by the National Assembly, promulgated the new Constitution. Its first section regulated the structure and function of the state. Although the reigning monarchs had been removed, and the princes no longer had to be considered, as in the days of Bismarck, the states remained as *Länder,* though their states' rights

President Ebert, with an entourage of generals, inspecting troops

Bettmann Archive

were curtailed. The second legislative chamber, besides the *Reichstag*, was the *Reichsrat*, composed of representatives of the *Länder* governments. The *Reich* President had extensive executive power. He was the supreme commander of the *Reichswehr*, and had the right to suspend any or all fundamental rights (civil rights) if public security and order were in danger, and, if necessary, he could use the armed forces to enforce his decisions (Article 48). As a further measure, he was permitted to dissolve parliament (Article 25). This last provision, in conjunction with Article 48, was later to become extremely important.

The nature of the government was most clearly characterized by the fact that not only the Chancellor was dependent upon the confidence of parliament, but that this was true of every single minister. "Any one of them must resign if the *Reichstag*, by formal resolution, withdraws its confidence from him" (Article 54). This provision, while essentially in agreement with democratic procedures, made it particularly easy for extremists at both ends of the political spectrum—while sharing no other goals or ideas—to join forces at any time and overthrow a government, thus endangering political stability.

While the Constitution of the Empire had not formally enumerated any civil rights, the Weimar Constitution followed the abortive Constitution of the National Assembly convened in St. Paul's Church [in 1848] and included a catalogue of fundamental rights and fundamental duties (Part II of the Constitution, Articles 109–165). It was thereby modeled on the American and French constitutions, and numerous other related basic laws influenced by them.

The day of August 11, when the Constitution was inaugurated, was declared a national holiday, but it never won the hearts of the German people as did the anniversary of the battle of Sedan, or the Kaiser's birthday in Wilhelminian Germany. This Constitution had not been born after a hard struggle; it was a privilege won without effort, and was thus "like children whom the stork brings: what the stork brings, the fox or the vulture may carry off in turn. Only a mother who bears a child will not let it be stolen, and, in the same way, a nation will not allow itself to be deprived of the rights and institutions for which it had to shed its blood. It can be truthfully said: the energy and love with which a people embraces and maintains its rights is proportionate to the labor and the effort it had expended to win them." [9]

Above all, the young Republic lacked democrats, that is men who were willing not only to accept those responsibilities necessary for democratic government, but to follow the rules of democracy by subordinating their own interests voluntarily to the common good. Democracy was widely considered a form of government which would function automatically, requiring neither effort nor dedication. That this was wrong and fraught with dire consequences will be shown later in more detail.

Even during war, Left Social Democrats, led by Karl Liebknecht and Rosa Luxemburg and known as the "Spartacus group," had pursued their own radical policies. On January 1, 1919, the group followed the Russian pattern and called itself

During the Spartacus uprising in Berlin, 1919   *Bettmann Archive*

"the Communist Party of Germany" (KPD). It attracted a relatively stable percentage of votes, about 10 per cent, rising to 14 per cent and 17 per cent during the Weimar Republic's years of crisis.

The Communists were open enemies of democracy. They called for a dictatorship of the Soviets on the Russian model, and during the restless post-war period, attempted more than once to achieve their goal by violence in Munich, Saxony, and the Ruhr district. They never joined a coalition government during the Weimar period, and specifically agitated against the Social Democrats, whom they denounced as traitors and, later on, as "social fascists." Such tactics, clearly influenced by Moscow, soon proved disastrous, for they merely aided the Nazis. Although Communists taught that Fascism originates when capitalists and large landowners join to stem the tide of revolution, the Communists in the

Reichstag joined the radical right most of the time in voting against all legislative proposals.

The Communists in Germany never enjoyed as much influence as their voting strength suggests. The KPD was by no means a revolutionary elite party on the Leninst model. This emerged especially when the Nazis seized power in 1933, and the KPD failed to trigger any strikes in protest. It was by no means "rooted in the masses" as it had claimed. But the large number of Communist voters afforded the Nazis a welcome pretext to scare people with "the red menace," which only Hitler would stop.

After 1918, the old conservative factions flocked especially to the German National People's Party (DNVP). Although the German Nationalists had first accepted the Republic, their program by 1920 included a demand for the restitution "of the German monarchy founded by the Hohenzollerns." They thereby acknowledged that they opposed the Republic, even though they granted parliament "a share in decision-making, and effective supervision." The *Reichstag* was to be supplemented by a chamber of "estates" based upon occupation. All those who scorned political parties and embraced the so-called "idea of the organic state" were attracted by this notion. Its basic anti-democratic attitude also induced the DNVP never to accept governmental responsibility, but to remain in opposition during the first hard years of the Republic. They continually mouthed the term "Fatherland" but did not want to lend a helping hand to this "Fatherland" to achieve its very limited political possibilities. For many years, the German Nationalists polled between 10 per cent and 20 per cent of the vote. By 1930 their share had dropped sharply to only 7 per cent of the vote under the impact of Nazism. They never recovered from this setback.

The National Socialist German Workers' Party (NSDAP) had grown out of a small group, which met in Munich in 1920 and called itself the Workers' Party. After attending some of its meetings, Adolf Hitler joined the executive committee of this party as member number seven. It was an obscure *Verein,* but Hitler seized on this very fact to take over its leadership and impose his ideas. Larger and more established parties would have offered him little chance of this kind. Since he was especially

1914—"Gentlemen, the whole people is behind us. We have the power! We are the Fatherland! So, a toast to His Majesty!"

1920—"The others have the power, why should we worry about the Fatherland? Let them do their own dirty work. Cheers!"

P. J. Hoffmann

Hitler with Julius Streicher at a meeting in Nuremberg, 1923

gifted in arousing the crowd, and had no scruples in choosing his methods for doing so, he succeeded in gaining further adherents, and soon he was filling even large halls. Slowly other, less dynamic *völkisch* (super-nationalist)* groups joined Hitler's

* The words *Volk* and *völkisch* were used by German nationalists in a way which renders them untranslatable. They carried overtones of a mystical and irrational kind, which evoked the Teutonic past, racial unity, collective memories of blood and soil, nationalism, and antisemitism. The words, as used by these groups, also denoted a vague romanticism and a glorification of military exploits and comradeship. *Trl.*

movement. The party now adopted the name NSDAP, and Gottfried Feder drew up a "program" for it which Hitler formally declared unalterable. With this program, the NSDAP did not immediately attack the Republic and democracy; it recognized, for example, the absolute authority of a central political parliament for all Germany.

For his own part, Hitler very clearly declared war on democracy from the very beginning. He gave free vent to his anti-democratic feelings in his book *Mein Kampf,* written in 1924. After reading this political concoction, nobody in Germany should have entertained the slightest doubts about Hitler's intentions. He called democracy an "institution beloved only by the most mendacious vagabonds operating under cover of darkness," and he denounced the *Reichstag* as an "association of babbling parliamentarians." Majorities, he declared, "always represent the stupid and the cowardly." Yet, on his side, he did not wish to dispense with the idea of democracy. He contrasted an allegedly "Jewish" democracy with "true Germanic democracy," which he defined "as freely choosing the Fuehrer who, in turn, must accept each and every responsibility for his actions. Under it, majorities will not vote on any single question; only one man will make the decisions and then stand up for them with his life and all else he possesses."

Here and in many other places, Hitler spoke quite candidly of his planned "leadership state" (*Führerstaat*). One might properly have asked why Hitler himself founded and led an opposition party, since he strictly opposed multi-party states. This, too, he explained openly and publicly in a speech in 1930:

> For us parliament is not an end, but a means to an end. . . . In principle, we are not a political party; otherwise we would fly in the face of all our convictions. We are a parliamentary party by necessity, and are forced to be so by the Constitution. . . . We do not fight for seats in parliament for their own sake, but for the day when we can liberate the German nation.

It goes without saying that such views made a coalition—implying co-operation within the existing state—out of the question. The NSDAP stood for opposition at any price. The party scored its first triumph at the polls (albeit in alliance with other groups of a similar hue, and under a false name) in 1924, while Hitler was in prison. At that time, it captured 32 seats in the *Reichstag* and 6.5 per cent of the vote. Before the year was out, a setback occurred from which it did not recover until the depression took hold in 1930. Then the party made its first real breakthrough; it received 18.3 per cent of the vote and 107 seats in parliament.

Thus, right from its inception the Weimar Republic was exposed to a crossfire coming from the two radical wings. It was vital then that it be able to rely upon those institutions which were not directly involved in the power struggle and upon whose services the Republic depended.

The first such institution was the judiciary. The independence of the judiciary, inherited from the Empire, was formally guaranteed by Article 102 of the Weimar Constitution. So much did the young Republic trust the independence of that body that it made no personnel changes in it. The new government failed, for example, to retire judges known for their anti-democratic attitudes, and to replace them with judges loyal to the Republic.

It soon developed, unfortunately, that the government's confidence had been misplaced. Politically rightist judges often used their discretionary powers in a way that was practically an abuse of power. This is illustrated by the sentences imposed for political crimes and *Putsches*. If the murderers or rioters belonged to the right, proceedings were frequently suspended or premature pardons granted. Where the defendants were left-wingers, however, maximum sentences were imposed. Of 354 political assassinations committed by rightists, 326 went unpunished, while only four of the 22 leftist assassins escaped punishment. Of 775 officers implicated in the radical-right Kapp *Putsch* of 1920, 91 were given leaves, 57 transferred to other commands, and 48 relieved of their duties, while proceedings were suspended in 486 cases.

Court decisions of this kind not only tended to undermine the people's sense of justice, but also were strong incitement to the radical right to further acts of violence. In this respect, the Weimar system of "political" justice prepared the way for the total breakdown of legal standards which was to follow. It must be noted, however, that no one was arbitrarily imprisoned, pro-

Ebert and Noske at amalgamation of the Bavarian Army
with the *Reichswehr*, 1920

Historisches Bildarchiv Handke

ceedings were conducted properly, and the right of the accused
to proper defense was not curtailed. In spite of some biased
judges, the Weimar Republic remained based on law (a *Rechtsstaat*).*

That no real revolution had occurred in November 1918 is
illustrated most aptly by the fact that the Republic also took over
the Empire's civil service without making any drastic changes.

---

* According to the *Staatslexikon* (Herder Verlag, Freiburg: 1961, 6th
rev. ed., VI, pp. 686-705), the concept of a *Rechtsstaat* implies a government (or state) limited in every action by statute law. This resembles the
traditional Western idea of a constitutional state. When it was first used in
its modern sense (by Robert von Mohl, a German political scientist of the
mid-nineteenth century), it carried overtones of Western libertarian ideas,
as for example elaborated in Germany by Immanuel Kant, Wilhelm von
Humboldt, and in the early writings of Fichte. With the advance of legal
positivism, however, the libertarian and constitutional implications were
de-emphasized. By the beginning of the twentieth century, a *Rechtsstaat*
was a state in which the rights and duties of citizens were clearly defined—however small the area of such rights may have been. It thus became
equated with formal legality, as opposed to an arbitrary tyranny, or a
"power-based state" (*Machtstaat*). More recent speculations on the *Rechtsstaat* tend to include elements derived from the natural rights tradition—
clearly a reaction to the Nazi experience. *Trl.*

It thus guaranteed that the bureaucratic machine would continue to function smoothly. But it also proved difficult, and frequently impossible, to breathe a democratic spirit into officials educated by an authoritarian state. Bureaucrats found many ways of vitiating progressive decrees through passive resistance. The state could not be made democratic by officials who were inherently opposed to democracy. These contradictions between political form and political loyalties affected the education of the young in an especially tragic fashion. Many teachers, still resenting the disappearance of the Empire, joined those who heaped contempt on the Republic, and even those of good will frequently lacked the skill to educate their young subjects in responsible citizenship.

The Versailles Treaty had allowed Germany an army of 100,000 men, the *Reichswehr*. In view of the nation's experiences with political generals in the First World War, it was now of the utmost importance that the new *Reichswehr* be firmly placed under political control. Therefore, it had to be provided with a corps of officers upon whom the Republic could rely in all circumstances.

Since the size of the army had been sharply reduced, it should not have been difficult to select, from among the rank and file returning from the front, a competent and reliable Officers' Corps. But even during its first few days the government of the Republic needed the support of the army to suppress Communist unrest. This led to a kind of agreement between the provisional government, led by Ebert, and the old army. The army presented its conditions as follows: "The Supreme Command expects the government to co-operate with the Officers' Corps in suppressing Bolshevism and in maintaining the discipline of the army."

Thus the moment had passed for shaping a new Officers' Corps. The army had indeed sworn fealty to the Republic, but how this oath was interpreted was demonstrated as early as 1920, when the East Prussian Provincial Director General, Kapp, a right-wing radical, attempted a *Putsch*. Instead of protecting the government and taking action against the regiments supporting Kapp, the Commander of the Army, General von Seeckt, declared: *"Reichswehr does not shoot at Reichswehr!"* He kept the troops in the barracks, and even offered to serve as an intermediary between the government and the rebels, as if the *Reichswehr* were some

Lieutenant-General Hans von Seeckt
Historisches Bildarchiv Handke

neutral power able to throw its support at will onto one side or another.

But when violence erupted shortly afterwards in the Ruhr through Communist instigation, the *Reichswehr* moved without hesitation, and the officers swung into action as soon as they had to march against left-wing *Putschists*. Thus the *Reichswehr* functioned as "a state within the state." It also secretly and independently sought to evade the disarmament clauses of the Versailles Treaty, thus undermining the efforts made by Foreign Minister Stresemann in London and Geneva. At every critical juncture, political leaders had to ask: "Will the *Reichswehr* back us up?" instead of relying upon its loyalty.

Thus the democratic forces could not rely on those institutions whose manifest duty was to stay out of party politics and remain absolutely loyal to the Republic. Yet, the democratic position was not totally unfavorable at the start. Forces friendly to democracy formed a compact and promising majority. In the first parliament of 1920, the democratic parties collectively had captured 82 per cent of the popular vote; in the last free *Reichstag* election of 1932, a mere 39 per cent remained. These two figures reveal the tragic fate of a democracy which could find no middle way between impractical dogmas and overly narrow egotistical interests.

Of all democratic parties in the Weimar Republic, the Social Democratic Party (SPD) attracted the largest number of members. Its tenets were based on long historical tradition, and it was a close-knit organization, consisting of party workers and leaders, many of whom had proven their worth in the trade-union movement. Its program, originating from Marx and Engels, advocated a classless society and equal opportunities for all. In the course of several decades the party's program for achieving these goals had changed several times. Since a large portion of votes had gone to the SPD, a revolution was unnecessary, as the peaceful conquest and penetration of the state appeared to be within reach. Along these lines, the SPD pursued a very moderate and sober policy, and gave some internal stability to the democratic Republic after 1918.

When the Communists, under Moscow's control, began to organize themselves and gain influence, the SPD's struggle for the labor vote faced new difficulties. The Communists claimed that they alone interpreted Marxist theory correctly, whereas the SPD "betrayed" the dogma of the revolution as well as the workers. Under such competitive pressures from the left, the SPD failed to adjust its traditional views of the class struggle to the new social realities. At times this created the situation where SPD deputies in the *Reichstag,* in deference to their Marxist voters, were obliged to vote against proposals made by ministers of their own party.

The gulf between ideal and reality was felt especially by younger people. Many of them were attracted by Communist logic and the opportunities for a rapid rise to political leadership. Demagogues of the right-wing parties made their own use of this by equating Social Democrats with Communists and frightening the citizenry with the "Red menace." Thus it was possible that as the years went by, the SPD which had entered the Weimar National Assembly with 38 per cent of the vote was reduced to 20 per cent in the election of November 6, 1932, in spite of its excellent organization and a faithful core of voters.

The second largest party—the Center Party—was also the most stable. As a Catholic party, it drew votes from all strata of society. This forced it to compromise between various interests *within* the party, and made it typically a moderate, middle-of-the-road party. It played an important part in the Weimar Republic, since its position in the center of the political spectrum meant that no government could be formed at any time against its interests, or without its participation. A frequent ally of the Center Party was the Bavarian People's Party, which had been founded by Bavarian deputies of the Center Party and which favored states' rights, at times to the detriment of common party interests. In all parliaments of the Weimar Republic, the Center Party and the Bavarian People's Party together controlled about 15 to 20 per cent of the votes.

In sharp contrast was the liberal German Democratic Party, which counted among its ranks some of the most outstanding personalities—Friedrich Naumann, Theodor Heuss, Max Weber, and Walther Rathenau. It had controlled 19 per cent of the votes in the National Assembly, but soon lost half of its votes and declined to an insignificant minority. In the last free *Reichstag* elections, the German Democratic Party, under its new name of State's Party (*Staatspartei*), did not even poll 1 per cent of the popular vote. German voters had little love for the liberal program offered by the party, and so it turned into a so-called "party of notables" attracting some top brains, but few members.

A somewhat more right-wing liberalism was for a while, with visible success, represented by the German People's Party which had gathered up the former National Liberals and had attracted Gustav Stresemann as its most outstanding political leader. In the National Assembly, it had won only 4 per cent of the vote and, as early as the *Reichstag* elections of 1920, voted in large numbers for the Nationalists. For a time the party retained 8 per cent to 10 per cent of the vote, until 1932, when it shared the fate of the German Democratic Party and was crushed between extremists.

All the hopes of the young democracy rested on these four parties—the Social Democratic Party, the German Democratic Party, the Center Party, and the German People's Party. They

A ballot paper for 1932 showing 27 party choices

entered into various changing coalitions with each other, and formed altogether 17 governments, including the Brüning government of 1932. Seven times, the SPD was represented in these governments, but the government was composed more frequently of parliamentary minorities obliged to rely upon the SPD—not itself a member of the government—for support if it wanted to retain office. Such an ill-defined situation, which knew no clear lines of responsibility nor a loyal opposition (both left and right opposition parties were destructive), did little to win the voting masses for democracy.

Even more confusing was the distressingly large number of small, even minute, splinter groups clinging to the major parties. They did not advocate programs hostile to the Republic, or to democracy, but used the opportunities offered by universal suffrage for the sole purpose of exploiting the *Reichstag* as a sounding board for their special interests. Among these notorious 27 or 28 parties in the Weimar Republic there were some whose aims had nothing to do with genuine politics. This is demonstrated by titles such as "Revalorization Party," or a "Tenants' League," a "House- and Land-Owners Party," or a "Peasants' and Vintners' League," etc. The largest of these groups, the "Economy Party," represented the interests of the middle classes. The large parties often needed these groups to form their coalitions, with the result that the influence of these groups in politics was out of all proportion to their true importance.

A glance at a ballot of this period explains why the voters were appalled by this turmoil, why they felt that parties did not represent the will of the people, but merely served as a pretext for selfish interests. Hitler's task was rendered easier by the already deep dissatisfaction with the existing party system.

A description of the politics of the Weimar Republic would be incomplete without mentioning the para-military organizations which played an increasing role in the political wars. At first they helped to recruit new members for certain parties and served as "security guards" for meetings (*Saalschutz*), or as strong-arm squads. In the end they turned into centers for the unemployed and, eventually, more or less well-armed private armies of the party leaders.

Among such organizations, the first and largest was the *Stahlhelm* (steel helmet), founded as a veterans' organization as early as 1918. It immediately drifted to the right, called the November upheavals "swinish," and poisoned political battles by heaping scorn upon the "black-red-and-gold" flag of the Republic. They ridiculed it by calling it "black-red-and-mustard," and themselves flew the [old Imperial] black-white-and-red flag on every occasion. Unfortunately the governments of the Republic tolerated such provocations, and took little notice of the controversy about the flag.

Meanwhile, Republican sympathizers soon came to understand that they had to counter the *Stahlhelm* with a similar organization. Thus, in 1924, they founded an "Association of German Veterans and Republicans" which became known as *"Reichsbanner Black-*

Spirited campaigning in Berlin: Some members of the right-wing Young German Order (in cars) encounter a *Reichsbanner* group
Ullstein

Red-Gold." The *Reichsbanner* originated with workers' guards close to the SPD; they were joined by sympathizers from the Center and German Democratic Parties, and thus gained a broad organizational base.

Hitler, meanwhile, had introduced Storm Troopers (*S.A.*) into his meetings as early as 1921. They were organized along military lines by Ernst Röhm, a former captain whom Hitler made Chief of Staff of the Storm Troopers. Hitler regarded the Storm Troopers as the "physical" expression of the party's power.

The "Red Veterans' League" completed the circle of these paramilitary groups. It was under Communist control, and followed the party line also in considering the *Reichsbanner* as its main enemy and competitor. It was always outnumbered by the other organizations.

During the last years of the Weimar Republic, when election or party rallies were held, these para-military troopers usually controlled the entrances to halls and lined up on both sides of the rostrum so as to protect the speaker. A political opponent who wanted to speak at such a meeting either had to have lots of courage, or adequate protection of his own. At the end, election campaigns turned into veritable battles in halls and in the street. Thus verbal battles had given way to brutal terrorism.

Politically, the first years of the Weimar Republic were full of leftist revolts and *Putsches* attempted by the right. Meanwhile, its economy declined progressively as its currency deteriorated. This inflation, which resulted in a depreciation of the mark to a worthless value, seems unmitigated madness to economists today. It probably would never have grown to such proportions if the ignorance of influential financial experts about monetary policy had not been compounded by economic egotism, particularly of the big industrialists, and by the paralyzing burden of reparations which dispelled the last vestiges of economic common sense.

The Weimar Republic inherited considerable inflation as an inevitable legacy of the war. Even by 1918, Germany was hit harder by it than, for example, England, where the costs of the war had been financed through increased taxation. The English knew they would never see a penny of this money again, for who has ever heard of a state refunding taxes? But the Germans had invested in war bonds throughout the war years; investors now owned certificates for which they expected to receive interest, and which they assumed, at some future day, would be redeemed by the government. Owners of war bonds thus fancied themselves as rich as ever before. The English system was fashioned for free citizens, of whom painful sacrifices could well be demanded, while the Germans saw only subjects who had to be duped into compliance.

By 1918, the mark had already lost two-thirds of its value as against the dollar. And government expenditures were not

Inflated German money

financed through taxes but through newly printed money. The faster money was printed, the quicker it depreciated. Although Matthias Erzberger, on coming to the thankless position of Finance Minister in 1919, did impose drastic new taxes, he did not stop the printing presses, and so depreciation continued. Banking experts such as Havenstein, the president of the *Reichsbank,* were sadly ignorant, and justified their measures by pontificating that Germany had to import more than it exported, and was thus forced to print bank notes in order to cover its international trade deficit. Havenstein even boasted before the *Reichsrat* of his technical efficiency which made possible a daily output of 46 billion printed marks! On this occasion, an English observer remarked that such a man would be hanged in any country where sound views on monetary policy prevailed!

Industrialists who perhaps should have known better, and probably did, failed to protest because they owned extensive real estate, and thus profited from monetary collapse. They were allowed to pay their debts with depreciated money, for the courts still

Waiting at a soup kitchen in a Berlin tenement, 1922

compounded the madness by ruling that "mark equals mark." As a result, conversions into gold mark were not legal. A debt of 100,000 Reichsmark, which two months previously would have bought a house, could be repaid with 100,000 Reichsmark, which, at the time of payment, might just buy a bureau or a loaf of bread. At that time, Hugo Stinnes built up his trust by buying up weaker companies, thereby concentrating an economic power in his hands which was unequaled even in America. Many others followed his example.

The main victims of the inflation were people who subsisted on interest from savings. These unfortunate people, their assets dissolved, had to put aside their pride and seek public assistance. Civil servants, employees, and workers, too, were affected. Wages agreed upon only a few days previously often lost half their value by payday. For this reason, officials and employees were not paid at the end of the month any longer, but in instalments. The flood of money rose, calculations continually had to be revised, and prices changed daily, as the ratio between mark and dollar shifted. In the end, the dollar preoccupied German minds so exclusively that even schoolchildren knew its precise value.

The question arises today as to why a whole nation let itself be exploited by such policies. To answer this, we must recognize a nationalist motive which existed along with the general lack of sophistication in monetary policies. Some people believed that the complete collapse of the currency would persuade the Allies to terminate reparations payments. The burden of reparations, too, certainly added to the inflation, but it was by no means its only cause, as is often maintained. It is against this background of economic pandemonium that the political events of the period 1919 to 1923 were enacted.

The unrest instigated by the Communists during the first few months after the revolution culminated in the proclamation of a Soviet Republic in Bavaria. Then, in March 1920, the first attack from the right came when the *Ehrhardt Brigade,* a former free corps, and some regular detachments of the *Reichswehr,* led by Director General Kapp, occupied Berlin, and drove out the government, then headed by the Social Democratic Chancellor Bauer. The people in general did not join in; the *Reichswehr,* instead of fighting for its government, remained "neutral." Trade unions, however, sided with the threatened Republic and proclaimed a general strike. It was carried out in a disciplined manner and, after four days, led to the collapse of the *Putsch.* The civil service, to its credit, also refused to co-operate with the rebels and rebuffed Kapp, when the self-styled chancellor asked the *Reichsbank* for 10 million marks in order to continue his treasonable activities.

Of greater consequence than this wholly amateurish and foolish *Putsch* was the turmoil which seized the workers after their successful general strike. The Communists, taking advantage of this confusion, then decided to test the strength of the government. Armed Communists attempted to occupy a few cities; people were massacred and mistreated; there was plundering; and the population in general was terrorized. "Communist elements clearly aimed at destroying the whole fabric of governmental powers," said Carl Severing, then Federal and State Commissioner in the Ruhr. The unrest was finally controlled with troops, who, in their turn, frequently engaged in arbitrary and one-sided reprisals. Historical experience again proved that "one form of terrorism is as bad as another." Further Communist outbreaks followed in central Germany and in Hamburg a year later, but newly strengthened police power proved strong enough to suppress the rioters.

During that same year of 1921, negotiations continued in Paris and London to determine the amount of reparations to be paid by Germany. At first, the amount was fixed at 269 billion gold marks, payable over a period of 42 years, then at 132 billion marks payable in 37 years. The harassed German government, under the pressure of reprisal (the French occupation of Düsseldorf, Duisburg, etc.), was compelled to accept this "financial ultimatum." Thus began a series of conferences about the problem of reparations, and the Allies soon realized that any lack of cooperation was due not entirely to German ill will but to the simple fact that money was not readily available. Payment schedules were discussed in Wiesbaden during the same year (1921), followed by discussions in Cannes and Genoa (1923), and, at frequent intervals, in London.

The Weimar Republic achieved its first success in foreign policy with the Rapallo Treaty, which Foreign Minister Rathenau concluded with the Soviet Union in April 1922. The treaty provided for the re-establishment of diplomatic relations, and declared as void all claims arising out of the war between Russia and Germany. The treaty aroused strong feelings and suspicion among the Western powers because Germany and the Soviet Union had broken out of their isolation for the first time. And, indeed, this treaty owed its existence to the fact that Allied inflexibility had maneuvered Germany into a desperate situation. Even today, whenever there is concern in the West that Germany might once again seek a separate understanding with the Soviet Union, "Rapallo" is frequently cited.

Two months later, after concluding this treaty in Germany's interest, Rathenau was assassinated. A year earlier, Matthias Erzberger had been murdered by two former officers of the *Ehrhardt Brigade,* who had escaped to Hungary. Erzberger paid with his life because, as the representative of the German government, he had signed the Armistice which Ludendorff and Hindenburg had

Walther Rathenau in the car in which he was assassinated

so urgently demanded. The partisans of the stab-in-the-back legend never forgave him for this.

Walther Rathenau, one of the "most intelligent, educated, and
far-seeing Germans," suffered the same fate. Being both Jewish
and an ardent patriot, he was the object all through his life of
antisemitic prejudices, especially from nationalistic groups in Germany. On June 24, 1922, misguided young antisemites killed him
with guns and grenades. One of the assassins was shot when apprehended, the other committed suicide soon afterwards. A third
accomplice, Techow, was brought to trial. What he said about
his motives during his trial reveals his total lack of a sense of reality and the world of fantastic hallucinations in which he lived.
Rathenau, said Techow, was a "creeping Bolshevist," one of the
300 "wise men of Zion," who wanted to apply the theories of the
"Jew Lenin" to Germany. (The so-called Protocols of the Wise
Men of Zion, an antisemitic forgery revealing an alleged global
conspiracy of Jews, were then being widely disseminated in Ger-

many.) Such were the muddleheads who "dared take politics into their bloody and violent hands."[10]

The workers demonstrated their horror of Rathenau's murder by holding a 24-hour strike and by organizing mass meetings. The cabinet decided to invoke Article 48 of the Constitution and asked the *Reich* President to promulgate a "law for the protection of the Republic." It must be admitted, however, that the revulsion was by no means universal. As in the case of Erzberger's assassination, certain political groups saw nothing improper in disposing of a political enemy in this infamous manner, and regarded the assassins as heroes and martyrs. This prepared the way for an even more extreme brutalization of the mind.[11]

During the summer of the same year, the mark declined ever more threateningly. The dollar had reached a thousand times its pre-war value. From then on, the value of the mark fell at an ever increasing rate. Several times Germany asked for a moratorium on payments, but was refused because France still hoped that defaults in payment would allow her to realize her long-standing plan of separating the Rhine-Ruhr area from the rest of Germany. Poincaré, then French Premier, cited the fact that Germany had defaulted on deliveries of coal, lumber, and telegraph poles as his reason for sending French troops into the Ruhr on January 11, 1923.

Since armed resistance had no chance of success, the *Reich* Government called upon the population to resist passively. The Germans were of one mind and were willing to make sacrifices in this hour of need. In the Ruhr area, workers refused to load the coal, and the railroad men would not move it to France. They were tried before French military courts, or deported from the French zone of occupation. The rest of Germany cordially received these expellees; and strikers even received financial aid from the government.

Passive resistance was a dignified measure, well-suited to demonstrate abhorrence of acts of violence and extortions. But it was hardly a weapon which could decide the issue in this situation. To a certain extent, the French overcame the resistance by such measures as running the railroads with their own personnel. To a certain extent, too, the measures backfired against the originators;

74

French troops occupy Essen in the Ruhr, January 1923 *Ullstein*

hundreds of thousands lost their jobs wherever the mines closed down. To provide money for the unemployed, the printing presses worked overtime. At the height of this madness, 62 printing firms worked around the clock, printing paper money! Every single month, from August to October 1923, money in circulation increased tenfold. By this time, even big business was calling for sound currency.

Gustav Stresemann, who formed a new government in August 1923, was willing to take the unpopular measure of breaking off passive resistance. The historian Erich Eyck acclaimed this step with the following words:

> Not only clear insight but also a high degree of courage would be required by any statesman who, under these circumstances, decided to give up the passive resistance in the Ruhr. Stresemann possessed this bravery as well as this vision. On September 26 a proclamation of the President

75

and of the cabinet announced the end of the resistance in the Ruhr. "To preserve the life of the nation and the state, we are confronted now by the bitter necessity of ceasing our struggle." This was by no means a rhetorical exaggeration. It was the simple description of a frightening set of facts. All the screams of protest that these words evoked, all the rebellious stirrings that they unleashed, in no way alter the fact that at this moment Stresemann showed himself a true stateman who should be honored by his nation for having taken the right step when to do so was as difficult as it was necessary.

With the collapse of passive resistance in her zone of occupation, France offered support to some separatist adventurers who wanted to split off the Rhineland from the German *Reich*. This maneuver, however, met with failure in both Aachen and the Palatinate. The population did not join in, and the English who had followed a "wait and see" policy when the French marched into the Ruhr, now definitely condemned France's actions. For the

Rollcall of a separatist group, 1923

present, however, France continued to occupy her "productive securities" in the Ruhr for two more years.

Another important step taken by the Stresemann government was to stop the printing of paper money. The new rates made 1,000,000,000,000 Reichsmark equal to one new *Rentenmark*. Since Germany lacked sufficient gold reserves to return to its previous gold standard, confidence in the new currency was created by basing it on a mortgage-like security imposed on all German real estate. Later on, when more gold reserves had been accumulated, the *Rentenmark* was replaced again by the Reichsmark. At last, Germany had a currency that served as a universal means of exchange and retained its value in savings accounts. Prior to this, people had resorted to barter trade, and had spent their paper money as quickly as possible, in order to avoid losses. This point marked the beginning of a real economic and political recovery in Germany.

Shortly thereafter, an incident occurred which, although of little significance at the time, was instigated by men who were to play a disastrous role at a later stage. Adolf Hitler, whose National Socialist Party had already been mentioned, had by means of incessant propaganda increased the number of his followers. At that time there were many such failures who fancied they had a special bent for politics. Former officers like Ernst Röhm and Hermann Göring joined disillusioned intellectuals like Josef Goebbels or Alfred Rosenberg to find common ground in fanatical Nationalism and antisemitism. They recognized early that Hitler's talent for propaganda could enhance their own futures.

Hitler had been the only party chief who had not accepted the spontaneous political "moratorium" (*Burgfrieden*) self-imposed by the German parties. Instead, he kept hammering into the heads of his followers that his motto continued to be not "Down with France!" but "Down with the November criminals!" As a result, Prussia and some other *Länder* dissolved his party under a law for the protection of the Republic. In Bavaria, however, the nationalistic government under Kahr gave Hitler free rein to spread his propaganda; this emboldened him to ally himself with General Ludendorff and a few hundred volunteers (the so-called *Hundertschaften*) in an attempt to overthrow first the Bavarian, then the

Hitler and associates on trial: Pernet, Weber, Frick, Kriebel, Ludendorff, Hitler, Brückner, Röhm, and Wagner *Copress*

Reich government. His *Putsch* collapsed even faster than the Kapp *Putsch*. And it did so not through a general strike, but by means of a police force smaller than the armed bands with which Hitler and Ludendorff marched on the Munich *Feldherrnhalle*. One volley of gunfire and the threat melted. One would have thought this "mad and hopeless foolishness" sufficient to discredit Hitler politically for all time.

In April 1924, the *Putschists* were brought to trial before a people's court in Munich. Shortly before, it had sentenced a young man, Felix Fechenbach, to eleven years hard labor for high treason because he had made public a telegram that had been years old and was hardly secret any longer. Now the same judges saw fit to sentence Hitler to five years of mild imprisonment, and promised him parole after six months, in spite of the obvious fact that Hitler had skillfully exploited the trial and boasted loudly of his high treason. Here once again, German judges carried the torch for right-wing radicalism.

The younger generation may regard the period of the Weimar Republic as sad and disillusioning because it ended in failure, and because Hitler was allowed to blacken its image with the propaganda slogan of "fourteen years—a field of ruins." Such stereotyping, however, obscures the rich intellectual life that developed during these very years of recovery.

Heinrich and Thomas Mann, Hermann Hesse, and Ricarda Huch wrote their great works in this era. Many brilliant writers like Stefan Zweig, Bruno Frank, and Leonhard Frank, lyric poets like Franz Werfel and Stefan George and his "circle" were widely read and admired. The Berlin *Deutsches Theater* gained fame far beyond the borders of Germany. Great conductors like Otto Klemperer, Bruno Walter, and Wilhelm Furtwängler inspired their audiences. Painters and architects met in "the Dessau *Bauhaus*" and created a new and purer style for plastic arts. Great educators with their enthusiasm stimulated adult education classes, school communities, and progressive boarding schools. Journalists engaged in sharp and brilliant political debates. Small independent periodicals of the left, like *Die Weltbühne* or *Das Tagebuch* (the latter about the size of a school note-book), countered events with effervescent comments and criticism, which amused the readers and spared nothing and nobody. At the same time, they unwittingly provided ammunition for those who denounced such pub-

Ricarda Huch

Thomas Mann

Archiv für Kunst u. Geschichte

lications as "destructive" and "typical" of the so-called *System* of the Weimar Republic. On the right—although they did not want to be politically classified as such—outstanding writers like Ernst Jünger, Ernst Niekisch, and others acquired both loyal followers and indignant opponents. These literary groups did not suffer from hardened intellectual arteries or a sense of alienation. They committed themselves to specific ideologies, philosophies, and theories. Yet, while committing themselves completely to ideas, they failed to strike those hard-headed bargains which are the life blood of politics. The day was not far off when all this wonderful intellectual life was to be trampled underfoot by pure activists.

The years of recovery were with good reason regarded as "the Stressmann Era," for the distinguished statesman of the Weimar Republic well deserved such recognition. He was one of those political figures able to profit from history and their own experiences, and point toward new goals and new directions. During the First World War, Stresemann had supported the Pan-German policy of annexations. Afterwards, he definitely renounced all ideas of this kind and turned to a sober and moderate policy of reconciliation within the country and abroad.

Stresemann was only Chancellor for a few months. His cabinet was overthrown in November 1923 because the Social Democrats, in deference to the feelings of their voters, withdrew their support, although they knew full well that no other Chancellor would co-operate with them as smoothly as Stresemann had.

For six years thereafter, Stresemann held the position of Foreign Minister in every German cabinet. Patiently and persistently he worked for German-French reconciliation during this period. But it was one of the tragic events in his life that his own party, the German People's Party, and the German Nationalists whom he had courted so frequently continually obstructed his efforts. His policy which benefited Germany so greatly had to depend increasingly on the support of the Center Party and the Social Democrats.

The Dawes Plan was the first sign that common sense was again returning to economic life. This plan is named after the American financial expert, Charles Dawes, chairman of an international commission of specialists who convened to re-open the reparations question in 1924. The new principle was: "Business, not

Politics." Therefore, precise distinctions were introduced between the "capacity to pay" reparations and their transfer to debtor countries. Nothing else would prevent the German currency which had been restored with such effort from losing value once again. Germany merely had to deposit the goldmarks agreed upon in the account of the Agent General for Reparations; their transfer or "conversion" into the currencies of the debtor countries was to be arranged through him. Annual rates were fixed at 2.5 billion marks, the full amount to be payable beginning with 1928. Until then, recovery was to be stimulated by keeping the annual rates low. The German state-owned railroad was to be transformed into a corporation, and a share of its earnings earmarked as securities for reparations. The occupation of the Ruhr was condemned, and through another recommendation Germany was granted a loan of 800 million goldmarks for her return to the gold standard.

Quickly recognizing the advantages of this plan, the German business associations unanimously recommended its adoption. In the *Reichstag,* however, the German Nationalists kept up an irresponsible opposition, and declaimed against "enslavement" and the "war guilt lie." Only when the *Reich* President, as a last resort, threatened to dissolve parliament unless it voted for the Dawes Plan did 48 out of 100 German Nationalists switch sides and vote for its adoption. The German Nationalists had wavered because they had feared to lose votes in a forthcoming election.

While foreign relations were gradually improving, German domestic affairs were changed by an event whose far-reaching significance was only appreciated much later. Friedrich Ebert, the first President of the Republic, died on February 25, 1925. Although his untimely death at the age of 54 was not caused by the bullets of political assassins, it was hastened, in the opinion of his friends, "by the infamous vilifications which an utterly biased press heaped upon him until his dying day." All along, certain circles of society had looked down on the former upholsterer, while others spoke or wrote contemptuously of "Fritze* Ebert." His political enemies even accused him of high treason, because in January 1918 he had participated in a strike of munitions workers. These accusations

* A derogatory Berlin colloquialism. *Trl.*

81

The funeral of President Ebert: Potsdamer Platz, Berlin, 1925

never ceased, even though it had been proven in the courts that Ebert had advanced the interests of national defense, for by joining up with the strike-leaders he had helped bring the strike to a quick close. Now once again the German Nationalists smeared him with accusations of complicity with the Barmat brothers, who were at the time on trial for corruption. As he wanted to clear his name, Ebert postponed necessary surgery. When he took his doctors' advice, it was too late.

In the view of Gerhart Hauptmann the writer, Ebert was a warmhearted and courageous man who had saved Germany in her greatest hour of need. Ebert, said Hauptmann, had faced problems that could no longer be ignored, and solved them with quiet strength, unceasing compassion, and firm determination. The historian Erich Eyck wrote that Germany had reason to feel proud because "a man who excelled in political common sense, mature judgement, and moral integrity had risen from the lower ranks." Yet, even the workers did not always respect the man who had risen from their ranks. Stresemann may well have been right when he observed: "The truth is that the German people want no President in a top hat . . . He must wear a military uniform, and plenty of decorations. . . ."

A general wearing plenty of decorations was in fact elected as the second President of the Weimar Republic on April 16, 1925. In the first vote German voters had a choice among seven candidates, ranging from Thälmann, on the extreme left, to Ludendorff, on the extreme right. Jarres, the Mayor of Duisburg, who was backed by the parties of the right (German People's Party and German Nationalist Party) received the largest number of votes, but not the majority of the votes cast. This made a run-off election necessary, which would be decided by a simple majority. Only the strongest combination of parties could hope to win.

FIRST VOTE (VOTE IN MILLIONS)		PROJECTED VOTE BEFORE RUN-OFF ELECTION	ACTUAL VOTE IN RUN-OFF ELECTION
Ludendorff (NSDAP)[1]	0.2		
Jarres (DVP,DNVP) [2,3]	10.7	Hindenburg 11.9	14.6
Held (BVP)[4]	1.0		
Marx (Center Party)	4.0		
Hellpach (Democrats)	1.5	Marx 13.3	13.7
Braun (SPD)[5]	7.8		
Thälmann (Communists)	1.8	Thälmann 1.8	1.9

[1] NSDAP–National Socialist German Workers' Party (Nazis)
[2] DVP–German People's Party (Right Center)
[3] DNVP–German National People's Party (Conservative)
[4] BVP–Bavarian People's Party (Catholic)
[5] SPD–Social Democratic Party

With this in view, the Center Party, Democrats, and Social Democrats agreed upon a single candidate, former *Reich* Chancellor Marx. The right-wing parties believed that Jarres, a little known Mayor, could not win against this coalition, and offered the candidacy to Field Marshal von Hindenburg, who at the age of 78 was living in retirement in Hanover. He accepted, after some hesitation, and won the election by 14.6 million votes. Thus, a monarchist soldier secured a larger middle-class vote than the middle-class candidate Jarres. Rightist election strategy had proven correct. In the final analysis, however, Hindenburg's victory was due to the Communists, who had renominated Thälmann, although he had no chance of success, and thus had split the vote of the middle-of-the-road republican candidate.

How this vote would affect future events could not yet be anticipated. But, even at the time, it was clear that Germany now had a President who, while he would abide by his oath of office and do his duty, had no love for the Republic. Hindenburg, as confirmed a monarchist as there was, had never forgiven himself for advising his Emperor to flee to Holland on November 9, 1918. Having a military rather than a political mind, Hindenburg had originated the stab-in-the-back legend, because he needed to justify his military defeat, and by doing so had provided the enemies of the Republic with a potent weapon. In politics, he depended totally on his advisers, which was to prove disastrous during the last years of his presidency. With his election, the friends of democracy lost an influential office to their enemies. The Republic was still in its infancy and needed careful husbanding in order to strike roots in

Final session at Locarno, 1925

Aristide Briand   *Popper*

the hearts and minds of the people, but now it had a President who himself did not believe in republican government. Nowadays we are more aware of its significance since the late Federal President Theodor Heuss, elected under the new Basic Law, demonstrated that a true democrat can turn the office of President into a bulwark of democracy.

To return to the development of foreign policy under Stresemann's aegis: the Locarno Pact was another great step forward. The German government had taken the initiative and offered guarantees for its western frontiers in order to meet French security needs and thus contribute to an easing of tensions. French foreign affairs were directed at the time by Briand, who, like Stresemann, was not blinded by narrow national interests and whose ambition was to establish a peaceful Europe. He considered this of real urgency, as nobody could yet foresee how the Bolshevists would use their new position in Europe at a future date.

Thus the German offer to negotiate was well received, and the European statesmen convened in Locarno, Switzerland. The conference opened in an atmosphere of cold suspicion which only gradually thawed to mutual confidence. It ended in political compromise of the kind that imparts meaning to the letter and the spirit of a good treaty, where no party has its own way completely but meets the others half-way. The Locarno Pact included mutual guarantees of the German-French and the German-Belgian frontiers. This protected the Rhineland from French annexation while, at the same time, formally recognizing the cession of Alsace-Lorraine to France. Future disputes were to be submitted to arbitration.

It is not necessary in this context to list the detailed provisions of the pact. But it is sufficient that it was considered a significant contribution to peace and security throughout the world. Speaking of the European idea, Briand said: "If we want to move ahead, we must not fight each other; we must work with each other." Stresemann, on his side, considered it a beginning, which he hoped would lead at some future date to a great international conference which in turn would redraw the eastern frontiers on the principles of national self-determination.

As usual, nationalists in Germany as well as France proved stubborn and uncomprehending, and, by fair means or foul, created difficulties for their own statesmen. German nationalists failed to be impressed by Stresemann's prestige abroad, and raised their usual cries of "All or nothing." Fortunately, an attempt on Stresemann's life by an ex-officer failed.

Unmoved by the mudslinging against him, Stresemann pursued his course with admirable steadfastness, and succeeded, in 1926, in gaining Germany's admission to the League of Nations. The League, which owed its existence to the initiative of President Wilson, had been officially inaugurated at Geneva in January 1920. Its members undertook to assist each other against aggression and agreed to submit disputes among members to the judgment of the Permanent Court of International Justice in The Hague. Neither the United States nor the Soviet Union belonged to the League at this time.

Germany's admission as a member was unanimously approved by the Assembly of the League of Nations, and it received a permanent seat on the Council. Two days after the vote, the German

Stresemann addressing the League of Nations, 1929

delegation, headed by Stresemann, was welcomed by the Assembly with a veritable storm of applause. Judgments on the effectiveness of the League of Nations may indeed differ; this first attempt to create an international meeting place for all nations undoubtedly suffered many setbacks. But the admission of Germany was a political success that added to its stature and increased public confidence.

One of the most difficult remaining tasks was the evacuation of the Rhineland, still occupied by French troops. Stresemann repeatedly urged the French Foreign Minister to meet him half-way and demonstrate French good faith by effecting the long-awaited evacuation. But on just this issue Briand had to face strong opposition at home. Articles in German nationalistic hate sheets were cited in which every French soldier leaving the Rhineland would be replaced by 10 *Stahlhelme* (steel helmets, i.e. German soldiers). Stresemann, on the other hand, recognized that it would take very few—perhaps only one—concession on the part of its former enemies to convince the German people that they were moving in the right direction. This achieved, an overwhelming majority of Germans would give their support to the men working for peace and reconciliation. Failing this, even men of good will would be driven into the arms of right-wing radicals by the continued occupation of the Rhineland.

Final evacuation was connected with the settlement of the reparations question (1929), an idea originating with the American Owen Young, and thus called the Young Plan. For months, the experts, assisted by Germans, wrestled over the new proposals. Payments were reduced below those stipulated by the Dawes Plan, and a time limit for reparations payments agreed upon. They were to run for 59 years; the total amount to be paid was set at 34.5 billion goldmarks. One determining factor in this decision was the debt of 22.8 billion goldmarks which the former Allied powers owed to the United States. The Dawes Plan had assigned the conversion of German reparation payments into foreign currencies to an Agent-General for Reparations. This provision was now dropped, and Germany regained its financial independence. But it did involve quite a considerable risk, for Germany was now responsible for its own remittances to the newly established Bank for International Settlement (BIZ) in Basle, Switzerland.

It may still seem harsh that Germany was thus obligated to bear the burden of the Versailles Treaty for another 59 years—the lifespan of almost two generations—but past experience indicated that this plan, too, would be further revised if the politics of reconciliation were followed with patient persistence. Stresemann had all the more reasons for hope since, at The Hague Conference of 1929, he had persuaded Briand in a dramatic debate to promise the withdrawal of French troops from the Rhineland in exchange for German adoption of the Young Plan.

In gaining this concession, Stresemann, already seriously ill, used up his last ounce of strength. He died of a heart attack on October 3, 1929, without living to see the liberation of the Rhineland, for which he had worked so hard. Even his contemporaries felt the loss deeply, and both the German and foreign press eulogized Stresemann as the greatest German statesman since Bismarck. But only posterity can judge the truly tragic effect on Germany of his premature death, for if Stresemann had lived to guide

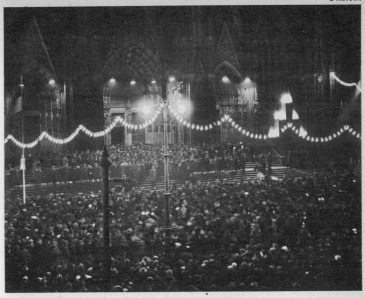

Celebrating the evacuation of the Rhineland, 1930

the German people through the approaching world depression, Hitler would, in all probability, never have become Chancellor.

As soon as the Young Plan was ratified, the so-called "Front of National Unity," led by Hugenberg (DNVP) and Hitler (NSDAP), called for a popular initiative (*Volksbegehren*) against it. It was signed by 4.1 million voters, the bare minimum legal number. The referendum (*Volksentscheid*) which was scheduled in accordance with the Constitution was approved by only 5.8 million voters; 21 million votes would have been needed to carry it. The leading force behind the whole operation was Alfred Hugenberg, a former director general of Krupp's, whose investments had assured him a controlling influence in many newspapers, and especially in UFA, then the largest German motion-picture company. His campaign against the "Young slavery" not only cost him money but also some of his followers, who left the DNVP and constituted themselves as People's Conservatives.

89

The restraint and moderation shown by the German voters must be admired especially in the face of the economic and financial storm signals which had been up since October 24, 1929, when Black Friday on the American stock exchange ushered in a world-wide depression. It was preceded by a feverish boom. Stocks had climbed to dizzy heights, and banks had extended excessive credits which stimulated excessive investments. Production had also risen, but purchasing power had not kept pace with this expansion. With the crash on the stock exchange, a correspondingly steep decline began.

An American historian describes the effects of the crisis on the United States in the following words:

> Millions of investors lost their savings; thousands were forced into bankruptcy. Debts mounted, purchases declined, factories cut down production, workers were dismissed, wages and salaries slashed. Farmers, already hard hit, were unable to meet their obligations, and mortgages were foreclosed, often with losses to all concerned. . . . Commercial failures increased from 24,000 in 1928 to 32,000 in 1932, and over five thousand banks closed their doors in the first three years of the depression. By 1930 there were a little over three million unemployed; in 1933 the number was variously estimated at from twelve to fifteen million. Factory pay-rolls fell to less than half the level of 1929 and the total wages paid out declined from fifty-five billion dollars in 1929 to thirty-three billion in 1931.[12]

From the United States the crisis spread relentlessly, causing chaos and unemployment throughout the world. In 1932, world unemployment stood at 30 million. A situation as desperate as this must inevitably affect politics wherever its presence was felt. Private enterprise alone could not repair the damages and, consequently, the powers of centralized governments increased everywhere, as they were more and more obliged to intervene in economic and social life. The classic example was provided by the U.S., where, in the darkest moments of crisis, the Democrats elected Franklin D. Roosevelt as President. Disregarding the time-honored tradition of American liberalism, Roosevelt successfully attacked the crisis by enacting an elaborate program of social and economic legislation which came to be known as the "New Deal."

It is perhaps just as well to bear in mind from the very beginning that the economic depression did not affect Germany alone. In no country could it be overcome without strengthening the regulatory powers of the state, which in many places included emergency legislation and extraordinary governmental powers, though by no means going as far as dictatorships or the suspension of fundamental rights. That Germany ultimately chose the latter way out was caused not only by the world depression, but just as much by the irresponsible escapism which characterized the German situation and affected even the *Reichstag*. Article 48 of the Weimar Constitution, which gained great importance with the onset of the crisis, allowed the parties to shift their responsibilities to the *Reich* President, while retaining their own freedom of action. But this lowered them still further in the esteem of the German people, who began to look upon them as superfluous and ineffectual.

Breadlines in New York, 1930 *Ullstein*

The first signs of the crisis in Germany appeared with the withdrawal of short-term credits by foreign creditors and with budgetary deficits. Then followed an extremely critical situation and the "Great Coalition" government, which included all parties from the SPD to the German People's Party, was split from end to end. Its extreme wings, the leftist Social Democrats and the right German People's Party, differed too widely in their economic views. To keep the national system of unemployment insurance solvent, the SPD wanted to raise contributions, while the DVP suggested lowering the rates of compensation. An additional reason for the desertion of the DVP was its desire to take better care of its extra-parliamentary interests.

As a consequence, Heinrich Brüning, a member of the Center Party, formed a minority government whose support ranged from the Center Party to the People's Conservatives. It had no majority in the *Reichstag* and could only function through emergency decrees issued by authority of the *Reich* President and Article 48 of the Constitution. Brüning's aim above all was to balance the

Communist demonstration in Berlin   *Historia-Photo*

Heinrich Brüning   *Ullstein*

budget, and he had the courage to carry out whatever unpopular measures were necessary, with or without the help of the *Reichstag*. They included tax increases, raises in tariffs (in order to protect agriculture and support grain prices), cuts in the social services, and lower salaries for government officials.

On June 30, 1930, foreign troops left the Rhineland on schedule. The German government issued a proclamation for the event which did not even mention Stresemann, whose relentless efforts had achieved this success. Two weeks later, the government promulgated the first emergency decree "for safeguarding the economy and the budget," since, despite all efforts, no majority could be found to support the new tax laws essential to solve the economic situation.

Thus parliament, as it were, had taken itself out of circulation, and shifted its responsibility to the *Reich* President. Brüning was quite willing to use the authority of the *Reich* President to steer the German state through the crisis. He might conceivably have succeeded, if he had remained steadfast in his determination.

But when the Social Democrats, supported by a narrow *Reichstag* majority, used their constitutional prerogative to demand that the emergency decrees be suspended, Brüning disregarded the advice of influential members of his government and dissolved the *Reichstag*.

It is true that the *Reichstag* was lamentably incapable of accepting compromises. The pettiest interests clashed in the Finance Committee, and one can indeed sympathize with the Finance Minister of that time, who publicly asked "whether the Germans were a bundle of interest groups or a state." What then was to be expected from another *Reichstag*? Did Brüning really hope that, at the height of the crisis, radical slogans would lose their attraction, and that he would now find support for his policy of strict, but absolutely necessary, sacrifice?

Whatever the answers to these questions, the results of the elections of September 14, 1930, exceeded the worst expectations. Hitler had opened the flood gates by his unscrupulous propaganda; he barnstormed up and down the country by air, denouncing the Young Plan as the source of all evil, and effectively discrediting the parties which had supported it. In the new *Reichstag,* the National Socialists no longer controlled a mere 12 seats, but a disciplined and uniformed troop of 107 representatives. Other changes were less noticeable, but together they left little hope for forming a new government on the basis of a parliamentary majority.

	REICHSTAG MEMBERS	
	1928	1930
NSDAP	12	107
DNVP	73	41
Right splinter parties	31	48
DVP	45	30
Center splinter parties	20	24
Center Party and Bavarian People's Party	78	87
Democrats	25	20
SPD	153	143
Communist Party	54	77

Cartoon by Wolfgang Hicks (1933): "They want to kill off half the population. Is that supposed to be a solution for the unemployment problem, or bring about the unification of the Germans?"

Nothing had really changed. Brüning continued to hold office, the only difference being that he could now count on not being opposed by the SPD, which had concluded from the Nazi victory that "all forces had to be marshaled if Germany was to be kept from degenerating into a Fascist dictatorship." The author of this sentence, the Prussian Prime Minister, Otto Braun, demanded accordingly that his party follow a responsible policy independent of public opinion.

Further emergency decrees became necessary. Salaries of government officials were cut and, at the same time, deductions for unemployment insurance (introduced a short time before the depression, in 1927) had to be raised. The Mayor of Leipzig, Goerdeler, was appointed Commissioner for Prices to halt spiraling prices. The government also considered instituting a labor service to take at least the unemployed youths off the streets and give them steady work. It had been pioneered by Silesian students under the leadership of Professor Eugen Rosenstock-Huessy, who voluntarily joined young laborers in public works projects during the day and held common debates and meetings in the evening.

Informed opinion abroad was obliged to acknowledge that in Brüning Germany had again found a statesman who could be expected to overcome the difficulties. His government was praised as the best answer for Germany at that time, while at home the demagogues with their cries of "Down with the hunger dictator!" won increasing support from the masses. It was unfortunate that Brüning was denied a decisive success in foreign affairs, which would undoubtedly have strengthened his domestic position.

The German and Austrian governments had discussed the possibility of a customs union, and announced their intentions of introducing one in March 1931. France immediately viewed this as a step toward the political union (*Anschluss*) of Austria and Germany and registered strong protests. At the suggestion of the British, the plan was submitted to the International Court of Justice at The Hague, which by eight votes to seven pronounced the customs union illegal. Austria, beset by financial difficulties as a result of the collapse of her *Kreditanstalt,* had by this time already abandoned the plan; but the train of events which revealed that Germany was still under the tutelage of the Allied powers served to fan the flame of national passions still higher.*

Brüning did, however, receive foreign aid in resolving another vital German problem. Even before he could make the difficult decision of asking for a temporary postponement of reparations payments, President Hoover of the United States proposed a moratorium "on all payments for inter-governmental debts." This Hoover moratorium was speedily accepted by all governments

---

* The strong French reaction to the German-Austrian plan of a customs union was in part due to the secretiveness with which negotiations had been carried on between the German and Austrian governments, and the suddenness with which the draft treaty was published in March 1931 (this suddenness may have been due to Austrian opponents of the proposal, who brought about its premature disclosure by taking a number of journalists into their confidence). The French feared a political *Anschluss* and, as a consequence, their attitudes toward the customs union and later toward the moratorium stiffened. *Trl.*

concerned. France alone had reservations, since she received the lion's share of German reparations, and feared with good reason that, even after the moratorium had elapsed, payments would never be resumed. In fact, the advancing economic and financial crisis soon liquidated this unfortunate legacy of the First World War.

In the fall of 1931, the Bank of England went off the gold standard, followed by a host of other countries. In June and July 1932, the Conference of Lausanne decided to liquidate the German reparations debt with a final payment of 3 billion Reichsmarks. This agreement, although never ratified, was nevertheless put into operation. At this time, however, the Brüning government had already been overthrown "100 yards before the finish line," as Brüning mournfully exclaimed in his last speech before the *Reichstag*.

For years, Hitler had been using the burden of the reparations as the butt of his propaganda campaigns. When they were abandoned (not on account of his propaganda, but because economic reason had slowly begun to prevail), it hardly affected the Germans at all; yet many Germans believe to this day that Hitler deserves the credit for ending reparations.

The campaign of hatred and vilification continued in high gear, fostering any and all dissatisfactions purely to keep the issue alive. True, rising unemployment in Germany, which passed the six million mark early in 1932, imposed heavy burdens, but other countries in a similar plight patiently and persistently sought reasonable means of overcoming the problem. Could anybody really expect that Hitler would work a miracle and solve it in one stroke?

Instead of trusting in patience, moderation, and good will, the people let themselves be dazzled by force. That Hitler sought power with such undisguised brutality appeared to add to his attraction. The political struggle was increasingly controlled by the para-military organizations mentioned previously. In October 1931, the German Nationalists, the Nazis, the *Stahlhelm* (steel helmet), and the S.A. joined a coalition known as the Harzburg Front. The *Reichsbanner* (Socialist), the workers' sports clubs, and trade unions countered with an Iron Front. These fronts became, as it were, the *raison d'être* of many unemployed people.

Iron Front rally in the Berlin *Lustgarten*   *Ullstein*

They were issued uniforms, called out for demonstrations, and did regular "tours of duty" in their respective meeting halls. A deeply rooted love for the life of the barracks was, once again, aroused and satisfied.

The second presidential election took place during this period, for Hindenburg's seven-year term of office expired in March 1932. The recent gains made by the Nazis, who nominated Hitler as their presidential candidate, left the republican parties only one choice; they had to agree on Hindenburg, who thus became the candidate for the center and the left—much against his own convictions— whereas in 1921, he had owed his election to the right. In the first vote, Hindenburg polled 18.7 million, Hitler 11.3 million, Thäl- mann 5.0 million, and Düsterberg, the German Nationalist candi- date, 2.6 million votes. Once again, a run-off election became necessary, and Düsterberg withdrew his candidacy. Hindenburg carried 19.4 million votes against Hitler's 13.4 million. Thälmann's strength was reduced to 3.7 million. The majority of the German people had cast their lot with the policies of the government, and against Hitler.

In accepting Hindenburg's candidacy, the republican parties had been forced to make the best of a difficult situation. They had tied their own hands by the miscalculations of 1925, and now they felt the effects of their lack of foresight. For on May 30, 1932, it was not parliament which caused the Brüning government to fall; parliament had continued to support him. His fall was engineered by Hindenburg. Brüning himself reacted with the greatest surprise and shock when Hindenburg, during a conference on May 29, rudely interrupted him a few moments after he had begun his report, and announced that from now on he could no longer sign emergency decrees. Hindenburg demanded that forthwith "there be 'an opening to the right,' and that the mess made by trade-union leaders and agrarian Bolshevists disappear." He ticked these three demands off a sheet of paper—for this was a well-thought-out plan. It was obvious that advisers acting outside the constitutional framework had preyed on the mind of the *Reich* President, and persuaded him that the *Osthilfe* (Aid to the East) planned by Brüning was "communistic" because it included a very modest measure of land reform, providing for the division of economically unprofitable large estates. Hindenburg himself had been given the Neudeck estate in East Prussia, and had fallen under the influence of his land-owning neighbors. The phrase "opening to the right" had obviously originated with his military advisers, primarily General von Schleicher. This soldier, who was fond of pulling political strings behind the scenes, and was once told by Brüning, after a heated controversy, that he would one day be caught in his own trap, now proposed that it would be wiser to channel the Nazi flood than store it behind dam-walls. He deluded himself into thinking that Hitler, in spite of his success, could serve his [Schleicher's] purposes and be brought under control. To this end, Schleicher considered Brüning's removal from the government a necessary step. After repeated visits to Neudeck, Schleicher succeeded in turning Hindenburg against Brüning with relative ease, since it already pained the old gentleman, in his own inimitable words, to realize that he owed his re-election to Sozis [Socialists] and "Cathols."*

After this memorable conference with Hindenburg, Brüning im-

* Derogatory abbreviation for Catholics. *Trl.*

Franz von Papen and *Stahlhelm* leaders   *Ullstein*

mediately informed the cabinet, which reacted by resigning to a man. The *Reich* President had his way. Groener, the Defense Minister, who knew the former Chief of the General Staff best, was stung to the quick and promised at this meeting to reveal Hindenburg's true picture to the world. Here, the legendary phrase which Hindenburg had misapplied was truly applicable. On May 30, 1932, Hindenburg stabbed a man in the back who served him faithfully, and with this act "killed not only the German Republic, but the peace of Europe."[13]

On Schleicher's advice, Hindenburg now called upon Franz von Papen to form a new government. Papen was a deputy in the

Prussian Diet and, although a member of the Center Party, stood ideologically far to its right. His political record was in no way distinguished, but he was ambitious; for this reason Schleicher believed that in him he had found a tool for his own purposes. In less than a year, the friend was to turn into a bitter foe.

Papen's new cabinet, composed exclusively of members of the German National People's Party and the German People's Party, was nicknamed the "Cabinet of the Barons." Hindenburg felt at home among the new cabinet members, in contrast to the preceding epoch, which he identified as the "period of the republican ministers." But in parliament, the cabinet had the support of a mere 71 out of 577 votes. No other course remained but to dissolve the *Reichstag* and to schedule new elections for July 31, 1932.

Until then, the "gentleman rider" (*Herrenreiter*) had time to indulge in some irresponsibilities of his own. As a first step he lifted the ban on the S.A. which the Brüning cabinet had decreed at the last moment, after much soul-searching, when terrorism on the streets had threatened to get out of hand. The suspension of this ban, which had been implemented without resistance, would —Papen presumably hoped—buy Hitler's sympathy and acquiescence.

As a next step, Papen deposed the constitutional Socialist government of Prussia by a coup d'état. In February 1932, the Social Democratic Party had lost its traditional majority to the Nazis in the elections for the Prussian Diet. One hundred and sixty-two Nazis and 57 Communists, together forming an absolute majority in the Diet, thus created a hopeless situation, since neither could conceive of joining to form a government. In line with the constitution, the Braun government (SPD) resigned, but it remained as a caretaker government until a new Prime Minister could be voted in. Several attempts at such a vote failed. Thereupon, Papen intervened with an emergency decree, installed himself as *Reich* Commissioner for Prussia, and deposed the ministers. When informed of this turn of events, Minister of the Interior Severing said that he would yield only if forced. Papen countered by proclaiming martial law in Berlin, and had the ministers driven from their office building by some newly appointed police officers.

Why, it has often been asked, did the Prussian government immediately yield without a struggle, when it could have called on the police, who were loyal to the Republic? It can only be presumed that these ministers did not wish to stir up a civil war, and detested any use of force, even to save themselves. Severing had voiced the feelings of a leading Social Democratic newspaper editor when he asserted that "You have no right to be brave at the expense of your policemen."

This was followed by an election campaign which aroused more passions and cost more lives than any other in the history of the Weimar Republic. The Storm Troopers goose-stepped more arrogantly and violently than ever before. Within a single month 99 people were beaten to death and 1125 wounded in street brawls and meeting hall skirmishes. The climax came with bloody battles on election day, primarily in Königsberg, where the Nazis ran wild during a "night of long knives," bombing and shooting their political opponents. In contrast to the so-called "bloody Sunday of Altona," during which the Communists had opened fire on the marching S.A., there was no trace of Communist provocation in Königsberg.

In the newly elected *Reichstag,* Nazi seats doubled while the Communists registered a much smaller gain. Among the moderate groups, only the Center Party gained some ground, while Papen's parliamentary support dwindled from 72 to 44 votes. We now know in retrospect that these were the free elections in which the Nazis amassed their largest vote of 37.2 per cent. They thus controlled fewer votes than the Social Democratic Party had controlled in the National Assembly [in 1919], and, at the time, the SPD had not demanded exclusive power for itself.

In the end, the great investment of passions and hatred, of propaganda and money, was "wasted, every shred." A gigantic election machinery had been set in motion to no avail, for Papen and his entire cabinet remained in office, and continued to govern by emergency decrees. The *Reichstag* met, was officially opened by its Communist senior member, Klara Zetkin, and then elected Hermann Göring as its presiding officer. The second session of this *Reichstag* was to be its last. The Communists proposed a suspension of Papen's latest emergency decree "for the re-activation

Street clashes between Nazis and police in Berlin, May 1932

of the economy," and moved a vote of no-confidence against the government. Papen did not even manage to get the floor this time. Göring, in the chair of the *Reichstag,* failed to recognize him with malice aforethought, and called for a vote, even though Papen slapped an order to dissolve the *Reichstag* which he had previously procured from the *Reich* President under his very nose.

Weary of elections, the German people were once again dragged to the polls on November 6. This time, fewer people voted, Hitler lost two million votes, the German Nationalists gained ground, and the Communists captured 100 seats. The new *Reichstag* was as incapable as the preceding one of producing a stable majority government. Coalitions between the Center Party and its previous allies, which had still been possible two years earlier, had now lost their foundation (see table below). The German voters had finally maneuvered themselves into a situation where the German parliament "was reduced to saying *Nein* writ large."[14]

Parliamentary Coalitions (% of *Reichstag* seats)

	MAY 1928	SEPT. 1930	JULY 1932	NOV. 1932
Harzburg Front (NSDAP and DNVP)	18.4	25.8	43.9	42.3
Brüning Block (SPD, Center Party, People's Conservatives)	89.2	56.2	42.7	40.0
Great Coalition (SPD, Democratic Party, Center Party, Bavarian People's Party, German People's Party)	61.2	50.4	39.6	38.2
Weimar Coalition (SPD, Democratic Party, Center Party)	48.6	40.0	34.9	33.1
Left wing (SPD and Communists)	42.0	38.1	36.5	37.8
Anti-republican Coalition (NSDAP and Communists)	13.5	31.9	52.5	50.7

It was no longer practical to let Papen muddle along any further. The *Reich* President ordered him to secure the confidence of parliament, and when Papen admitted failure, the "old gentleman" accepted his resignation with sincere regrets. Following parliamentary custom, Hindenburg now approached Hitler first as the leader of the largest party. There ensued a lengthy exchange of letters which were made public after negotiations had failed. Hindenburg asked Hitler to form a government based on a parliamentary majority, but Hitler wanted to head a "Presidential Cabinet" as Brüning and Papen had. This Hindenburg rejected, stating that such a cabinet, under Hitler's leadership, "was bound to develop into the dictatorship of a party, and to lead to an extraordinary increase of the tensions plaguing the German people." This was November 24, 1932. Two months later, the *Reich* President did exactly what he had previously, for such excellent reasons, refused to do.

Now Hindenburg would have liked to return to Papen, even if it meant disregarding the Constitution (i.e. postponing a new election of the *Reichstag* for an indefinite period after the inevitable vote of no-confidence would have made such an election necessary). In this situation, Defense Minister von Schleicher began to pull strings, with the result that more cabinet members sided with him than with Papen. This forced Hindenburg to offer the chancellorship to Schleicher.

Schleicher was not quite as reactionary as Papen. He had at least some political ideas for improving the muddled situation; he hoped to split the Nazi party with the help of Gregor Strasser, one of the strongest opponents of capitalism among its members. Strasser actually wanted to back the Schleicher cabinet, but was not strong enough to prevail against Hitler, nor to lure a sizeable number of his followers away from him. Schleicher further aimed at co-operating with the trade unions, primarily in a work program, and appeared to have some initial success in this area.

Schleicher exploited the setback suffered by the Nazis in November, which discouraged them from moving a vote of no-confidence against the government, and from agreeing to another dissolution of the *Reichstag*. They feared a further loss of votes, and spirits in the propaganda headquarters of the NSDAP were at low ebb during these weeks, as Goebbels described in his diaries. Funds had been exhausted, and the feeling persisted that the goal had moved farther into the distance than ever before.

Schleicher further managed to reap the rewards of many years of efforts expanded by his predecessors, from Stresemann to Brüning.* Now, at the beginning of December 1932, Germany's demand for parity in armaments was, at long last, recognized by the League of Nations in Geneva. But, as the chief German interpreter Paul Schmidt wrote in his memoirs, this great success was little recognized in Germany at that time. The public, the press, and the parties seemed in no way to realize—or did not wish to realize—the significance of what had been achieved. This made it that much

* At the Lausanne Conference of mid-1932, Papen had succeeded in obtaining a final agreement on German reparations. They were fixed at 3 billion marks. He also raised the German demand for equality in armaments but did not succeed in obtaining French agreement for it at that time. *Trl.*

easier for Hitler later on to claim that he had single-handedly restored Germany's equality and prestige.

The beginning of January 1933 saw the end of Schleicher's hopes of broadening his domestic base by adding the trade unions. Social Democratic leaders had passed the word to Socialist trade-union leaders that the SPD would refuse to co-operate with Schleicher because he had participated in the coup d'état against the Prussian government. Yet, was there anybody left who could have taken his place?

Meanwhile, Papen had re-entered the political arena and was preparing to take revenge for having been outwitted by his ex-friend, Schleicher. On January 5, Papen met Hitler at the home of the Cologne banker Kurt von Schröder. In his memoirs which [in German] bear the pretentious (and misleading) title *Make Way for the Truth,* Papen claims that he never hatched a plot against Schleicher. Yet, if other sources are also consulted, and if the result of this first meeting is considered, one is led to conclude that Papen had been scheming with Hitler for his political return.

There is no need to recount all the twists of this evil political intrigue. Hitler immediately saw his opportunity. Papen used his influence on the *Reich* President to persuade him that, by now, Hitler's demands were much more modest, and that he could easily be restrained in a coalition cabinet. Hitler, on his part, met the son of the *Reich* President and assured him, in a small gathering, of his undying loyalty to the Constitution.

For all this, Hindenburg had told General von Hammerstein as late as January 27, that he hoped people would not suppose that he would make a chancellor of the "lance-corporal from Bohemia." After Schleicher had resigned on January 28, Papen, in collusion with Hindenburg's son Oskar and the Secretary of State Meissner, overcame the reservations of the President. He assured him that Hitler's cabinet would include only two Nazis, and, for the rest, would be so well "packed" with German Nationalist ministers, among them Hugenberg, that "nothing could happen." It is probably not too farfetched to assume that Hindenburg had at last grown tired of the shabby maneuverings and wanted to be left in peace.

Thus, on the morning of January 30, 1933, he received the

Hitler's first cabinet with (l. to r. seated) Göring, Hitler, Papen, and (far r. standing) Hugenberg

new Hitler cabinet. The well-laid intrigue nearly failed at the last moment because Hitler had mentioned early *Reichstag* elections while waiting in the President's antechamber. Hugenberg, whose party stood to lose in elections, countered vehemently.

A violent altercation ensued. Finally, Hitler stepped up to Hugenberg and promised, on his solemn word of honor, never to separate from any of those present, whatever the election results would turn out to be. Papen, afraid for the unity he had brought about, then came to Hitler's aid, and addressed Hugenberg: "Herr Privy Councillor, will you really distrust the solemn word of honor of a German man?" In the end Hugenberg yielded, for time was running out, and Hindenburg had already been kept waiting for 15 minutes.

In such manner Hindenburg installed the government "of national unity" and brought about the end of the Weimar Republic.

Adolf Hitler (1889-1945)

III
The Third Reich

5: Did Hitler Come to Power Constitutionally?

Hitler was appointed *Reich* Chancellor by *Reich* President Hindenburg in the same way as his predecessors, Brüning, Papen, and Schleicher. The appointment had been made properly in accordance with Article 53 of the Weimar Constitution. Although intrigues and deceit had entered into it, Hitler did not come to power by military force, machine guns, or martial law. He squeezed every ounce of advantage from this fact. It became one of the key slogans of his propaganda that he had formed his government constitutionally and "by the will of the overwhelming majority of his people." He thereby catered to the tendency of the German people to consider as legal, right, and just, everything that agrees with the letter of the law.

It can indeed hardly be denied that the transfer of power to Hitler was "legal," if we narrow it down to his appointment as Chancellor on January 30 *alone*. Even so, one cannot absolve those who appointed Hitler from the reproach that they acted against the interests of the Constitution by placing the fate of the Republic in the hands of an avowed enemy of democracy. Hitler's appointment as Chancellor was only the first logical step toward totalitarian power, and the methods used to obtain this were by no means "legal" or constitutional. Those who believed that they could give Hitler the chancellorship, and take it away from him "legally" if at any future date a majority of the people should demand it, were soon to learn how badly they had erred. Like the proverbial devil, once Hitler was offered a finger, he took the whole hand.

The question persists whether this could have been foreseen. Were people really justified in mistaking this arsonist for an honest man who planned no evil? And, if it could have been foreseen, why did people allow themselves to be deceived? Or did they wish to be deceived?

The program of the Nazi party (already mentioned above p. 58) suggested the ultimate goal only in a few of its points. Nobody could have been the least mistaken about its demand to deprive the Jews of all official positions, and to place them under an "alien law." The hodgepodge of demands and assertions which made up the rest (including the assertion that the party embraced a "positive Christianity") allowed everybody to read into the program whatever he liked. Some of the economic points were total nonsense, for example the slogan calling for "breaking the fetters of interest." But there were so many party programs being floated around at that time that none was taken particularly seriously.

Hitler's book *Mein Kampf,* written in 1924, gave away a more substantial part of the story. In it, Hitler expounded not only on his *Weltanschauung* but also laid bare the methods and goals of his "struggle." Today, the reader is shocked into recognizing that, long before his seizure of power, Hitler had outlined his fanatical aims.

The Nazi *Weltanschauung* can be summarized in three sentences, using Hitler's own formulations: "Struggle is the father of all things. Moral excellence derives from the race. Leadership is inborn and decisive." This raised brute force to the level of a supreme principle. On the "iron logic of nature" the weaker had to yield to the strong. The Aryan race alone was, in Hitler's opinion, strong, creative, and "culture-bearing"; it alone was capable of idealism and self-sacrifice for the more valuable community. Jews, on the other hand, appear as the shadow, the counter-race, as bearers of all evils, "destroying" everything. "Der Stürmer," a Nazi party paper, reduced this "doctrine" every day to a simple

Dritter
Märkertag
29-30. Sept.
1928

Berlin voran!

Nazi poster—"Forward Berlin!" for the Third Brandenburg
(and eastern provinces) Rally, 29-30 September, 1928

Ullstein

formula: Here the "sun-drenched forms of the Nordic German" —and there the "hellish features" of the Jew!

It has already been recounted above (p. 58) how Hitler visualized leadership and the leadership state. With no less remarkable honesty Hitler's book revealed the methods he meant to use in his "struggle." His opinion of the masses whom he courted so assiduously was in fact very low: "By and large the popular masses consist of . . . unstable human specimens, given to doubt and insecurity. . . . The people, in their overwhelming majority, are so feminine in inheritance and attitudes that they think and act less from sober thinking than from emotions and sentimentality." Such people could not be reached by sober and judicious arguments, nor by lukewarm or changeable propaganda slogans. Whoever wished to stir these dull masses must "limit [his propaganda] to a few ideas, and must repeat these ideas again and again. . . . They will remember the simplest ideas only after they had been drummed into their heads a thousand times."

> The force moving the most gigantic revolutions on this planet lies at all times less with scientific knowledge dominating the masses, but rather in fanaticism imprinted upon their soul, and, at times, in hysteria whipping them on. Whoever wants to win the masses must know the key that will open the door to their hearts. It is not called objectivity, i.e. weakness, but will and power.

Such were the principles which Hitler, in fact, applied in his election campaigns. As a result, as he himself predicted in 1924, he "realized with astonishment one day what immense, hardly anticipated, results such persistence would yield."

Hitler went even further. He revealed not only his future domestic policies—persecution of the Jews, the leadership principle, abolition of all parliaments—but his book also proposed that the new *Weltanschauung*, if necessary, be forced down the throats of an entire population later on. The foreign policy he expounded in the last chapter of the book rested on the view that the leaders of a nation should also have the courage "to lead it beyond its narrow living space to new lands." The frontiers of 1914 "mean nothing for the future of the German nation. They neither gave protection in the past, nor will they provide strength for the future." Where, however, was the land to be found which was by right due to the "master race"? Hitler answered:

> If we speak of new land in Europe today, we think primarily only of Russia and the border states under its control. Fate itself appears to point the finger for us. By delivering Russia to Bolshevism it robbed the Russian nation of the intelligentsia which until now had guaranteed its existence as a state. . . . . The giant empire in the East is ready to collapse. . . .

The extent of fanaticism to which Hitler had managed to inspire his followers was illustrated when the so-called "Boxheim documents" reached the light of day in November 1931. Their name derives from the Boxheim estate, near Worms, where Nazi functionaries had held the conversations recorded in these documents. These men had drafted a plan of action for a Nazi seizure of power. It was to be put into operation following a hypothetical Communist revolution. The S.A. and the party were to exercise governmental authority, discipline the people into total submission, and execute all those disobeying orders. Drum-head military courts were to pass summary sentences, food was to be turned over to the government, and all interest payments suspended: "Private income has ceased to exist until further notice." Nobody had a right to be fed who did not serve in a "national draft" (beginning at 16 years of age).

Although the documents were signed by Werner Best, subsequently *Reich* Commissioner for Denmark, and were certainly known to the party, Hitler publicly disavowed them, and reiterated the "legality" of his party. Anybody in his right mind, however, could have drawn the inevitable conclusions.

Even without this there was enough material available to reveal the future plans of the Nazis. It could not easily escape notice that such party papers as the "Völkische Beobachter" and the "Angriff" were by no means moderate, and that the party leaders generally spiced their speeches with outrageous mudslinging. Unbridled abuse of the political opponents was a systematic part of Nazi propaganda, and it was customary to call members of parliament belonging to other parties, especially the Marxists, by such

113

names as dopes, babblers, bunglers, blackguards, criminals, crooks, scoundrels, trash, cheaters, half-wits, or assassins.

Their actions proved as crude and hate-filled as their thoughts. Any lingering doubts should have been removed by August 1932, when, in Potempa, Upper Silesia, five S.A. men forced their way into the apartment of a Communist worker, Pietrzuch, tore him from his bed, and beat him to death before the eyes of his mother. Here is the police report:

> The body bore the marks of 29 wounds, the deepest ones at the neck. The carotid artery was completely torn. The larynx was kicked in and had a gaping hole. Death occurred by suffocation as the arterial blood had entered the lungs by way of the larynx. Besides these wounds, Pietrzuch's body showed marks caused by severe beatings. He was beaten severely on the head with a blunt axe or a club, and had other wounds probably caused by having the top of a billiard cue thrust in his face.

The five murderers of Potempa were tried before a court in Beuthen, and sentenced to death. After the sentence was pronounced, Hitler sent a telegram with the following message: "My comrades! In the face of this monstrous and murderous sentence I stand absolutely loyal at your side!" On the same day, he issued a proclamation printed in the "Völkischer Beobachter" in which he praised the murder as a step advancing the nation's struggle for "its eternal rights," and declared war "and more war" on Papen's "blood-stained objectivity." At least now, if not before, anybody who retained even a rudimentary sense of justice must have recoiled in horror. For here was an open admission that murder was murder no longer if the murderer happened to belong to the "Nazi movement," and the victim was on the other side.*

Goebbels used the occasion to remind his readers once again that crime and guilt did not matter, but only race:

> The hour will come when the public prosecutor will have other duties than to protect traitors acting against the nation. Never forget this, comrades! Repeat it to yourselves a hundred times a day until it haunts you in your deepest dreams: The Jews are guilty!

---

* The five convicted murderers were released after Hitler seized power in 1933. *Trl.*

Hate slogan "Death to the Jews" smeared on a synagogue
wall in Düsseldorf

Now nobody could fail to realize that antisemitism was not
only a hobby horse of the Fuehrer but part and parcel of the Nazi
Weltanschauung. Hatred of the Jews was carried into the smallest,
most distant village by such slogans as *"Juda verrecke!"** by gory
songs, posters, and leaflets. Physical violence was as yet rare but
hate-mongering went on without restraint.

If all this was public knowledge, which it undoubtedly was, why
did large sections of the German people look to Hitler as their
leader, or, at least, not consider him a danger? Why did they expect their salvation from him? Why did they cheer him? These
questions have many facets. They must be considered in the light
of the general decline of culture in the Western world against
which Albert Schweitzer had raised his warning voice decades
earlier. As the view spread that life was nothing but a "struggle

* "Death to the Jews." No translation will catch the vulgarity of the phrase.
Verrecken—slang for the death of animals. *Trl.*

115

for existence," violence for its own sake was glorified. The belief in reason and in effective ethical ideals lost its power; what impressed people was "the pure will," even if it willed evil.

Over and beyond this moral decadence was the wear and tear caused by years of unemployment, by insecurity, and economic struggles. Against this somber background, the delusions, misunderstandings, and mistakes which led to the catastrophe of 1933 can to a certain extent be explained.

The broad middle-class stratum which provided Hitler with most of his voters expected that he would take political responsibility off their shoulders. Bedeviled by the multi-party system, they considered it more of an unwelcome burden than a precious privilege. That the movement was violent was more attractive than repellent to them; they had been searching for a "strong man" who would cut through the tangles of their many worries and economic ills, instead of patiently unraveling them.

The intellectuals among Hitler's followers were deceived by the truth which Hitler himself called the greatest camouflage. What offended them they simply repressed, or considered clever tactics. Admiring the demagogue who could move such large masses, they willingly overlooked the means used in favor of the ends; and these too were often tailored to their own wishful thinking. Some saw Hitler as a sincere man of the people, and a force for social harmony, while others regarded him as an ardent patriot who would restore the fatherland's honor among the nations. Hitler, in their opinion, knew nothing of violent excesses of any kind. They thought of him as a head-in-the-clouds idealist.

The young also suffered from similar delusions. They were attracted primarily by Hitler's radicalism. The very single-mindedness with which Hitler declared war on existing political institutions struck a chord in the minds of young people. His appeal for sacrifices and loyalty satisfied their craving to dedicate their lives for a great cause. The Weimar Republic had neglected to utilize this craving and had been unable to arouse the enthusiasm of the young for the ideals of liberty and democracy.

Another effective slogan, finally, was Hitler's call for a "people's community" (*Volksgemeinschaft*). The ideology of the class struggle was out of date. The young, more than everybody else, were tired of it, and—not entirely without reason—blamed the parties because the old clichés of "proletarians" and "capitalists" and their irreconcilable mutual hostility were still in circulation. It was easy enough to talk the young into believing that parties had to be abolished so that the German nation could finally unite as a harmonious people's community.

The business community, which in the past had often contributed to Hitler's ebbing party funds, nursed the illusion that they could control a man because they had bought him. Because Hitler was seen primarily as a check to the trade unions, his socialism was not taken seriously. Many of the leading business men had a simple-minded desire for "order in the state," irrespective of the means by which this was to be achieved. Alfred Krupp, for example, expressed this view before a Nuremberg tribunal in the following words: "The entire nation identified with Hitler's major goals. We at Krupp merely wanted a system that would function well, that would give us the opportunity of producing without being disturbed. Politics is not our business."

Even many political figures of the Weimar Republic who certainly should have understood the dangers of Nazism grievously mistook the totalitarian character of the party. Although Mussolini had already demonstrated the pattern of fascism in Italy, many of Hitler's political opponents believed that "the responsibility would ruin him," and that the sooner his movement came to power, the sooner the specter would be banished. The phrase "At most six weeks, and all will be over" made the rounds in these circles. Since these ideology-oriented politicians never had a developed sense of power, they lacked understanding for Hitler's elementary will to power, as it appeared in an answer he gave once to an American journalist: "What will you do after you have seized power?"—"Keep it!"

Still others believed that once Hitler was responsible for leading the government, he would become "reasonable" and have done with tactics necessitated by the struggle for power. Only a minority understood, or knew better, but their warnings were ignored. In 1932, Theodor Heuss, who represented the German State's Party in parliament at the time, wrote a pamphlet "Hitler's Way" which had a truly prophetic tinge. Nobody listened to these voices, however, and Hitler did not wait long to silence them.

German people of all classes fell under the spell of their new

Parade through the Brandenburg Gate, 30 January 1933

leader, and Josef Goebbels, "the devil's great propagandist," saw
to it that the customers were satisfied, now that government funds
were at his disposal. Under his aegis, on January 30, 1933, toward evening, Storm Troopers marched on Berlin from the surrounding areas and put on a gigantic torchlight parade. Two radio
reporters, overwhelmed by this brilliant feat of organization,
transmitted their own enthusiasm to their listeners:

> Cheers continue to well up. Adolf Hitler stands at the win-
> dow. His face is serious. He was torn away from his work.
> There is no trace of a victory mood in his face. He was in-
> terrupted. And yet, his eyes shine over the awakening Ger-
> many, over this sea of people from all walks of life, from
> all strata of the population, who parade before him, work-
> ers of the mind and of the fist—all differences among
> classes have been erased. It is a picture which may have
> been seen once before, in 1813, when the word rang out:
> "The king called out, and all, all came! . . ." A wonderful
> picture, the likes of which we shall not see again soon!
> These outstretched arms, these calls of "Heil!" . . . I hope
> that our listeners receive just an idea, an inkling, of this
> great spectacle, of how immeasurably great this moment is!

Two days after Hitler took over the *Reich* Chancellery, Hindenburg dissolved the *Reichstag*. On this occasion Hitler issued a proclamation which illustrates his appeasement tactics, and also the distorted image of history he projected from then on. It can be summarized in the words: "Fourteen years—a field of ruins!" He said too:

> Fourteen years of Marxism have ruined Germany. One year of Bolshevism would destroy Germany. The richest and most beautiful cultural centers of the world would be turned into chaos and a field of ruins. [Hitler in fact achieved exactly this twelve years later!] In these hours when worries about the existence and the future of the German nation have become overpowering, the venerable leader of the World War called upon us men from national parties and associations to fight once more at home, as once in the front lines, in unity and loyalty for the salvation of the *Reich*. . . . The legacy which is ours is awesome. The task we have to solve is the most difficult German

Hitler, the new Chancellor, greets the Chancellery guard 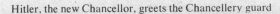 *Feltrinelli*

statesmen have faced within living memory. . . . Above status and class, the national government shall return to our people an awareness of its national and political unity, and of the duties arising therefrom.

Hitler presented a moderate and peace-loving foreign policy. He even spoke of conscientiously fulfilling Germany's obligations toward other nations, whereas, previously, he had been abusing the political figures of the Weimar Republic as weak-kneed opportunists.* The elections were to give the Germany people the opportunity "of co-sponsoring the act of reconciliation." The proclamation ended with these words:

Now, people of Germany, give us four years, then judge and pronounce your sentence! We shall begin, faithful to the command of the Field Marshal. May Almighty God receive our work into his grace, make our will just, bless our minds, and give us courage by honoring us with the confidence of our people. For we do not want to fight for ourselves, but for Germany!

This proclamation was a masterly achievement in the art of satisfying everybody. Hitler had the astonishing capacity of believing precisely in what seemed a tactical necessity of the moment, and he managed by such talk to convince many who would by no means have approved of his true intentions.

The elections had been scheduled for March 5, 1933. Hitler could not yet afford to permit the German people to decide freely whether to accept his government or not. Before he could be certain of their loyalty, Marxism had to be dealt a decisive blow. Accordingly he drew up laws to deal with this and looked for a convincing pretext which would allow him to bring them into force. On the night of February 27, the Berlin *Reichstag* caught fire. The flames spread with incredible speed and consumed the great central hall and the dome. A 24-year-old Dutch national, Marinus van der Lubbe, was picked up at the location of the crime and arrested. It was established later that he had, at one time, belonged to the Communist Party.

With amazing promptness and unanimity the press and radio informed the German people in the early hours of February 28

* *Erfüllungspolitiker:* see footnote on p. 46.

The *Reichstag* fire

that the *Reichstag* fire was to have been the signal for a Communist uprising, and that worse had been averted thanks to the "iron energy" and "use of all powers of the state" [sic]. Still on the same day, a draft decree, prepared by the government, was placed before the *Reich* President for him to sign, and immediately issued as a "Decree of the *Reich* President for the Protection of the People and the State." By this decree, the most important civil rights were suspended "until further notice": personal liberty, in-

121

violability of the home, the privacy of postal communication, freedom of the press, of assembly, and of association, and the constitutional guarantee of private property. In addition, death penalties were imposed on a number of crimes which heretofore had been punishable only by imprisonment.

"Legality" was thus suspended a mere month after Hitler had been made *Reich* Chancellor. It was true that this decree had been "promulgated as law," and was thus formally legal. Its content, however, dealt a decisive blow to the Constitution, and its motivation was not in the least convincing but a web of lies and propaganda. The Communist Party had nothing to do with the setting of the fire, and had not been preparing any uprising. On the contrary, it had received explicit instructions from Moscow to refrain from any such thing. (The alleged "uprisers"* and conspirators were arrested in large numbers in their apartments, and taken straight from their beds on February 28.) The trial before the Supreme Court established that Marinus van der Lubbe had been acting on his own. His co-defendents, the Communist deputy Torgler and three Bulgarian Communists, were able to prove that they had not been involved in the crime. But the *Reich* President and the German people alike were duped into believing that Hitler and Göring had that night saved the nation from immeasurable dangers.

Very soon afterwards, a rumor began circulating that S.A. men, on Göring's orders, had entered the *Reichstag* through a passageway from the home of the *Reichstag* President [Göring] and set it on fire. The fact that Hitler exploited the fire with such baffling speed to his own advantage gives much credence to this rumor. But to this day, definite proof has not been forthcoming. The undeniable fact remains that the Nazis used the fire to deceive the people and to rob them of their freedom.

That February night saw the demise of the German constitution and the imposition of a state of emergency, which, according to the proclamation, would be maintained "until further notice" but which actually lasted until May 8, 1945. Terrorism was now rampant; a wave of arrests engulfed the entire country, carrying off not only Communists, but all those who had previously dis-

* *Aufständler*—semi-ironic neologism. *Trl.*

pleased the party and the Storm Troopers. The latter saw their chance to take revenge on their opponents. In cellars and guard-houses, prisoners were beaten and tortured in scenes anticipating later concentration-camp practices. Although the victims of these acts of vengeance were bullied into the strictest secrecy, and often made to sign affidavits to that effect, the news filtered through, creating an atmosphere of dread which paralyzed the will to resist of many honest and decent Germans. Even more suffocating was the censorship of the press which kept the masses in ignorance of events occurring in the back-rooms of the "Movement." Official propaganda followed the line Hitler had established by the proclamation cited above.

Nevertheless, the elections of March 5, 1933, fell far short of Nazi expectations. Hard as they had tried, the NSDAP did not gain an absolute majority, but a mere 44 per cent of the votes cast. Only after 52 seats of the German Nationalist People's Party had been added, did the National Coalition headed by the NSDAP manage to control 340 of 647 seats. Compared to the previous *Reichstag,* the Social Democrats had lost only one seat, while the Communist Party, having been exposed to a wave of persecu-tions, had lost 19 seats. The Communist Party had been barred from nearly all effective participation in the campaign, since most of its officials had been arrested, and its press shut down.

But Hitler was not too concerned about election results, for he already had enough power to secure control. The new *Reichstag* was to function on only two occasions. On March 21, it opened ceremoniously in the Garrison Church at Potsdam. Hitler had selected this location to suggest symbolically that he, the "savior of the *Reich,*" was the last link in an unbroken tradition from the great Prussian king Frederick I down to Bismarck and Hinden-burg. *Reich* President von Hindenburg was intentionally ma-neuvered into the center of the solemn ceremony, and princes of the House of Hohenzollern also played their prominent parts, in order to persuade many monarchists of long standing that the restoration of the monarchy was imminent.

Two days later, Hitler sent to the floor of the *Reichstag* (meet-ing in the Berlin Kroll Opera House) the so-called "Enabling Act" which, in actuality, aimed at the total emasculation of the *Reichs-*

Hitler and Hindenburg at the *Reichstag* opening, 21 March 1933

dpa-Pictorial

tag. The legislative powers vested in the *Reichstag* by the constitution were to be handed over legally and formally to the *Reich* executive, which was to combine executive and legislative powers in a single body. In foreign affairs, too, treaties were to be concluded without necessarily obtaining the approval of the *Reichstag*. In his declaration of policy, Hitler was again the wolf in sheep's clothing. He explained that the government aimed at creating conditions for a deeply felt and truly personal religion, that it placed the greatest value on friendly relations with the churches, and that the German nation wanted to live in peace with the world.

Since the proposed act involved a change of the constitution, Hitler needed a two-thirds majority. He obtained it with the help of the parties in the center, especially the 92 votes of the Center

Party and the five votes of the State's Party, which allowed him to act with apparent legality. The representatives of these parties decided to vote for the Enabling Act because they believed that otherwise Hitler would usurp these powers through a coup d'état. The fact that this would in all likelihood have happened is nonetheless insufficient excuse for handing the dictator the easy justification of having "acted constitutionally" in every way.

The decision made by the parliamentary group of the Social Democratic Party to vote against the proposed act is thus even more admirable. Some of its members were already under arrest. All seats once occupied by the Communist Party were empty. The Communists were in prison, or else had fled the country to escape persecution. The Kroll Opera House where the *Reichstag* met was surrounded by massed Storm Troopers who, in unison, roared threatening propaganda slogans. In this atmosphere, it fell to the Social Democrat Otto Wels to explain the vote of his party. His brave stand for justice and liberty was the last free word uttered before a German parliament for a long time to come:

> Never in the history of the German *Reichstag* have the elected representatives of the people been so radically excluded from controlling public affairs as now. The new Enabling Act would exclude them even more strongly. The concentration of all power in the hands of the government must have even farther-reaching effects since the press, too, has been stripped of all freedom. . . . This is a vain attempt to turn back the wheels of history. We Social Democrats know that the facts of power politics cannot be undone by mere assertions of the law. We recognize that your control, at present, is a fact of power politics. But the sense of justice in the nation is also a power in politics, and we shall not desist from appealing to the national sense of justice. We German Social Democrats pledge ourselves solemnly in this historic hour to the principles of humanity and justice, of freedom and socialism. No Enabling Act gives you power to destroy ideas which are eternal and indestructible.

This speech provoked Hitler to such a paroxysm of anger that he betrayed his true nature in the ranting tirade with which he replied.

Once the Enabling Act had removed the legal foundation of

the state, Hitler, with ruthless determination, destroyed whatever stood in the way of total control by the NSDAP.

On March 31, 1933, the states of the *Reich* were stripped of power (*gleichgeschaltet*),* which meant that the federal structure which the Weimar Republic had taken over from the Bismarck Empire was torn down. Even earlier, *Reich* commissioners had been placed in control of the *Länder* police. On May 2, trade union buildings were occupied, the unions dissolved, and their entire property was confiscated. By June, the political parties had ceased to exist. The Social Democratic Party was suppressed; the other parties, including the German Nationalists, disbanded voluntarily. In July, a decree forbade any reconstruction of political parties.

The logical outcome of these events was the dissolution of the *Reichstag,* which had not been convened since March 23. In the "elections" of November 12, no one but Nazis was on the ballot. A great many voters were driven to the polls by an overwhelming barrage of propaganda, and 92 per cent of the vote was cast for the "unity list." The new *Reichstag* was convened only when Hitler felt the need to give his decrees or declarations an aura of solemnity. Members of parliament reported in party and S. A. uniforms for the occasion, cast "unanimous votes," and concluded their labors with the national anthem, now augmented by the Nazi *Horst Wessel* song. (Some satirists spoke of the *"Reich's* most expensive choral society.")

In the Secret State Police (Gestapo), brought into being and directed by Göring, the Nazis were shaping a dreaded weapon with which to control the thoughts and deeds of the citizens. Sentences passed by judges who still upheld their independence could be circumvented by the Gestapo, which had power to bury people in concentration camps without trial or sentence for years on end.

In one respect alone Hitler's power was not yet complete: the army, by its oath, was loyal to the *Reich* President as its supreme commander. Hitler had to wait for the "old gentleman's" death to bring this important power factor fully under his control.

* *Gleichschaltung* was a favorite Nazi term. It was used to describe how in many-sided activities the Nazis brought all aspects of German political and associational life under the control of the party or the totalitarian state. The term originates in physics where it is used to denote the transformation of one electrical current into another. *Trl.*

Hitler and Röhm with the S.S.   *Copress*

In deciding on the role of the army and whether the Storm Troopers were to be incorporated into it, Hitler differed with Ernst Röhm, one of his earliest comrades in arms, and the only one among his friends with whom he used the familiar *Du*. From the very beginning, Röhm had been in charge of organizing and training the Storm Troopers. The ex-army officer dreamed of a future when Hitler's private army would combine with the armed forces to make a great "people's army" under his own supreme command.

Röhm's plan met with determined resistance: the *Reichswehr* command, for one, wanted no part of it. Hitler himself could hardly be expected to favor it, since his plans for a strong army could, in his opinion, only be realized by allowing old traditions to continue unbroken. In addition, Ernst Röhm, the chief of staff of the Storm Troopers, had to reckon with Heinrich Himmler, the leader of the S.S., a new and dangerous rival. In March 1934, Himmler had taken charge of Göring's Gestapo and built up his own security service known as the *Sicherheitsdienst* (S.D.). The black-uniformed S.S. had risen from 30,000 to 100,000 men and, in theory, was under the supreme control of the chief of staff Röhm, as the (brown-uniformed) S.A. was. In truth, however, the S.S. had become Himmler's private armed force. Members of the S.S. considered themselves "elite troops" because their racial pedigree was investigated when they enlisted, and by reason of this distinction they despised the S. A. Even by that time, Himmler had acquired the dreaded Reinhard Heydrich as his assistant. Now Himmler patiently awaited the day when the S.A. could be brought under his control too. He saw his opportunity in the coming conflict between the S.A. and the army.

As far as can be understood from the mass of obscure back-stage maneuvers which went on during those weeks, it is considered certain that although Röhm was consumed by high ambitions for his Storm Troopers, he never planned a *Putsch* against Fuehrer and *Reich*. Instead, Röhm had agreed to send the S.A. on leave for four weeks, beginning in late June. "Information," probably fabricated by Heydrich, was fed to Hitler and to influential commanders of the *Reichswehr* alleging secret orders by Röhm and the establishment of arms caches. Hitler was about to eliminate all socialist elements from his party, most of which were centered in the Storm Troopers; consequently these machinations accorded well with his own plans to strip its leaders of their power in favor of the *Reichswehr*.

The decision was made after some hesitation and implemented

in a bloody show of gangsterism. On June 30 and July 1, hundreds of people on a prepared list were liquidated without indictments, trials, or sentences. Hitler himself flew to Munich, then drove by car to Wiessee where Röhm and some leading figures of the S.A. had stopped. He had some of them shot in their beds; others were arrested and subsequently executed. A gun was placed in Röhm's cell, and he was told that "the Fuehrer wanted to give him the chance to carry out the sentence with his own hand." Ten minutes later, the murder squad returned, and shot down the "Fuehrer's best friend."

That same day, the German nation was treated to the most astonishing revelations by its newspapers. Suddenly, the homosexual tendencies exhibited by Röhm and a large number of his comrades were brought to light, just as if Hitler and his entire inner circle had previously not known about them. Thus moral defamation was added to murder. Slowly it became apparent that the orgy of executions had not stopped with members of the Storm Troopers, but had also provided the occasion to "liquidate" innumerable other people out of favor with the regime. They included the former *Reich* Chancellor Schleicher and his wife, General von Bredow, Papen's collaborator Edgar Jung, the president of the Berlin Catholic Action Erich Klausener, Gregor Strasser, and many others. In quite a few cases, *Gauleiter* and other NSDAP chiefs seized the opportunity of settling their private accounts with former opponents.

But the mere fact that such a mass slaughter could be staged was not enough. Hitler, using his notorious methods, now set out to give it the appearance of a "legal act." On July 3, 1934, the *Reich* government pronounced the following decree: "The measures taken on June 30, and July 1 and 2, to repel the treasonable and mutinous attacks are legal and in accordance with the state's right to self-defense."

With this butchery the S.A. ceased to play an active role. From now on, Hitler relied primarily upon the S.S.: Himmler and Heydrich had thus achieved their goals.

On August 2, 1934, *Reich* President von Hindenburg died at the age of 87. Even before he had breathed his last, the *Reich* government had decided on his successor by incorporating the

Recruits take the oath to Hitler

office of *Reich* President with that of the Chancellor. That very
day, the armed forces were made to swear an oath of loyalty to
Hitler:

> I swear by God this sacred oath that I will render uncondi-
> tional obedience to Adolf Hitler, the Fuehrer of the Ger-
> man *Reich* and nation, the Supreme Commander of the
> Armed Forces, and that I shall be ready, as a brave soldier,
> to lay down my life at any time for this oath.

With this new formula all soldiers swore loyalty to Hitler in
person rather than, as previously, to the national Constitution. The
oath created many a severe conflict of conscience for members of
the armed forces later on and, in the end, led many resistance
fighters to the recognition that they could succeed only if they
removed Hitler.

One month after Hindenburg's death, Hitler, at the Party Congress in Nuremberg, spoke of the "final stabilization of National

130

Socialist power in Germany." He declared the revolution at an end and the German way of life definitely established. "There will not be another revolution in Germany for the next thousand years."

6: Who Were Germany's "Leaders"?

With the transfer of the *Reich* presidency to Hitler the "seizure of power" was complete. All countervailing forces, any method of limiting his power had vanished. Germany resembled a giant robot in which everything, down to the last cog, was "synchronized." What would the manipulators of power do with this robot whose movements they controlled? What were they really like? And where did they come from?

Adolf Hitler was the son of an Austrian customs official who, as an illegitimate child, had borne his mother's maiden name Schicklgruber for the first 40 years of his life. Only at this unusually late date did his presumed father recognize him and change his name to Hitler.

Twelve years later, on April 20, 1889, Adolf Hitler was born in Braunau on the Inn, his father's fourth child of a third marriage. He first attended public school, then the state high school, from which he was forced to withdraw before obtaining his intermediate certificate (*Mittlere Reife*).

Hitler had a burning desire to become an artist, a painter. He applied to the Vienna Academy of Fine Arts, but was turned down twice for lack of talent. Deeply hurt by this rejection, he gave up all further attempts at training for a regular trade. For a while he drifted in Vienna, living in "flop houses" and like places.

He eked out a very poor living with such jobs as painting and selling picture postcards. Since he led an extremely frugal life—he neither smoked nor drank—he was able to support himself without too much exertion. When reading the newspapers and arguing about politics he was aroused to great emotion; already his way of talking politics was characteristic. He did not seek discussions and avoided strenuous debates; all he wanted was an audience for his

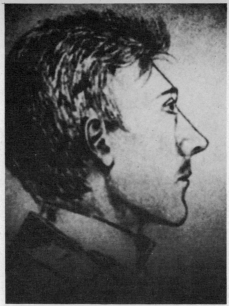

Self-portrait, Vienna, 1907

monologues. He would talk himself into a frenzy and be maddened by contradictions, to which he reacted with instantaneous and uncontrolled wrath. This manner was to stay with him until his death, as all those who met him, friend or foe, were to testify.

In *Mein Kampf* he speaks of the amount he read during this period, and this is very probably true, since he could read the newspapers for nothing in cafés where he indulged his sweet tooth, could borrow books from public libraries, and buy anti-semitic pamphlets (the mainstay of his intellectual arguments) at any bookstall for a few pennies. He read indiscriminately, picking varied subjects, and above all exploring the mystical sciences, such as hypnotism, occultism, and astrology. As a result, Hitler became half-educated, lacking a solid grounding in any subject, but he could be brilliantly persuasive for a brief period because of his excellent memory. Of the books he read, he retained only those ideas which fitted his preconceived notions, a method he openly boasted of in *Mein Kampf*. He read for the sake of political propaganda.

Probably the most enduring consequence of Hitler's period in Vienna was his encounter with antisemitism. From then on he believed he had found the key which would unlock the riddles of the universe. "The Jew" took the place of the medieval devil as the source of all evil. Anything Hitler hated—and hatred was the driving force within him—he ascribed to Jewish origins: the Jews were blamed for socialism, capitalism, modern art (called "decadent" by Hitler), internationalism, parliamentarianism, pacifism, and the rest. In antisemitism, Hitler found not only a scapegoat for all evil, it also enabled him to feel himself a member of the chosen "Aryan master race." Since he was, at the time, close to the bottom of the social ladder, this feeling of belonging to a superior race must have given him deep satisfaction.

Shortly before the First World War, Hitler moved to Munich. In 1914 he volunteered for the army; he served as a dispatch runner at the French front during the entire war and was decorated

Hitler in the crowd at the Odeonsplatz, Munich, at the outbreak of the First World War *Ullstein-Copress*

Two views of Hitler speaking   *UP*

with the iron cross second and first class. Yet, in spite of the great need for officers, he never advanced beyond the rank of a lance-corporal. His solitary nature, his unbalance and eccentricity, his distrust, and his contempt for people probably rendered him unsuitable for higher command positions. Toward the end of the war he suffered gas-poisoning and was confined to the military hospital at Pasewalk in Pomerania. It was there that he first learned that the army and the monarchy had collapsed. The German defeat dealt a severe shock to his intense and narcissistic nationalism. Before long, he had passionately identified himself with the stab-in-the-back legend.

How he would earn a living, however, after being demobilized worried him much less, since he was quite ready to resume the irregular pattern of his pre-war life. Now, however, with fresh inspiration, he decided to "go into politics." He returned to Munich, where for a time he was employed as an "education officer,"

UP

i.e. he spoke before soldiers against socialism and democracy. Through this, and later on through the German Workers' Party (cf. pp. 55-8), he discovered his abilities as a speaker, his talent for hypnotizing large masses of people and expressing with incredible sensitivity those ideas which touched their emotions and aroused them to action. This talent was so astonishing that Alan Bullock, his British biographer, has called him "the greatest demagogue of all time."

Thanks to this talent he talked himself into the leadership of the largest party in Germany. Still, an economic crisis had to occur before the soil was ready for his demagoguery. Until 1928, he had no more than mild success (2.6 per cent of the popular vote).

His rise to power was decisively aided also by another of his talents, the ability of involving others in his struggles, of winning their unconditional loyalty, and exploiting their strength for himself without allowing anyone to grow strong enough to endanger his own position. Whether a normal human being would call it friendship that tied these men together may justly be doubted. Considering that he had his old comrade-in-arms Röhm, the only one familiar enough to use *Du* when talking to him, murdered in cold blood, the ties that usually bind one man to another could hardly have played a role in this closely knit circle of political mercenaries. Hitler may have had some sympathies for his adjutants, his driver, his secretaries, simple people all of humble origins, with whom he could drop his defenses because he was sure of their unbounded admiration. And the same was true later of his wife, Eva Braun.

The inner clique of leaders—if the term "leaders" applies to anybody besides the "Fuehrer"—was, however, a most peculiar group in which each person used another for his own purposes. Hitler exploited all these strategists of power, these propagandists, and ideologues as long as they were useful to him, playing one off against the other. If they showed human failings like Röhm, or had Jewish ancestors like Heydrich, Hitler used these factors to control them with greater ease. He did not mind Göring's dishonest appropriations of funds as long as he did a good job of gearing the economy to war. If need be, such men could be used later against collaborators who had outgrown their usefulness, as in the case of Röhm.

Conversely, his comrades knew that, despite all their own strong drives for power, they were totally at the mercy of Adolf Hitler's personality, and that no one was capable of playing a role of his own apart from him or without him. Petty jealousies notwithstanding, they remained his willing tools, and, in their own way, promoted the "Hitler legend," since Hitler's mystique reflected back on their own positions. The Fuehrer was the star to which they had hitched their own fortunes.

Leading Nazis included an astonishing diversity of types: old soldiers, frustrated poets, petty trades people, dissatisfied adventurers, white-collar officials and intellectuals, the refined and the crude, the well-to-do and the failures. But it was primarily in three prototypes that the nature of the movement was best expressed: the propagandists, like Goebbels; the manipulators of power, like Göring; and the doctrinaires, like Himmler.

Josef Goebbels came originally from Rheydt, in the Rhineland, and was discovered by Gregor Strasser for the Nazi movement. He had studied philology, and had written his doctoral dissertation under Friedrich Gundolf, a Jewish professor. Then he had published an unsuccessful novel, *Michael,* and had written film scripts that would not sell. Soon after Gregor Strasser had given him a job as his confidential secretary, his abilities as a journalist and public speaker began to emerge. Hitler was then in prison, and the Strasser brothers were busy building a party organization of their own in northern Germany. Goebbels only met the Fuehrer later during a debate between Hitler and the "socialist Strasser wing." Hitler recognized the young intellectual's ability, and played cleverly upon his vanity. At the beginning, Goebbels had little liking for Hitler's political views (at one point in his diary he calls him a "reactionary.") But he soon accepted Hitler as the "only captain with whom one can conquer the world!" and was more than willing to separate from Strasser and to join him.

Hitler reciprocated by appointing him *Gauleiter,* or district leader, of Berlin. For, already at that time, substantial donations from industrialists allowed the party to pay some of its workers regular salaries. As *Gauleiter,* Goebbels founded a daily paper, called "Der Angriff" (Attack), in 1927, which can only be described as a scandal sheet. In it he faithfully adhered to Hitler's prescription for successful propagandists (cf. p. 112). He hammered and abused, he beat the drum and railed against all opponents left or right, and he even ridiculed his later allies, the German Nationalists, by giving the nickname "Hugendwarf" to the party chairman, Hugenberg. As for his physical person, Goebbels was certainly not the best advertisement for the racial doctrines he spread with such zeal. He was neither blond nor tall, and he had a clubfoot, an inherited defect according to medical science. Such a disability would have been left unmentioned if Goebbels himself had not preached the doctrine of the Germanic superman day after day, and drawn attention to the contrast.

At the same time, Goebbels used his uncommon shrewdness to feed another line of propaganda: he concocted the "positive images" of the party to appeal to the fancies of the masses. It was Goebbels who created the popular Hitler image. In his diaries, Hitler is always "intelligent, of crystal-clear logic, tough, resolute,

Josef Goebbels with his family   *Brown Bros.*

great, inspiring, eternally persevering, unflinching, and poised." Since this image would only stimulate admiration, not love, Goebbels also provided the emotional appeal: "Who ever has the good fortune to be often in the Fuehrer's company grows more fond of him day by day. Not only does he always make the right decisions on every question, but he is also a person of quite unusual kindness, and such a splendid comrade that he captures everybody who comes within his sight." In similar fashion, Goebbels described his fellow party member Göring as an "honest soldier with the heart of a child"—an image gladly and eagerly accepted.

After the debacle of 1945, Hitler's closest entourage gave in official evidence a totally different image. The former *Reich* press chief, for example, reported on Hitler's frequent temper tantrums, which seized him "whenever events went counter to Hitler's wishes or predictions, when he would be goaded by his unceasing, ever-ready distrust and suspect sabotage. (He liked to resort to cries of sabotage if he wanted to avoid admitting failure.) He reacted in a similar manner when he felt unduly upset by human weaknesses." In states like these, small errors and misdemeanors would be magnified into the most damnable crimes. Executions and confinements to concentration camp were caused as frequently by his unrestrained ravings as—to use his own words—by "ice-cold calculations." These historically documented temper tantrums were later turned into "carpet chewing" by enemy propaganda, but this, too, belongs to the realm of invention.

Goebbels, of course, did not fail to build up his own popular image as well. He projected himself as the supreme commander of propaganda battles, staggering under his work while pining for sleep, sun, and light. Photographs of him always showed the family man, surrounded by numerous daughters, despite the fact that all Berlin knew of his liaisons with actresses.

The party included some other effective propagandists besides Goebbels. One was Julius Streicher, who published an unspeakably filthy antisemitic weekly "Der Stürmer." He bears heavy responsibility for the later persecution of the Jews. Less odious was Walther Darré, the peasant "Fuehrer," who knew nothing of agriculture but surrounded peasant life with a romantic glow, glorified "blood and soil, customs and mores," and organized the peasants for Hitler. Robert Ley reached a peak of tasteless adulation for the Fuehrer by permitting his Labor Front to identify the Christian credo with Hitler in its "training letters": "In this world, we Germans believe only in Hitler!"

Whatever these propagandists wrote was always a means to an end. How far they believed it themselves cannot be known for sure, especially in the case of Goebbels, the supreme master of the art. Ernst Niekisch, who lost his eyesight during years of confinement for his resistance to Hitler, offered about the best characterization of the Propaganda Minister:

> The masses are his puppets; he makes them feel, believe, laugh, and cry, as his fancy strikes him. What they hold sacred serves him merely as a challenge to test his virtuosity, and to exert his power. He is hardly touched by the concerns, wishes, and beliefs of the masses; it is enough for him to subject them to his control because they are concerned, they wish, and believe. His whole being is, as it were, immersed in a flood of untruth, insincerity, and dishonesty; he is all lie when he chooses his words and recites them, when he emphasizes some over others . . . when he smiles and lets a shadow move across his face, when he knits and unknits his brow, when he turns about and bends his arm . . . he lies in everything and admires himself for it, and he mocks the masses who fall for him.[15]

This description of the Goebbels of 1937 already anticipates the Goebbels of 1944 who whipped up excitement for total war among the masses in the Berlin Sports Palace—while clearly anticipating Germany's total defeat.

A thoroughly different type was the later *Reich* Marshal Hermann Göring. Born of a good family, he attended military college, became an officer, and was awarded the highest decoration for bravery under fire, the *pour le mérite,* while commanding an air squadron in the First World War. After the war, he worked in Sweden for a time, piloting airplanes for a Swedish company, and met his first wife Karin, the daughter of a Baron von Fock.

In 1923, patriotic sentiment made him return to Germany. He settled in Munich, where he met and joined Hitler. What attracted him was the fusion of nationalism and socialism in Hitler's pro-

Hermann Göring after his marriage to the actress Emmy Sonnemann, 1935

Ullstein

141

Hermann Göring after his marriage to the actress Emmy Sonnemann, 1935

Ullstein

gram. Following the abortive *Putsch* of 1923, Göring lived for some time in Austria and later in Sweden, from whence he returned in 1927. Elected to the *Reichstag* in 1928, he was placed in charge of his eleven Nazi fellow deputies by Hitler, who could not run for office as he did not become a German citizen until shortly before his appointment as Chancellor. Göring, from then on, proved of inestimable value to Hitler and the NSDAP by establishing connections with other parties, public figures, and primarily social classes whose sympathies or tolerance the party valued. Göring was sociable, and knew how to move in the drawing rooms of the "better social strata." He was able to laugh with abandon—at times at himself, whereas Hitler lacked all sense of humor. Of all Nazi leaders, Göring was most liked by the people for these character traits. They considered him a man who "lived and let live."

Göring was in fact less of a radical and a fanatic than Goebbels and less contaminated by lunatic racism than Himmler. But he wanted power, was determined to have it, and, with unsurpassed lack of scruples, removed all obstacles from his path. A speech he delivered in Essen on March 11, 1933, well reveals his mentality:

> I thank my creator for not knowing what objective means.
> I am subjective. I stand only and exclusively by my nation;
> all else I reject. . . . When people say that here and there
> somebody was picked up and mistreated, one must answer:
> You must break the egg to make an omelette. . . . Although we make many mistakes, we at least act, and keep
> cool. I prefer shooting short or far off the mark, but, at
> least, I shoot. . . .

Another of Göring's slogans was: "I have no conscience. My conscience is Adolf Hitler."

Showmanship and lack of scruples were Göring's main traits. He went about lining his own pockets without any shame or caution. When he married the actress Emmy Sonnemann in 1935, the list of his wedding gifts filled a medium-sized book. To simplify matters, "contributions for a gift" were deducted from the salaries of Berlin civil servants. These deductions amounted to 40,000 marks, which the city commissioner presented to Göring with his congratulations. Everything of value could be found here, from a villa to valuable paintings, tapestries, silverware, jewels, carpets, and candlesticks.

Among the Nazi leaders, Göring's type was the most common. He was quickly joined by all the parasites who wanted to profit from a share in power. Foreign Minister Joachim von Ribbentrop, who belonged in this group, handled foreign affairs as unscrupulously as Göring handled domestic matters. One could also mention people like Sauckel, who organized a thriving business with slave laborers during the war, and, indeed, most of the *Gauleiter* for the party down to petty officeholders in county and local branches who basked in power, and used it more or less innocently, as the case may be. To grow rich quickly was one of the less harmful ways of exploiting a position of influence; as a rule it cost no human lives. No one in these circles worried too much about a *Weltanschauung*.

The manipulators of power were driven by their lust for power without continually keeping the Nazi *Weltanschauung* in mind. The propagandists used the *Weltanschauung* as a crutch for their publicity. But there were also doctrinaires who believed this *Weltanschauung* and strove to translate its every word into deeds.

One of the first doctrinaires who appeared in Hitler's circle was Alfred Rosenberg. A refugee from the Baltic, he had studied architecture, and set down his *Weltanschauung* in a voluminous manuscript which, later on, was published as *The Myth of the Twentieth Century*. The book established him as a not overly original follower of the French writer Gobineau, who had interpreted world history from a racist point of view, and as an imitator of Houston Stewart Chamberlain, another Gobineau disciple then living in Germany. Rosenberg taught the myth of "racially pure blood," and impressed Hitler with his pseudo-scientific and pompous style. When Hitler was arrested in 1923, he made Rosenberg his deputy ("From here on you shall lead the movement!"), for he knew full well that Rosenberg was no man of action and would merely fill in for him.

In this respect, Rosenberg differed from Heinrich Himmler, who rose to importance in the party as late as 1929. Himmler not only blindly believed in the race theory but had the energy and the nerve to translate it verbatim and with bureaucratic pedantry into stark and bloody reality. He turned madness into method. Before Himmler joined the Nazi movement, he had graduated from an agricultural school and operated a small chicken farm. Hitler gave him the task of organizing the S.S., and as their *Reichsführer* he rose to one of the mightiest positions in the state. In contrast to the exhibitionist Göring, Himmler was not given to ostentatious use of power. Even as *Reichsführer* of the S.S. he lived the life of a petty bourgeois. All observers could detect the schoolmaster in him, his narrow mind, and his penchant for pedantry.

Himmler lacked the cold cynicism of Goebbels; he always acted with dreadful seriousness and a persistence bordering on lunacy. The S.S. admired deeds and not words and despised Goebbels as a boaster whose propaganda was just hot air. Himmler was by nature a religious fanatic who would stop at nothing in order to save the world in the way he saw it.

He had the responsibility for ordering and supervising the extermination of the Jews as if they were vermin. He had human beings subjected to the most heinous medical experiments, and listened "with interest" to reports about them, as if they concerned experiments with cultures of bacteria. On his orders, his Central Office for Questions of Race and Settlement developed giant projects for the "colonization of Eastern space," i.e. Russia. They contained references to the "re-folking" and the "Germanizing"* of the inhabitants, to the sterilization of entire ethnic groups, and to mass abortions to be performed by midwives especially trained for the job! Here, death and extermination were being planned as methodically as other countries planned public health measures for the benefit of the population.

Such projects could only be thought up by people who had severed all ties with the moral traditions of the Christian West. Himmler moralized before his S.S. men as follows:

> An S.S. man must embrace one principle absolutely: he
> must be honest, decent, faithful, and a good friend to
> members of his own blood and nobody else. What happens
> to Russians, what happens to Czechs, leaves me totally in-

* Nazi neologisms. *Trl.*

Heinrich Himmler with the S.S.

different. What the nations can offer in the way of our kind of good blood we will take, if necessary, by kidnapping their children and by raising them here with us. Whether other nations prosper or starve to death interests me only insofar as we need them as slaves for our culture: I am interested in nothing else.

Humanitarianism he considered a "Christian softness of the spinal cord," pity was equivalent to weakness. The slogan "Praised be what makes me hard!" was, on his orders, printed and hung on the walls of nearly all S.S. offices.

Himmler's personal physician, Felix Kersten, who used his unusual position to save the lives of many people, reported that Himmler always depended on Hitler for the ideas behind his deeds. Hitler indeed was propagandist, manipulator of power, and doctrinaire in one, a fact which assured him decisive superiority over his "sub-devils." The former president of the Danzig Senate, Hermann Rauschning, has recorded statements made by Hitler during his conversations with him:

> We must free ourselves of all sentimentality and become hard. When I give the order for war one day, I shall not worry about ten million young men whom I thus send to their death. . . . What impresses is cruelty, cruelty and brute force. . . . If someone is so effeminate that he cannot endure seeing somebody writhe in pain beside him, he must join a monastery, not my party comrades.

Hitler also originated the idea of genocide: "We have the duty to 'depopulate,' much as we have the duty of caring properly for the German population. We shall have to develop a technique of 'depopulation.' You will ask what is 'depopulation?' Do I propose to exterminate whole ethnic groups? Yes, it will add up to that. Nature is cruel; therefore we may be cruel too."

In Himmler, Hitler discovered the executioner for his unrestrained destructive urges. And Himmler soon surrounded himself with such insensitive, calculating technicians of genocide as Heydrich, Globocznik, Kaltenbrunner, Eichmann, and Höss. Some doctrinaires remained outside the S.S. however, such men as Hans Frank, who carefully recorded in 38 volumes of diaries the crimes he committed while he was Governor General of Poland. He spoke in one breath of exterminating lice and Jews in Poland, and noted under the date of January 14, 1944: "After we have won the war we can make mincemeat out of the Poles and the Ukrainians and all the vagabonds around here. We can do with them as we please."

Although this "elite" of the Nazi party leaders only *began* their "careers" in 1934, their characters already revealed what was to happen in the future. Kurt von Schleicher, who was assassinated during the "Röhm revolt," predicted it only too well when he told a friend a day before Hitler was appointed:

> The entire German people will be ruined, not merely a few Communists and Social Democrats. This lance-corporal from Bohemia will destroy the *Reich*. . . . It will have a horrible end!

7: Life in the Third Reich

In 1932, a writer, Arthur Möller van den Bruck, published a book with the title *The Third Reich*. It was a nostalgically conservative, antidemocratic, and antiliberal tract. The author considered the Holy Roman Empire of the German Nation, which had been ruled by the great emperors of the Middle Ages, as the "First Reich" of the Germans. The German Empire founded by Bismarck was called the "Second Reich," and now he dreamed of a future "Third Party" which would found a "Third Reich" and lead it to grandeur and supremacy in Europe. Before coming to power, the Nazis had appropriated this grandiose and mysterious-sounding label and had applied it to the Germany they planned to build in the future.

Young people in Germany often receive contradictory information about the true conditions of life in the Third *Reich*. History books, documents, films, and magazines describe it as ugly and horrible, and make it hard to believe that such a thing once happened in their fatherland. Their elders, on the other hand, often tell them that most people lived well in the Third *Reich,* that people had jobs and earned good money, and that those were the best years within memory, at least up to the war. Nothing much could be felt of the terror.

The rostrum at the Nuremberg stadium, built as part
of Hitler's work program

Puzzled by these reports, young people may well ask that these contradictions be resolved.

When Hitler seized power, the world depression had in fact already passed its peak. Conditions everywhere had begun to improve more or less quickly. Nevertheless, unemployment did not disappear by itself, and generally government intervention provided the means of revitalizing the economy without endangering the currency of the country.

In Germany, the construction of the *Reichsautobahn* (superhighway) was begun as one of these government ventures. The first relevant decree had been enacted by June 1933, but publicity for building such highways had begun as early as 1924. In 1926, an association founded exclusively for this purpose advanced a proposal for an autobahn from Hamburg to Basle. By 1932, a superhighway linking Cologne with Bonn was opened for traffic, although without the great, nation-wide fanfare which became the custom later on. Hitler took up existing plans, but, for military reasons, placed his main emphasis on building an east-west connection. An outstanding civil engineering expert, Dr. Todt, built the autobahns and achieved great technological success. No doubt, Hitler also hoped to build himself a monument for future generations in the *Reichsautobahn*. And, indeed, even today there are people in Germany who remember Hitler primarily as the "builder of the *Reichsautobahn*," and refuse to believe that he murdered millions of innocent people, started a world conflagration, and rent Germany in two.

In order to create the capital necessary for the *Reichsautobahn*, Hjalmar Schacht, Hugenberg's successor as Minister of Economics invented a system of MEFO-bills. These bills could be drawn on a company founded exclusively for the purpose, "Metal Research, Inc." (*Metallforschungs GmbH.*), and guaranteed by the state. Usually companies under contract with the armed forces were empowered to write such bills in order to finance their production. MEFO-bills could be extended for up to five years, and thus took the place of cash.

With equal shrewdness Hjalmar Schacht directed Germany's foreign trade. Germany needed large quantities of foreign foodstuffs but, due to insufficient exports, lacked the foreign currency to buy them. Schacht therefore concluded a series of commercial treaties, especially with Balkan countries, which made a foreign trade balance unnecessary by substituting barter deals, i.e. exchanging German finished products for food and raw materials. Though merely an emergency measure, this direct barter trade worked surprisingly well.

From the start, re-armament played a great role in creating new jobs. Before Hitler even assumed power, Germany had been granted parity in armaments. Hitler followed it up by re-introducing universal conscription in 1935.

A few months later, the Compulsory Labor Service Law was enacted, which obligated each young German, in the public interest, to serve for six months in the Labor Service. For this purpose, an organization called the *Reich* Labor Service (*Reichsarbeitsdienst* or RAD) was established. Compulsory labor service also extended to women, drew a considerable number of unemployed workers off the labor market, and thus provided cheap labor for jobs which did not attract a sufficient number of free workers. Women, for example, were directed mainly to do housework in peasant homes. It also served as pre-military training for young men. The Labor Service embodied Hitler's ideal of subjecting men to total service and of thoroughly militarizing all areas of life. This latter aspect of the Labor Service affected men more than women, for the latter often found it a truly enriching experience to spend six months with women of the same age from all walks of life and all occupations.

In September 1936, Hitler was able to announce to the *Reich* Party Congress that unemployment had been reduced from six million to one million. This made a lasting impression on the population at large. Anybody who had been out of work and starving for years could easily believe that another "golden age" had arrived, for he now held a regular job and received secure pay. Such personal reminiscences tend to make people ignore the fact that the economy could have recovered without a dictator (as demonstrated by other countries), or that the re-armament factor might well become a threat to peace in the future.

This trend could already be observed in the Four Year Plan which Hitler announced at the same *Reich* Party Congress. He called for German economic self-sufficiency (autarky) in a maximum number of fields: "Within four years, Germany must be made independent of foreign countries in all those raw materials which, with German efficiency, our chemical and machine tool industries as well as our mining concerns can produce by themselves."

This program of self-sufficiency led to the mass production of artificial rubber (called buna) and synthetic gasoline. Since this policy was principally dictated by military rather than economic considerations, Göring, the airforce expert, and not Schacht as Minister of Economics, was put in charge of its execution.

Schacht recognized the road of the future very soon. Germany aimed at arms superiority over its rivals, rather than a limited re-armament which would have given her parity with other European nations; Schacht quarreled with Göring, who used his newly acquired authority to interfere continually in matters controlled by the Economics Ministry. When Schacht therefore asked to be

The RAD on the march

relieved of his office, Hitler agreed with reluctance, since Schacht's expertise enjoyed great prestige both in Germany and abroad.

Hitler, however, obstinately refused to follow any advice on the matter, and Schacht's resignation in November 1937 removed all restraints from a policy of "guns instead of butter" (Göring's phrase). When the MEFO-bills fell due in 1938, Hitler ordered the *Reichsbank* to make unlimited credits available to the government, since payment from government funds would have meant curtailing re-armament. The *Reichsbank*, of course, was only able to comply by printing paper money. This increased money in circulation from year to year, and started the depreciation of the currency toward inflation.

The economic recovery, maintained with such splendid results so far, now became economic disintegration. In Schacht's words:

Unlimited armaments ruined not only the German currency, but also cut down the production of sufficient high-quality consumer goods to such an extent that foreign producers were deprived of the opportunity of buying German goods. . . . The excessive drive for self-sufficiency pushed up production costs and wasted material and labor. The exorbitant production of armaments deprived the consumer of many standard items, and, at the same time, diminished exports. All these factors together steadily lowered the standard of living. Rationing of consumer goods (food and clothing) had already begun before the war, and the quality of these goods was dropping rapidly.

The masses, meanwhile, were hardly aware of these facts, for they were enthralled by foreign policy, and primarily concerned with the preservation of the peace during the 1938-39 period. The economic consequences of the policy of re-armament were only felt by the individual after the climax had been reached, and war was in progress.

When Hitler declared May Day (May 1) a "Day of National Labor" and a nation-wide holiday, he not only proved himself an uncommonly shrewd manipulator of the masses but also revealed the principles of his social policies. Since 1889, May 1 had been an international day, dedicated to the struggle of the workers, a day of demonstrations for higher wages and better working conditions. True, after 1918, it had lost some of its fighting aspects, and had generally become a day of peaceful parades for trade-union solidarity, followed by outings to the countryside. Employers and people not affiliated with unions, however, did not take part in the day. By appropriating a cherished tradition of the workers, Hitler emphasized his special interest in winning labor for the "national awakening." But by stripping this holiday of its traditional working-class character and, at the same time, by turning it into a holiday for "all people at work in city and country," a day of rest for "all workers of fist and brain," Hitler emphasized the fact that he no longer recognized the traditional organizations of the workers.

This became apparent a bare 24 hours after labor and management, peasants and craftsmen, students and professors had marched side by side in the May Day parades: in the morning of

May Day ceremonies in the Berlin *Lustgarten,* 1937   *Ullstein*

May 2, the buildings of the free trade unions were occupied by
S.A. and S.S. commandos all over the *Reich*. Leading officials
were taken "into protective custody," and all trade-union property
was confiscated, while the bulk of union officials was ordered to
stay on their jobs under the supervision of commissars appointed
by the National Socialist Factory Cell Organization (NSBO).
These raids sufficed to bring the rest of the unions (Christian,
"yellow," etc.) into "voluntary subordination." In order to create
a favorable climate of opinion for these steps *ex post facto,* the
Reich Minister for Public Enlightenment and Propaganda, Josef
Goebbels, launched a propaganda campaign to discredit the "great
Red super-bosses of the unions." Daily bulletins reported on
"corruption growing to unheard of proportions," mismanagement,

embezzlement, and waste of union funds. Since most of the accused were in prison or had been deprived of their own newspapers, they had no means of protesting their innocence.

Lower union officials had been retained, so it appeared at first as if a mere "co-ordination" (*Gleichschaltung*) had taken place, that is, only a change of leaders. But the following year, the Law for Regulating National Labor revealed the long-range design. In essence, the law applied the leadership principle to private enterprise. Management was made the "leader of the enterprise," while labor was turned into the "followers," and was expected to "remain loyal to its leader, such loyalty being grounded in the community of the enterprise." Thus, concepts were grafted upon modern industry which had originated in medieval or even Teutonic Germany. The "New Order" of the Nazis was surrounded with a romantic halo so that labor would be made to forget that it had ceased to speak independently for its own rights. It followed that the German Labor Front (*Deutsche Arbeitsfront* or DAF), in which the former labor unions and white-collar associations were combined in October 1934, included management associations as well. Paragraph 7 of the relevant decree reads:

> The German Labor Front must secure labor peace by creating in leaders of enterprises an understanding for the legitimate demands of their followers, and in the followers an understanding for the situation and the possibilities of the enterprise. In line with National Socialist principles the German Labor Front has the task of establishing harmony between the legitimate interests of all concerned.

It goes without saying that strikes, the last weapon of the economically weak, had no place in this system. This, however, at once turned the alleged balance of interest into an illusion. In reality, the German Labor Front was primarily a means to win the working people over to the Nazi *Weltanschauung*. Few people realized at the time the future importance of the fact that the German Labor Front had deprived the workers of the most important weapon with which to fight for better conditions. After years of unemployment, people concerned themselves only with job security, and showed no interest in fighting for better wages or other issues.

As one of its major assignments, the German Labor Front was to spread the idea of a "people's community." People from all walks of life liked this slogan, for the parties of the Weimar Republic had failed to impress public opinion with the basic unity of all the political parties, from the Social Democratic Party to the German People's Party, on important matters of common democratic principle. Instead, they had over-emphasized their ideological differences. The theory of the class struggle had lost its hold over the workers, and so it was easier for the National Socialists to instill into many German minds the idea that Hitler had ended "discord among Germans" and created the "people's community." "Common weal before private gain!" was to many the new ideal. They forgot that in Hitler's state only the Fuehrer decided what the "common weal" was!

To foster the new "people's community," firms conducted holiday excursions where laborers and foremen, white-collar workers and office managers, packers and engineers met over bockwurst, beer, and dancing. "Strength through Joy," a branch of the Labor Front patterned after the Italian *Dopo lavoro,* enabled not only businessmen to spend their vacations in Tenerife, but also laborers and employees to go on Caribbean cruises on specially built "Strength through Joy" boats. A campaign to improve working conditions in the plants was launched under the slogan of "the Beauty of Labor." Employers who distinguished themselves in this campaign received gold medals for their firms.

In order to take a balanced view, we must consider these facts and compare them with the social achievements of the Weimar Republic, which included the introduction of the eight-hour day, a law on workers' councils, and unemployment insurance. It is also true that today a much greater variety of trips at an equally cheap rate are offered by private organizations than those offered by "Strength through Joy." All that has survived the Third *Reich* is the holiday on May 1, and an occasional company excursion. It is thus hard to understand why many Germans believe the greatest social advances occurred primarily during this period.

This mistaken opinion can be understood only as an effect of propaganda. While the newspapers of the Weimar Republic rarely mentioned its great social gains, and used to criticize rather than

The movie actress and director Leni Riefenstahl collecting for Winter Aid

praise, Goebbels ordered his newspapers and radio stations to build up these "gigantic achievements" in enthusiastic and flowery language. He thus persuaded many contemporaries that they were witnessing striking social progress, and some still believe it to this day. For the historian's appraisal, however, only facts matter, not delusions.

Such fields of social policies as "social work," or "social welfare," had traditionally been reserved for independent private agencies. Now the Home Mission, the Workers' Welfare [Agency], and Caritas [a Catholic agency] were suppressed or restricted, and a special body created, the National Socialist People's Welfare. Besides caring for the needy, it concerned itself primarily with problems of population and strains of healthy heredity, which meant family case work and the "training of mothers."

156

Funds were raised mainly through public collections. Each year, great drives were organized. Winter Aid (*Winterhilfe*) and money were collected on the streets, especially on Sundays. Donors placed coins in collection boxes and received buttons for their lapels. All associations and occupational groups had to make their personnel available, and at centrally located points in the cities famous "stars" of the party, the motion pictures, and the theater collected money. Newspapers used to report the amounts collected in blaring headlines. It is no wonder, once again, that quite a few contemporaries believed that never before had there been so much charity or such a benevolent government in Germany.

In an analysis of life in the Third *Reich* cultural policies may appear comparatively secondary; for the population at large was more interested in securing jobs and adequate incomes than in questioning whether writers were allowed to publish, or painters to paint abstract pictures, for example. A comprehensive view of a period must, however, include its intellectual, as well as its economic, military, or technological achievements.

There was one respect, admittedly, in which cultural policies coincided directly with the interest of the nation as a whole. That was in the production of the kind of information it obtained from its newspapers. Insufficient, biased, false, or exaggerated information will create an untrue image of reality. Readers of this type of information are misled and easily manipulated by the authorities. Aided by the so-called Editors Law, Goebbels through his Ministry of Popular Enlightenment and Propaganda was in absolute control of the German press. The German people were told only what he approved of. He had perfected the technique of "regulating the language" so well even before the Second World War that he prescribed to the press, down to minute details, whether and how an item was to be presented or emphasized. Hate campaigns, political slander, or purposeful lies could thus be "produced" and spread at any time in any manner as desired.

Poets and writers fared little better than journalists. The book-burning which was organized at the Berlin Opera Square on May 10, 1933, and considered important enough for radio coverage, had sounded the keynote for the cultural policies of the Third

Books being collected for burning by the Nazis

Reich. Mouthing campfire slogans, students threw into the fire works of those authors who had been derisively labeled as "racially alien," including Karl Marx, Sigmund Freud, Erich Kaestner, Erich Maria Remarque, Friedrich Wilhelm Foerster, the Nobel prize winner Carl von Ossietzky, and many others. Later on in September, the control of the Propaganda Ministry was extended to all areas of cultural life through a law which created a *Reich* Culture Chamber, to be presided over by Goebbels. Artists were forced to join one of the branch chambers controlled by this Chamber (*Reich* Literature Chamber, *Reich* Music Chamber, *Reich* Radio Chamber, etc.). Exclusion from a chamber, in effect, meant the end of all professional activities. When the artist Schmidt-Rottluff was ordered to stop painting, compliance with the order was enforced by the Gestapo!

These devices served primarily to exclude the Jews from cultural life. As a result, untold numbers of poets, writers, musicians, conductors, actors, architects, and painters fled abroad. The emigration of Jewish artists not only inflicted a great loss on all areas of German culture but also disgraced Germany before the entire world. In Germany only a few voices were raised in protest against this lunatic persecution. Wilhelm Furtwängler, the great conductor, wrote a letter of protest to Goebbels. Ricarda Huch, the poet, resigned from the Prussian Academy of Fine Arts when this institution, too, began to "dismiss" its Jewish members. She wrote as follows to the President of the Academy:

> That a German should feel German I take almost as a matter of course; but opinions differ on what German means, and how the German element is to be expressed. What the present government prescribes as national beliefs is not my kind of Germanism. Centralization, use of force and brutal methods, defamation of dissenters and boastful self-adulation I consider disasters. Since my views differ so greatly from the opinions which the state prescribes, I can no longer remain a member of a state academy.

Typical Nazi architecture: the entrance to Hitler's Chancellery in Berlin

If more people had spoken out with such force, intelligence, and courage at the beginning of Nazi rule, it might perhaps have had some influence on subsequent developments.

But Hitler and Goebbels were not satisfied with driving the Jews from German cultural life. They also wanted to influence German artists and artistic tastes directly. Goebbels ordered the production of motion pictures spreading antisemitism (e.g. "The Jew Süss"). He outlawed art criticism and wanted it replaced by "meditations on art," i.e. mere descriptions of subject matter. Some journalists made a virtue of necessity: their descriptions damned more effectively than any critical review!

Hitler fancied himself an expert in the fine arts. He hated not only abstract art but all modern painting. Dubbing them "degenerate," he had hundreds of pictures removed from museums and galleries. To house the new "racially correct" art, he built the House of German Art in Munich, where he sponsored annual exhibitions of art that suited his taste; these consisted mainly of Hitler portraits, outsized canvasses of Storm Troopers on the march, and Labor Service gangs carrying spades over their shoulders, idealized peasant scenes, pictures glorifying Nordic man, and sweetly sentimental nudes.

Such "art," together with political jingles by people like Anacker, the Horst Wessel biographies, the "blood-and-soil" novels, and the rest of the racially correct elaborations of Nazi culture, well deserve to remain forgotten. Race hatred and self-glorification have proved uncreative.

The great artistic peaks worth noting during this period were reached in spite of, and not because of, this system. The theater, for example, lacked good contemporary plays and, as a result, cultivated the classics with greater care. They often turned out to be breathtakingly contemporary. One could have heard a pin drop when Marquis Posa demanded freedom of thought from King Philip [in Schiller's *Don Carlos*]; the oath at the Rütli [in Schiller's *William Tell*]* called forth torrents of applause. And the public that watched Richard III (in the play performed under Fehling's direction at the Berlin State Theater) toss on his bed at

* Both plays, and particularly these two scenes, center around the spiritual and political conflict between freedom and authority. *Trl.*

"Hitler the standard-bearer"—an example of the trashy
idealization of Hitler in Nazi art

night because he was haunted by the ghosts of his victims felt
Justice herself breathing retribution down their necks.

The shameful persecution of the Jews extended equally to the
sciences. Jewish university teachers (including such outstanding
Nobel prize winners as James Franck, Albert Einstein, and Otto
Warburg) were driven from the country. Books by Jewish authors
were removed from the libraries, and references to them forbidden.
Contrary to the prevailing belief of free scientists in the universal
validity of the methods and results of the natural sciences, Nazi
university teachers claimed that natural science, too, was determined by race. Philipp Lenard, a Nobel prize winner, wrote a

German Physics in 1936: in spite of all this, research in the natural sciences continued to be carried out on the basis of discoveries by Jewish scholars such as Albert Einstein and Niels Bohr (who had a Jewish mother). Otto Hahn, for example, succeeded in 1938 in splitting the uranium atom, thus making a significant contribution to modern atomic science.

Nazi Germany paid special attention to racial science, a marginal field up to that time. But since the basis of all true knowledge —a maximum of objectivity and faith in facts—was lacking from the start, Nazi research on race was confined to "proving" the fancies which their *Weltanschauung* prescribed.

Whether a social scientist or humanist—a historian, legal scholar, linguist, or economist—conformed to the prevailing trend was, to a large extent, a matter of moral strength. The Nazis made only two demands: nothing could be said in favor of the Jews, or in opposition to the Nazi *Weltanschauung* of the Fuehrer.

Nobody forced university teachers to write on specific subjects, and those who wished could avoid controversial subjects. University researchers who scoured books for quotations by Jewish authors, or bowed to the doctrine of "Nordic blood" and the leadership myth, did so as voluntary contributors and fellow travelers determined to climb to the top. It was disgraceful, for example, that Bonn University deprived Thomas Mann, then a refugee in Switzerland, of his honorary doctorate. No professor who set out to give a philosophical underpinning to Nazi doctrine, no jurist who justified Nazi injustices, or no literary scholar who tried to rewrite the history of literature from a racial point of view can ever claim that he had to yield to unbearable pressures. Things were much more difficult for younger scholars, who were indoctrinated by the party in "Instructors' Camps," and had their *Weltanschauung* checked before being appointed or promoted.

Despite much interference, however, the universities retained a certain independence, and the Nazis continued to watch them with untiring suspicion. Schools were much worse off than universities. Teachers were "co-ordinated" in a National Socialist Teachers' League, and the intimate face-to-face group of a department provided fanatics with many opportunities to make things hard for the unconvinced and the dissenting. Pupils, on their part, might turn teaching into a nightmare by raising embarrassing questions and, finally, forcing their teachers to resort to lies. Textbooks, written from a Nazi point of view only, were permitted, and this created moral conflicts for many teachers and publishers.

Hitler himself had relatively little use for learning and education. Where Lenin had issued the order "Learn, learn, learn!" (it decorates the walls of all Soviet schools) and thus placed a premium on effort and ambition, Hitler summarized his ideas on education as:

> My pedagogy is hard. The weak must be chiseled away. In my "Order Castles"* young people will grow up who will frighten the world. I want a violent, arrogant, unafraid, cruel youth, who must be able to suffer pain. Nothing weak or tender must be left in them. Their eyes must bespeak once again the free, magnificent beast of prey. I want my young people strong and beautiful. I shall train them in all kinds of athletics, for I want youth that are athletic—that is first and foremost. Thus will I erase a thousand years of human domestication. Thus will I face the pure and noble raw material. Thus I can create the new. I do not want an intellectual education. With knowledge I will spoil the young. I would vastly prefer them to learn only what they absorbed voluntarily as they followed their play instinct. They shall learn to overcome the fear of death through the most arduous tests. This is the [historic] stage of heroic youth.

The promotion of such educational goals was primarily the function of two state-controlled organizations, the Hitler Youth (*Hitler Jugend* or HJ) and the League of German Maidens (*Bund Deutscher Mädel* or BDM), which replaced the dissolved youth organizations. Since Hitler did not care for learning, athletics took first place in the Hitler Youth. But the "beast of prey" Hitler wanted to train would of course not be free at all. Hitler had written in *Mein Kampf* that a young man needs to learn to suffer injustice silently. While visiting the "Order Castle" of Sonthofen Hitler had once formulated his principles succinctly as "blind obedience and absolute authority."

---

* "Order Castles" (*Ordensburgen*) were training schools for the future Nazi elite. The name was derived from the medieval castles built by such orders as the Teutonic Knights, and it played upon adolescent romanticism and perverted youth movement traditions. *Trl.*

163

The Hitler Youth   *Ullstein*

The leadership principle was accordingly applied to the Hitler
Youth and the League of German Maidens too. All leaders were
nominated from above. The spirit prevailing in a group of HJ or
BDM depended to a large extent on the attitudes of the leading
boys or girls. Most boys and girls felt happy if they were with
decent and bright young people who were close to the group, and
did not abuse their "power of command." They felt themselves to
be the "guarantors of the future," in the service of a great cause.

One of the slogans drummed into their ears day after day was
"Common weal before private gain!" Were there any objections
to it? Were young people to know what adults had not realized in

time: that it was dangerous to let only one man in the land determine the common weal? Another slogan proclaimed: "You are nothing. Your nation is everything!" This, too, sounded noble and provided a ready-made *raison d'être*. How could these boys and girls suspect that Hitler cared as little for his nation as he cared for the individual, and that he was driven only by his lust for power? These young people believed that the great ideal of nationalism demanded sacrifices. They saw that one did not have to become old before being entrusted with "positions of leadership." They were convinced that Hitler wanted to build a new world pri-

League of German Maidens   *Ullstein*

marily with this youth, and that he wanted to restore Germany to her past greatness at the same time. The future was to be wonderful! Is it fair to expect that the young should have recognized a fraud that had seduced so many adults?

Some people, to this day, are fond of praising the Hitler Youth for keeping the young off the streets. That's why there was no juvenile delinquency problem then. They forget altogether that, although training in the Hitler Youth fell far short of Hitler's "ideal," it contributed much to lowering the respect of the young for adults. And it should not be denied that children were taught to spy on their parents, and that Hitler Youth leaders considered it their prime objective to alienate the children from the churches. This touches upon another important aspect of Nazi cultural policies.

In no field did Hitler disorient the minds as thoroughly as in his approach to the relations between Nazism and Christianity. "Positive Christianity" was already on the party program. After seizing power, too, Hitler never failed to inject protestations of religion into his speeches (see p. 124). Because of this, many people were induced to believe in all seriousness that Hitler had saved Christianity from "Red persecutions," and he would allow the free exercise of religion. Hitler further confirmed Christians in this belief by declaring, in so many words, that he was concerned only with the state and politics, not with the supernatural.

As a result Hitler succeeded in concluding a Concordat with the Vatican in July 1933. Negotiations for the Concordat had begun before he even entered the government. By concluding them speedily Hitler wanted to assure himself of "an atmosphere of confidence," by impressing world public opinion with this recognition of his regime. He therefore formally guaranteed the freedom of Catholic education and of communications between the German bishops and the Holy See. The Catholic press was to remain uncensored, and in exchange Catholic priests were to swear loyalty to the state and refrain from all political activities.

The conclusion of the Concordat was Hitler's first diplomatic success, and he was immensely proud of it. The Catholic Church wanted thereby to secure its rights within the state, but in fact Hitler reaped all the advantages by gaining in prestige; he planned to fulfill the obligations only as long as they appeared useful.

Signing the Concordat in the Vatican, July 1933; (l. to r. seated)
Papen and Cardinal Pacelli, later Pope Pius XII

Feltrinelli

From the very beginning Hitler failed to come to an understanding with the Protestant Church. It was true that Protestantism included a large number of so-called "German Christians" who worked hard to harmonize belief in Christ with the "laws of blood and soil" and the leadership myth. But the very subservience of this group to Hitler produced its antithesis, the Confessing Church, which wanted to keep the Evangelical faith pure. The Confessing Church refused to obey the *Reich* Bishop sponsored by Hitler and thereupon convoked the Fraternal Council of the Evangelical Church in Germany.

Confessing Church resistance was principally aroused by the demand made by the Church authorities, under the domination of "German Christians," that the "Aryanization clause" be implemented by driving pastors of Jewish descent from office, and the further requirement that clergymen swear loyalty to Hitler's person. It now became obvious that a Christian who took his faith seriously was bound to run into unavoidable conflict with a state which claimed the total human being for itself. To exclude legitimate pastors from preaching the gospel merely on account of their "blood" would have implied recognition of the race doctrine. In this manner, the Church would have taken over the Nazi belief that man cannot be saved by faith, but is damned or saved by race alone. The oath to Hitler, required from the clergy, was nothing less than an attempt to subject their religious functions to state control, too.

Hitler's real plans were well known to his inner circle, where he dropped all pretense: "The churches may take command of the German in the hereafter. The German nation, through its Fuehrer, takes command of the German in this world!" Hitler told Rausch-ning that he would completely stamp out Christianity in Germany. "Whether the German people retained its Jewish faith in Christ, with His soft morality of pity, or whether it believed strongly and heroically in god in nature, god in the nation, god in destiny, god in the blood" was a question which would decide its very destiny.

The great contribution made by the Confessing Church was that it understood and declared unerringly that Christian doctrine was incompatible with Hitler's *Weltanschauung* and politics. What this resistance against the omnipotent state required of the Church, and how bravely it was carried on, will be described later.

The Catholic Church did not long enjoy the peace it had been promised by the Concordat. It soon met with numerous vexations, prohibitions, obstructions, and provocations, against which it protested in vain. The dispute erupted into the open when Count von Galen, Bishop of Münster, attacked Rosenberg's anti-Christian view (see p. 143), and the Fulda Conference of Bishops then supported him with Episcopal letters. The Nazi rulers went on the offensive. They closed numerous monasteries, arrested many monks, placed a number of them on show trials, and sentenced them on trumped-up charges of immorality and of smuggling foreign currency. Goebbel's propaganda machine ran at high speed to arouse disgust among the German people for the "moral morass" of the Catholic Church.

As yet the Church had refrained from an open break, for it hoped that more could be achieved through the Concordat than by an open declaration of war. But this hope proved vain and, in March 1937, Pope Pius XI issued an encyclical, *Mit brennender Sorge* ("With burning sorrow"). In this encyclical, the Pope

The attempt to create a Nazi religion: *Ullstein*
"In the beginning was the word," by H. O. Hoyer

charged the Nazis with having violated the Concordat on many occasions, and sharply condemned the Teutonic folk heresies, promoted by Rosenberg, and Nazi ideology.

The Nazi struggle against the churches ended with the outbreak of the Second World War. Hitler shied away from public controversies, for he feared they might impair the morale of his soldiers. Yet, he did not lose sight of his final goal and ordered plans to be drawn up which aimed at the final annihilation of both faiths.

What did all this mean for those inhabitants of the Third *Reich* who went to church more frequently than just at Christmas, paid more than lip-service to their faith, and saw in their religious affiliation more than a demographic accident? To them, Hitler's rule brought moral conflicts, anxiety, and temptations. For them, all comfortable illusions had ceased.

These problems lead us to a key question: what was the position of the judiciary in the Third *Reich,* and what did the people know of the injustices all around them?

The law is one of the means by which power is checked and limited. It is therefore hardly surprising that Hitler, with his lust for power, hated and despised the law above all else. At best, he considered it a means of controlling the populace. To him, the human conscience was a Jewish invention, and he boasted in his "secret conversations" that he would not hesitate to commit perjury, or conclude and break treaties "in cold blood" many times a day. Hitler's contempt for the law contrasted sharply with his respect for the Germanic tribes: the ancient Germans held the law sacred, whether customary or statutory, and would rather have killed their kings than broken their laws.

Hitler was, of course, shrewd enough not to reveal to the masses that he "despised justice and morality." Instead, he tried to hide his misdeeds behind a screen of legal verbiage. To this end, he very cleverly adopted a technique of pseudo-legality which was well calculated to play upon the German mind. Most Germans believed that a law or command per se had to be just. It was by such pure legal formalities that "unjust laws" were accepted in Germany. Such laws were not based on the idea of justice but on the principle that "law was what was useful to the nation." Again, it was up to Hitler alone to determine how this usefulness should be applied. As early as 1936, the *Reich* Law Leader Frank had formulated the guiding principles which expressed quite unequivocally official rejection of previously accepted values:

> The judge must not be placed above the citizen as representative of state authority. He is one of the members of the living community of the German nation. It is not his task to apply a legal system which is superior to the people's community, or to realize universal values. Instead, he must preserve as it is the real order of the existing *völkisch* community, exterminate obstructionists, punish anti-social behavior, and resolve conflicts between members of the community.

To interpret the law "correctly," judges were ordered to consider the Nazi *Weltanschauung,* the utterances of the Fuehrer, and

"Trial" before the President of the People's Court, Freisler

the so-called "healthy sense of the people." Any arbitrary decision could be rationalized with such principles.

Despite this, the population did not recognize the abandonment of justice, and this may in part be explained by the fact that civil law remained practically untouched by this collapse of legality. Litigation over a legacy, a commercial contract, or an eviction still brought a fair verdict according to existing laws.

This new evil left an undeniable mark in the field of criminal law. As a first measure, penalties became ever more severe, an increasing number of offenses were made capital crimes (their number had risen to 43 at the end), and death sentences were almost invariably carried out. During the war years, in particular, the number of executions rose to frightening heights. Secondly, special courts and people's courts were established and staffed with judges of proven loyalty to Nazism. Appeals from their sentences were not permitted. These courts adopted procedures whereby the accused now had to prove their innocence, instead of enjoying the right of innocence until guilt was proved. Defense

171

became a farce since sentences were usually decided upon before the trials opened. Judges became prosecutors and abused the defendants, an outstanding example being the disgustingly base trial of the men who attempted to murder Hitler on 20 July, 1944, which was presided over by Roland Freisler.

Still more pernicious was the way in which an ever increasing number of people were tortured or executed without trial or sentence for no worse crime than unorthodox opinions or "impurity of race." This development took place before the eyes of the entire German people.

What, then, of concentration camps? When they were established, people might have believed in good faith that they were needed for the "restoration of public order and security," to quote Article 48 of the Constitution. However, when the Nazis had firm control of all effective power—the police, the armed forces, the civil service—after all political opponents had totally disappeared from public life, after elections had "proved" that 98 per cent of the people favored Hitler—why were concentration camps still kept up? Why were they even increased in number?

And what happened on June 30, 1934? Was it necessary to shoot opponents in their beds? Had they mounted the barricades? Could they not have been brought to trial? Should they not have been allowed their day in court? Was not the traitor Hitler allowed to organize a thorough and extensive defense at his trial in 1923? Were there in fact people in Germany at that time who did not know of these injustices? Those who lived through this period must examine their own consciences, and admit, at the very least, that they were too easily duped.

It was not due to either negligence or accident that concentration camps continued to exist past the time when people no longer had any reason to fear the "Red danger." They formed a well-calculated part of the system. To quote Hitler:

> Terrorism is an effective political tool. I shall not deprive myself of it merely because these simple-minded bourgeois "softies" take offense. These so-called atrocities render it unnecessary for me to conduct hundreds of thousands of individual raids against mutinous and dissatisfied people. People will think twice before opposing us, if they know what awaits them in the camps.

The exact fate of these unfortunate victims—the political opponents, the trade-union leaders, the clergymen, the monks, Jehovah's Witnesses, and pacifists—was only hinted at among people in the Third *Reich*. Those who returned from these hells had to keep silent to avoid renewed danger to themselves. In all probability, their stories would not even have been believed. Yet, it was known, or could have been known, that prisoners were sent to camps without a trial and for indefinite periods, and that there was no right of appeal.

In this day, the trials before German courts of former concentration camp commandants and guards have given all of us an insight into the grisly realities of these camps. Hundreds of witnesses have revealed how limitless power unleashed evil instincts. "In the camps, everything human disappeared. We were merely objects. No normal mortal can imagine how we were treated," said one of the witnesses. Blows, beatings, and kickings were part of the daily routine, so much so that one of the accused camp-torturers declared during his trial that such measures did not constitute mistreatment! Prisoners had to do "gymnastics" until they fainted with exhaustion, or, for hours on end, had to give the Saxon salute, i.e. remain in a deep knee-bend with arms laced behind their heads. These were merely the harmless "jokes" indulged in by the camp guards. Prisoners were whipped for the slightest offense—or for none at all; they were strapped on a rack, and ordered to execute knee-bends after being whipped; no less frequently prisoners were trussed up with hands tied behind their backs.

The life of a prisoner counted for nothing. Prisoners disliked by the guards were arbitrarily selected for injections (*abgespritzt*), which means they were murdered through injections of Phenol or Evipan, only one of a number of methods of killing. Prisoners were often trampled to death with nailed boots, or drowned in cesspools, or driven into the electrically charged barbed-wire fences of the camps, or, in an especially bestial manner, hosed to death with high-pressure water hoses. Innumerable witnesses have placed all these ghastly details on court records during many months of trials, and the defendants have admitted them.

In this system human beings had turned into "things" to such an extent that the administrative S.S. bureaus concerned "calcu-

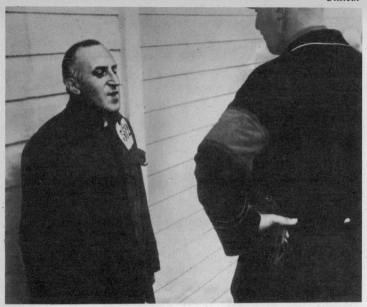

Inside Sachsenhausen concentration camp—
the 1935 Nobel Peace Prize winner Carl von Ossietzky

lated the profitability" of prisoners. A prisoner was expected to live on average for nine months. During this time, according to calculations, the productivity of each prisoner was calculated to yield 1,631 Marks for the Nazi state (the total includes the profit gained from the "careful utilization of the corpse").

The trials conducted against Hitler's underlings in Ulm, Bayreuth, and Bonn have induced many Germans to ask: "How was it possible? Were there so many unrecognized sadists, criminals, and murderers among us?" There is only one answer: if the state had been based on law (a *Rechtsstaat*), they would not have found the opportunities to indulge their base instincts with impunity. The Nazi state, based on injustice (an *Unrechtsstaat*), gave them these opportunities. It handed them the victims after depriving the latter of all right and protection, and it placed a premium on sadism and cruelty. It was the bullies and the murderers who advanced in this system, not the decent citizens.

One of the camp guards (revealingly nicknamed "Iron Gustav") testified at his trial: "In 1939, Sachsenhausen was visited by the President of the People's Court, Freisler [then the highest jurist in the country]. We showed him everything, the rack, the whipping, everything. Upon leaving Freisler said: 'Your prisoners strike me as still rather cocky. You simply have a recreation home here.' This was a confirmation for us. Everything was O.K."

Physicians on duty in the concentration camps lost all sense of values in the atmosphere of general lawlessness. They killed thousands of innocent human beings by injecting poison, or performed senseless and painful medical experiments on helpless victims who died miserably as a result. Thus had physicians abandoned their proper profession as healers.

While all these horrors took place, only a few people knew about the full extent of the atrocities. Yet, the mere two letters KL (*Konzentrations-Lager*)—the abbreviation used by the S.S., instead of the popular KZ—inspired terror, exactly as Hitler had wanted it, as his own words bear testimony. The terror threatened anybody who dared to offer even the slightest resistance to the two main doctrines. Those ready—or at least pretending—to believe that "the Jews are our misfortune," and that "the Fuehrer can do no wrong," were able to stay out of danger.

Erwin Rommel (1891-1944)

IV
The Second World War

8: Who Was Guilty for the Second World War?

The accusation that Germany alone was guilty of causing the First World War has been refuted, and today, as a consequence, many uninstructed people still believe that the guilt for the Second World War can be refuted in a similar way. On the other hand, anti-German propagandists state: "Germany has always been disturbing the peace, it has plunged Europe and the world into two world wars within a very short time." This, too, is false. Neither view is acceptable as historical truth, but the following will show that Hitler's responsibility for the Second World War is, unfortunately, only too clear.

When Hitler seized power, a French political figure said, "Hitler—ç'est la guerre!" German opponents of the Nazis expressed their fears in the same words, "Hitler—that means war!" But they were a small minority, and Hitler's dictatorship silenced their voices. It is all too probable that in any event nobody would have believed them, for Hitler, as he manipulated the emotions of the masses with expertise, never tired of professing his peaceful intentions during his first four years in power (see p. 120). He found moving words to describe the horrors of modern war, and proclaimed so emphatically the German people's desire for peace (for once speaking the absolute truth) that he quieted not only the fears in his own country, but also anxieties abroad. One example will illustrate this effect: on October 19, 1933, the London *Daily Mail* printed an interview Hitler had granted the journalist Ward Price. It quoted Hitler as saying:

> Almost all of us leaders of the National Socialist movement were actual combatants. I have yet to meet the combatant who desires a renewal of the horrors of those four and a half years. . . . Our youth constitutes our sole hope for the future. Do you imagine that we are bringing it up only to be shot down on the battlefield?

Such was the tenor of all of Hitler's speeches during this period. It was most effectively linked with a demand for an end to the discrimination against Germany imposed by the Versailles Treaty. With this approach he succeeded more easily, as opinion in England and France had for some time been veering toward the view that the Versailles Treaty could not be maintained without revisions. Unfortunately, these revisions came too late to save the last governments of the Weimar Republic, and it was Hitler alone who reaped the benefits. This was to influence him in all important steps of his foreign policy.

In October 1933, Hitler withdrew the German *Reich* from the League of Nations, and declared that a totally disarmed Germany would not be able to achieve the equality granted her in principle, as long as her heavily armed neighbors refused to take so much as the first steps toward disarmament. The member states of the League deplored this step but took no counter-measures, and so Hitler was confirmed in the belief that Germany's re-armament would meet with no serious resistance.

On March 16, 1935, Hitler announced the introduction of compulsory military service, providing for a peacetime army of 550,000 men. Conveniently, a few days earlier, the French had doubled the length of their compulsory military service in order to make up for the small number of draftees born during the First World War, a period of low birth rates. This enabled Hitler to explain his decree as a defensive move against the warlike threats of his neighbors. The Eastern European powers protested, and the League of Nations denounced Hitler's act, but it needed more forceful protests than these to convince Hitler that, in the future, he would have to act with more caution.

In Germany, the introduction of military service was generally welcomed with joy. People, not suspecting any aggressive intentions, saw it as a restoration of national honor. By January 1934, Hitler had concluded a non-aggression pact with Poland. In addition, when the Saar was returned to Germany early in 1935, as scheduled, he formally declared that Germany would make no more territorial demands on France. Finally, Hitler concluded an Anglo-German Naval Agreement in June 1935, which provided for the limitation of German naval strength to 35 per cent of the British navy. Did this not establish him clearly as wiser and more moderate than Wilhelm II?

Therefore, when Hitler denounced the Locarno Pact in March 1936, and sent German troops into the demilitarized zone of the Rhineland, German opinion considered it his crowning political achievement, for it put a final end to the Versailles Treaty. The troops re-occupying the Rhineland were almost buried under mountains of flowers. Nobody seemed to appreciate the bluff called by this exploit, which was a clear violation of the Treaty of Versailles and the Locarno Pact. Hitler himself told his interpreter Paul Schmidt later on:

> The forty-eight hours after the march into the Rhineland were the most nerve-racking of my life. If the French had then marched into the Rhineland, we would have had to withdraw with our tails between our legs, for the military resources at our disposal would have been wholly inadequate for even moderate resistance.

This successful move had a decisive influence on Hitler's subsequent behavior toward his more cautious generals. He concluded that he had been right in relying on his own ideas rather than in listening to expert advice. If the Western powers had offered a more determined resistance at that time, much subsequent evil might have been averted. Resistance on their part, however, would have meant resurrecting the "spirit of Versailles" which had finally, though belatedly, sunk into its grave.

The peaceful atmosphere of those years reached its climax with the Olympic Games held in Berlin in August 1936. In the new arena athletes from all parts of the world were enthusiastically welcomed by German spectators: the French contingent received a rousing applause, and even the skeptics were inclined to hope for the best in regard to world peace.

Meanwhile, storm warnings were rising over the horizon. On July 17, 1936, civil war erupted in Spain. General Franco, the leader of the army revolt, addressed a personal letter to Hitler, who decided at once to aid the rebel general. The Fascist dictator Mussolini followed suit for Italy, while France and the Soviet Union supported Franco's opponents, allied in the left-wing Popular Front. Thus, in Spain, European powers rehearsed for the war to come. The German armed forces in particular were given an opportunity to test their tanks and planes. Germany's major contributions to Franco's war consisted of the volunteer Condor Legion, but this support for Franco was kept secret until victory had been won, since, officially, Germans were prohibited by law from taking part in the Spanish civil war!

Another fateful step occurred when Hitler made a pact with Italy, dubbed the Berlin-Rome Axis by Mussolini. Originally, Mussolini had not considered his German fellow-fascist as a natural ally, for he feared that Hitler planned to annex Austria to Germany (by *Anschluss*), and to pursue an anti-Italian policy in the South Tyrol. His reluctance was increased by the assassination of the Austrian Chancellor Dollfuss by Austrian Nazis on July 25, 1934. Hitler, however, had already expressed a desire for alliance with Italy in *Mein Kampf,* and had let not opportunity slip to do favors for *il duce.* When Mussolini launched his attack in Ethiopia, which he considered as the final consummation of Italy's long-standing imperialist ambitions, Hitler offered his support. The British, concerned for their position in the Suez Canal and in Egypt, pushed economic sanctions against Italy in the League of Nations. After the conquest of Ethiopia, Hitler offered to recognize the newly created Empire of Ethiopia, ruled by the King of Italy. Mussolini was invited for a ceremonial visit and received a rousing welcome in Berlin. He was treated to parades by the new German armed forces, and was so awed by their fighting qualities that he carried away an indelible impression of Germany's military strength.

Action in the Spanish civil war   *UP*

Mussolini soon had occasion to return Hitler's favors, for in the spring of 1938 Hitler thought the moment propitious to incorporate the 6.5 million Austrians into the German *Reich*. Austria herself had already in 1918 expressed this desire. But it had been denied her by the Treaty of Versailles. Since Austria had been under a semi-dictatorial government since early in 1933, it is hard to decide whether, later on, the majority of the Austrians were willing to accept Hitler's dictatorship as the price to be paid for *Anschluss* with Germany.

A coup d'état led by Engelbert Dollfuss of the Christian Social Party had been followed by the gradual suppression of all parties, primarily the Nazis. Dollfuss himself had founded the Fatherland Front, which became his sole support. After his assassination, Dollfuss's policies were carried on by Kurt von Schuschnigg. The illegal Nazi Party, of course, received strong backing from Germany, where Dollfuss's murderers were celebrated as martyrs.

Yet, as late as 1936, Hitler had recognized the independence of Austria in a formal treaty.

Two years later, Hitler felt sufficiently strong to tear up this treaty. He invited Austrian Chancellor Schuschnigg to Berchtesgaden in February 1938, but the conversation consisted for the greater part of massive threats. Since Schuschnigg had no reason to expect that England, being poorly armed, or France would intervene "in a family quarrel of the Germans," he was forced to yield to Hitler's demands. Seiss-Inquart, a leading Nazi, took his place in the cabinet, and the imprisoned Nazis were granted amnesty.

In a last desperate attempt to gain moral support for Austria's independence, Schuschnigg scheduled a plebiscite; and it was this move which precipitated her violent integration with Germany. Hitler could not afford to sit back and see a plebiscite favor Schuschnigg's policies, so he massed German troops at the border.

The Austrian government was informed, in a series of lengthy telephone conversations between Vienna and Berlin, that neither the cancellation of the plebiscite nor Schuschnigg's resignation could stop the *Anschluss*. The question was merely whether German troops were to be met with resistance. In this situation, Schuschnigg announced over the radio that he wanted to avoid bloodshed, and so he ordered the withdrawal of Austrian armed forces. In order to preserve the appearance of legality, Seiss-Inquart was ordered by Göring to sign a pre-fabricated telegram in which the Austrian minister requested invasion by German troops "to restore peace and order" in Austria.

Throughout this undertaking Hitler had grave doubts about Mussolini's reaction. Under no circumstances would Mussolini welcome an increase of German power and the close proximity of the "Axis Powers" at the Brenner Pass. In private, Mussolini expressed shock and anger, but in public he announced his agreement to this move, whereupon Hitler sent word that henceforth he would "go with him through thick and thin" and would "never, never" forget the support he had given him.

And so Germany occupied Austria without resistance. Radio stations and newspapers broadcast enthusiastic reports about the jubilation in Austria. Hitler in person drove to Linz, where he had

Hitler addressing the masses from a balcony of
the Hofburg, Vienna, 15 March 1938

spent his youth, and where enormous crowds now lined the streets
to celebrate the consummation of the long-awaited dream of an
Austro-German union. Meanwhile, Himmler's S.D. men had gone
to work, and in Vienna alone 67,000 people were taken into
custody.

Austria's *Anschluss* took place without foreign intervention,
and it called forth no comment from the League of Nations. The
victors of Versailles were now tacitly prepared to grant the Germans the right of national self-determination which they had previously withheld. In Germany itself there was the growing view
that Hitler's policies aimed at uniting all Germans into a single
state: "One nation, one *Reich*, one Fuehrer" was the slogan. The
next logical step appeared to be incorporation of the Sudeten

Germans into what was now dubbed the Greater German Empire (*Grossdeutsches Reich*). Not until Czechoslovakia was occupied in the spring of 1939 did there exist unequivocal proof that Hitler's plans went beyond the right of German self-determination and ethnic unification. Only then was it revealed that Hitler was hatching considerably more far-reaching plans. What did he really want?

There is no doubt that Hitler wanted war, war under any circumstances, notwithstanding his frequent and loud protestations of his love for peace. Even if one disregards the belligerent references in *Mein Kampf* (see p. 110) as fantasies of a young hot-head, one cannot overlook the fact that Hitler repeated the same ideas a bare four days after seizing power (February 3, 1933) before the *Reichswehr* command, when again he spoke of the "conquest of new *Lebensraum* in the East, and its ruthless Germanization."

In his inner circle, Hitler liked to expound his favorite theme: war. Rauschning often heard him talk of the "duty to war": "I make war. I determine the proper time for the fight. Only one moment is right. I shall wait for it. With iron determination. And I shall not miss it. I shall concentrate all my energies on bringing it about. That is my task. If I bring it about, I have the right to send the young to their death."

This, indeed, sounded quite different from what Hitler told foreign correspondents and the *Reichstag*. Already in 1937, Hitler's war plans had matured sufficiently to be presented to the Foreign Minister and a small inner group of leading generals. Colonel Hossbach, who was present at the conference and took notes, composed immediately afterwards a memorandum which has since become known as the Hossbach Protocol.

According to this memorandum, Hitler began with the proposition that "the solid racial core" of the German nation gave it the right to more *Lebensraum*. Germany's future depended on satisfying its need for space. Expansion could never be carried out without breaking down resistance. The problem was how to gain the most at the smallest cost. Once the use of force, with its attendant risks, had been decided upon, its timing and execution were to be determined. The latest possible time at which such plans could be realized was between 1943 and 1945. All later changes would only work to Germany's disadvantage. In any event, the first objective was to overthrow Czechoslovakia and Austria, and it appeared probable that France and England already had tacitly written off Czechoslovakia. The conquest would probably involve the forcible removal of two million Czechs and one million Austrians from their home countries.

Hitler was totally obsessed with the idea that he had to wage "his war." Whatever restraints remained were gradually removed by the successes of his foreign policy. Mussolini's son-in-law, Count Ciano, Italy's Foreign Minister, noted in his diary in October 1938: "Hitler has his mind fixed on the idea of war, he wants war, his war. He does not know or say precisely where he wants to march. He neither names his enemies nor fixes his aims. But he wants war within the next three or four years."

On November 10, 1938, Hitler frankly and cynically explained to 400 selected journalists that tactical considerations alone had forced him to protest his peaceful intentions so frequently as a means of camouflaging re-armament. But since such peace propaganda might have the undesirable effect of misleading the German people with regard to the true goals of his government, the press had to help in gradually re-adjusting the psychology of the nation and conditioning it in such a way that it would spontaneously demand violent action. The people were to be prepared "to stand upright even if thunder and lightning struck."

The violent overthrow of Austria foreseen in the Hossbach Protocol had been averted. The *Anschluss* had succeeded not without pressure but without physical violence. Earlier than anticipated, Hitler was now able to prepare his moves against Czechoslovakia, for which he had felt an abiding hatred from early youth. Czechoslovakia had been founded as an independent republic in 1918 and comprised three national groups: 7 million Czechs, 3.3 million Slovaks, and 3.2 million Germans. The Czechs in the majority had not managed to enlist the co-operation of their minorities, so Hitler was able to use these Germans in Bohemia and Moravia as a welcome pretext to create a "Czechoslovak question." As early as March 1938, Hitler summoned Konrad Henlein, leader of the Sudeten German Party (one of the legal

Germany's expansion 1933-1939

political parties of Czechoslovakia), and instructed him to make continuous demands upon the Czechs which they would be unable to meet. This created the constant unrest Hitler needed as an excuse for intervention.

Soon afterwards, Hitler conferred with Keitel and made plans for the military overthrow of Czechoslovakia, under the code name "Case Green." The summary of this discussion reads—in abrupt military phrasing:

186

1. The idea of a sudden strategic attack without cause or possibility of justification is to be rejected. Because of the consequence: hostile world opinion, which may lead to [a] critical situation. Such a measure should be reserved only for the elimination of the last enemy on the Continent.
2. Action after a period of diplomatic haggling which will gradually become critical and precipitate war. (Case 2 is undesirable since "Green" will have taken security measures.)
3. Lightning action based on an incident (for example assassination of the German ambassador in the course of an anti-German demonstration).

These blunt sentences foreshadowed the style of the foreign policy: it was its aim, by provoking bloodshed and murdering its own practitioners, to fabricate a pretext for war which would be a prerequisite for satisfying Hitler's unlimited lust for power. The following introductory paragraph was added to Case Green by the Fuehrer on May 30: "It is my unalterable decision to smash Czechoslovakia by military action in the near future. To wait for, or bring about, the moment which is politically and militarily suitable is the task of political leadership."

To their credit, the leaders of the German armed forces did not support Hitler's play with fire in any way. The concentration of troops at the Czech frontier leaked out. England and France thereupon warned Hitler that any move against the Czechs might lead to general war. At this point, Ludwig Beck, Chief of the General Staff, summarized his misgivings in a memorandum and threatened to resign if Hitler disregarded them. A small group of conspirators even pushed its resistance to the point where they would have had Hitler arrested as soon as he gave the order to attack Czechoslovakia, but the situation never reached that point.

England and France adopted a policy of "appeasement," which, in fact, was also a blow to Hitler's plans. Carrying out orders, the Sudeten German Party had kept the masses "at the boiling point," and had set down its demands in eight points which were considered unacceptable. Nevertheless, early in September, President Beneš of Czechoslovakia declared his willingness to meet all the demands. Two days later, the *Reich* Party Congress of the NSDAP began at Nuremberg, and here, before his adherents and the world represented by the press, Hitler launched a brutal attack on Beneš, calling him a liar and branding the Czechs as irreconcilable enemies of Germany. His inflammatory speech led to riots in the Sudeten area, which forced the Czech government to declare martial law. Konrad Henlein reiterated his demand: "We want to return home to the *Reich!*" He and a few thousand of his followers crossed the German frontier and organized a free corps.

To meet this threatening situation (which, indeed, accorded precisely with Hitler's plans), Chamberlain, the British Prime Minister, offered his services as a mediator. At first, Hitler was as astounded as he was flattered, and he received Chamberlain at his mountain eyrie at Berchtesgaden. Chamberlain offered to mediate in the peaceful secession of the Sudeten area. Since Hitler did not expect the Czechs to accept this, he agreed to the offer, but continued his military preparations and fixed September 27, 1938, as the day for the attack on Czechoslovakia.

On September 22, Chamberlain met Hitler a second time at Bad Godesberg, and informed him that the Czech government had acceded to the demands. English and French pressures had left it with no other choice. This compliance in no way suited Hitler's designs, and he retorted: "After what has happened during the last few days, that solution has no meaning any longer." Chamberlain reacted with profound shock, especially since Hitler failed to give any valid reason for his change of heart. The real reason was that Hitler wanted "his war." He broke off negotiations by raising a series of additional demands, including the immediate evacuation, even before a plebiscite, of the area in question. A day later, he fixed September 26-28 as the latest date for invasion.

When Chamberlain brought this ultimatum back to England, Hitler's conditions were pronounced unacceptable, and preparations for war were set in motion. But Chamberlain made one final attempt, and informed Hitler in a personal letter that the conflict could still be resolved peacefully if Germany would agree to direct negotiations with the Czech government with English participation. After receiving this letter, Hitler delivered a speech on September 26 in the Berlin Sports Palace which surpassed all his previous abusive and angry tirades against the Czech chief of state. The German people held its breath. A day later, motorized

Neville Chamberlain returning
from Munich, September 1938

divisions on war footing paraded through Berlin. Hitler expected demonstrations of enthusiasm, similar to those that had occurred in 1914 at the outbreak of war. But the man in the street turned away in fear and silence.

This disappointment may not have been the least of the reasons why Hitler yielded. Mussolini, too, on British insistence, had offered to mediate, and Hitler, at the last moment, accepted a proposal for a conference. It convened at Munich. Chamberlain, Daladier (the French premier), and Mussolini gave Hitler everything he had already demanded at Godesberg. The Czechs had not even been invited to take part in the negotiations, which ended with the secession of their German-speaking areas.

In the streets of Munich, the population lustily cheered Chamberlain for having saved the peace. When he disembarked from his airplane upon his return to England, he brandished an agreement which, he believed, would guarantee the peace. Upon his arrival in Berlin, Hitler, in contrast, told his S.S. troops: "That guy Chamberlain has spoiled my entry into Prague!" Churchill, who was an M.P. then, judged the events much more realistically than his gullible colleague Chamberlain in his speech in the House of Commons on October 5, 1938:

> [At Berchtesgaden] One pound was demanded at the pistol's point. When it was given, two pounds were demanded at the pistol's point. Finally, the dictator consented to take £1 17s. 6d. and the rest in promises of good will for the future. . . . We are in the midst of a disaster of the first magnitude.

Very soon it would become apparent how right he was. World opinion wondered whether Hitler would help himself first to Memel, which belonged to Lithuania, or to the Free City of Danzig, where the problem of national minorities was to be resolved and the Treaty of Versailles revised. But the idea of smashing Czechoslovakia obsessed Hitler so intensely by now that he moved next in that direction.

A pretext for further blackmail was handed him by Slovak extremists agitating for the total secession of Slovakia from Czechoslovakia. Hitler recklessly supported their cause. By March 1939, their secessionist plans had advanced so far that the Czech government was forced to dissolve the [local] government of Slovakia. Thereupon Hitler summoned the deposed Slovak premier, Tiso, to Berlin, and handed him a Proclamation of Independence for Slovakia, written in the Slovak language. Hitler informed Tiso that Slovakia, on her part, had to adopt this Proclamation immediately or else he would leave Slovakia to her fate. Tiso flew back, and the Slovak parliament adopted the Proclamation.

By this act, Czechoslovakia disintegrated as a political unit, and England concluded that her guarantee of the Czechoslovak frontier had ceased to exist in the face of this "internal dissolution." Hitler had a free hand. As he had summoned Tiso, now he summoned Hacha, who had succeeded Beneš as president. Hacha was told bluntly that German troops would invade Czechoslovakia from all directions the next day, March 15. He had merely to decide whether resistance was to be offered, for "the world would not move a muscle," Hitler told him. When Göring spoke of bombarding Prague, Hacha fainted and had to be given a shot to revive him before the negotiations could be continued.

The Czech president Hacha confers with Hitler in Prague, March 1939

At 4 a.m.—two hours before German troops were to start the invasion—Hacha signed an agreement and "confidently placed the fate of the Czech people in the hands of the Fuehrer!" It was as if a mouse agreed to be swallowed up by the cat! German troops marched in, at the entreaties of the Czech president—to quote Hitler's handout to foreign correspondents in Berlin. Czechoslovakia became the German *Reich* Protectorate of Bohemia and Moravia. As German administrator a former *Reich* Foreign Minister, von Neurath, was appointed *Reich* Protector.

These events produced two significant though opposite effects. Hitler was intoxicated with his own successes. After Hacha had signed, he called out to his secretaries: "Children, this is the greatest day of my life! I shall go down in history as the greatest German!" The behavior of the English convinced him that they would never do more than protest, never act, and that English warnings could be taken lightly. Foreign Minister von Ribbentrop never ceased to confirm his views. He had been ambassador in England for some time, but he had not the faintest notion of English democracy or English politics.

In reality, England was just then about to change decisively the direction of her policy. By the spring of 1939, Chamberlain's appeasement policies had failed so miserably that Hitler's protestations of no more territorial demands proved quite hollow; therefore, the decision to stand firm could no longer be avoided, lest the entire continent fall under Hitler's sway.

Hitler's next action could be anticipated without difficulty. The return of Memel to the German *Reich* was effected en route, as it were, after Prague had been occupied. Lithuania was handed an ultimatum, and since this small state was even less able to defend itself than Czechoslovakia had been, it had to return Memel, which had been ceded to the Lithuanians by the Treaty of Versailles.

A little while later, the *Reich* government asked the Polish ambassador in Berlin to submit proposals for the solution of the questions of Danzig and the Pomorze (or Polish Corridor). As if pre-arranged, beginning in May 1939, German newspapers began to print reports on incidents in Poland. In fact, at a press conference Goebbels had formally given the green light to any reports on incidents in Poland. In June 1939, he complained that these incidents had not been played up sufficiently, but warned, on the other hand, against "blowing them up too big: matters are such that this business is to be kept at a low boil." In August, however, he instructed the press to headline Polish atrocity stories on the front pages in large type. The general staff of the press, now totally controlled, was lending its effective support to the Fuehrer's design for war.

This time the British government swung into action; it issued a formal declaration, in which it was joined by France, promising to support Poland in the event of an attack. Already as early as April 3, 1939, Hitler had ordered the armed forces to work out strategic plans for invading Poland. In May, the alliance between Germany and Italy was strengthened by the so-called Pact of Steel. In Article III of the pact, Germany and Italy undertook to assist each other, should "either power become involved in warlike complications with another power, or with other powers." The pact

Hitler and Goebbels with Mussolini, May 1938

was not merely defensive, since there was no pretense of its operating only in case of an attack on either party. Mussolini had truly chained himself to Hitler with steel clamps. Mussolini's motive for agreeing to this is particularly hard to ascertain in view of the fact that Count Ciano had fully recognized Hitler's warlike intentions, and had rejected them (see p. 185).

Before concluding the pact, Mussolini formally declared that he needed at least another three years of peace, but Hitler had no intention of respecting this, and demonstrated it 24 hours after the Pact of Steel had been signed. The occasion was a conference attended by fourteen people who had been summoned to the Chancellery to hear Hitler's military plans. According to notes taken by his chief adjutant, Schmundt, Hitler said:

War is inevitable. Danzig is not the object of the dispute at all. It is a question of expanding our *Lebensraum* in the east, of securing our food supply, and also of solving the problem of the Baltic States. . . . There is no question of sparing Poland, and we are left with the decision to attack Poland at the first suitable opportunity. We cannot expect a repetition of the Czech affair. There will be war. Our task is to isolate Poland. Success in isolating her will be decisive. . . . It must not come to a simultaneous showdown with the West.

No doubt, Hitler's mind was firmly made up. Only one unknown factor still upset his calculations; how Russia would react to a German attack on Poland. Since Hitler had never tired of writing or preaching his ideological opposition to Bolshevism, since he had frequently presented the Third *Reich* as a "bulwark against Communism," Russia was bound to consider an attack on Poland as the first step toward "colonization of the east."

Hitler knew that his Polish venture could become dangerous if England and France, who had been negotiating a military convention with the Soviet Union since April 1939, succeeded in bringing Russia into their system of alliances. The same train of thought occurred to Baron von Weizsäcker, Secretary of State in the German Foreign Office. In spite of his extremely difficult and exposed position, he did his utmost to save the peace and recognized Hitler's and Ribbentrop's intention of outmaneuvering the Western powers in Russia. If they succeeded, the east would be off their backs; then Poland would be lost, and war could no longer be prevented. In view of this, Weizsäcker, disregarding the great danger to his person, decided to send a secret warning to the British and to inform them of Hitler's plans for a German-Soviet pact. London reassured him that England would not allow herself to be outmaneuvered in Moscow.

Yet, this was precisely what happened subsequently. Not only had Hitler thrown all his ideological reservations to the wind, and convinced himself that a pact with Stalin would be considered as a stroke of genius and enhance his prestige, but the dictator Stalin had impressed him much more deeply than the emissaries of the Western democracies. Consequently, he dispatched first the German ambassador to Moscow and then Ribbentrop in person to explore the terrain.

Ribbentrop signs the German-Soviet Non-Aggression Pact, August 1939;
standing behind are Molotov and Stalin

Stalin, it emerged, was not averse to seizing Hitler's outstretched hand, primarily because he expected to make some solid gains which he had little prospect of obtaining in an assistance pact with the West. The German-Soviet negotiations were concluded in the latter half of August: Voroshilov, the Soviet Commissar for War, informed the Western powers that further negotiations would serve no useful purpose, since Poland refused to agree to the passage of Soviet troops in the event of war. A week later, an astonished world learned of the conclusion of a non-aggression pact between Germany and the Soviet Union.

The true significance of the German-Soviet Non-Aggression Pact emerged only after Poland had been defeated, and the Secret Additional Protocol to the pact had become operative. The German government recognized that Finland, Estonia, and Latvia belonged to the Russian sphere of interest. In the event of a territorial and political transformation of Poland, the new Russian frontier was fixed far to the west of the Russian border. "In Russia, nobody doubted Hitler's warlike designs on Poland. . . . It was thus Stalin who ultimately enabled Hitler to mount the attack on Poland."[16]

Now, indeed, all obstacles had been removed from Hitler's path. Neither Mussolini's announcement that he would stand by the Pact of Steel but could not furnish troops at this time, nor the absolutely unmistakable declaration by the British government that it would honor its commitment to Poland brought Hitler to his senses. His sole concern now was to justify himself in German eyes, and to create the impression that he had done all to preserve the peace. To this end, he made some conciliatory proposals, but before the Poles had a chance to accept them, they were told by Ribbentrop that the time for their acceptance had passed. Finally, he manufactured an "outrageous gangster attack on the Gleiwitz [Gliwice] radio station." The truth about it can be read in the sworn affidavit of ex-Security Serviceman Naujocks:

> On or about August 10, 1939, Heydrich personally ordered me to simulate an attack on the radio station near Gleiwitz, near the Polish border, and to make it appear as if the attacking forces consisted of Poles. Heydrich said: "Practical proof is needed for these attacks of the Poles for the foreign press as well as German propaganda." I was ordered

to go to Gleiwitz with five or six Security Service men and
wait until I would receive the code word (canned goods)
for the attack from Heydrich. My instructions were to
seize the radio station and to hold it long enough to permit
a Polish-speaking German, who would be put at my disposal, to broadcast a speech in Polish.

The Supreme Command of the Armed Forces (*Oberkom-
mando der Wehrmacht* or OKW) was ordered to provide Polish
uniforms for the attack. When Naujocks reported for "the canned
goods" on August 31, he was handed a concentration camp in-
mate dying from a lethal injection. Naujocks laid this prisoner at
the entrance of the radio station and left him there after the action
was completed as "proof" of the "Polish raid."

It can hardly be doubted that quite a few true incidents did
occur in the tense atmosphere of the last few months and weeks
before the outbreak of the war. Not all that Goebbels headlined in
big type on the front pages of the newspapers was invented. At
times, the Germans may have been more to blame, at other times
the Poles. The Gleiwitz case shows, however, that Hitler was not
concerned with true incidents. Instead, his one and only purpose
was to create an incident which would justify, in the eyes of the
world, the war he had planned.

German artillery moves into Poland, September 1939   *Brown Bros.*

On September 1, 1939, "the fire was returned"—as the official Goebbels press put it. German troops invaded Poland. This time, however, they met with resistance. In Germany—in contrast to 1914—there was no enthusiasm for war. The soldiers obeyed; the German people accepted the inevitable; and Hitler had his war.

9: Was Hitler a Great General?

A comparison of the situation prevailing on August 1, 1914, with that of September 1, 1939, reveals that in 1914 the nations stumbled into a war nobody wanted, while in 1939 Hitler expressed his fear that "at the last moment some *Schweinehund* [dirty pig] will make a proposal for mediation." Another significant difference of long-term importance was that, although Wilhelm II combined political and military authority in his person, he left it to the *Reich* Chancellor and the General Staff to make their respective decisions. Hitler, in contrast, now extended his previous authority over German politics not only nominally, but actually, to the conduct of the war as well. To dramatize the change, he moved his center of operations from the *Reich* Chancellery to military headquarters, and showed himself to the public only at ceremonial occasions, or when he made one of his lengthy speeches.

The disastrous consequences of the failure of political leadership in the First World War have already been described. This time the situation was reversed. Political leadership usurped military authority as well. Did it improve the results? Did Hitler have the abilities and the characteristics of a great general?

Poland was crushed in three weeks, in spite of the brave resistance of the Polish army. As early as September 17, 1939, the Russians invaded eastern Poland; on September 27, the capital Warsaw surrendered to the Germans; on October 6, the fighting was over. The campaign in Poland thus set the pattern for "lightning war" (*Blitzkrieg*). A few similar successes convinced Hitler of his own infinite superiority. It seemed to him that there was no longer anything beyond his reach.

The aid England and France had promised to Poland did not become effective in time to prevent defeat. Until the very last, Hit-

Hitler with his generals   *Ullstein*

ler refused to believe that these two states would keep their promises. When he received the British ultimatum, he at first sat at his desk in complete immobility, and, after a long pause, asked Ribbentrop, who had always confirmed him in his underestimation of the West: "What now?" Göring expressed his dismay with these words: "If we lose this war, may Heaven have mercy upon us!"

After achieving his lightning success, Hitler made a peace offer to England and France, for he assumed that they would "yield to facts" and abandon the defeated Poland forthwith. If this had been their intention, why did they declare war in the first place? People in England and France knew now that only tough and persistent efforts could stop Hitler's drive for conquest. The rejection of the peace offer was thus a foregone conclusion and, in some ways, even suited Hitler, who considered it poor military practice to keep troops inactive for too long, and pressed for an attack on France as early as November 1939.

German troops invading Holland, May 1940 *UP*

In this, he was opposed by his generals, who feared the great risks attendant on attacking the extremely strong French frontier fortifications, known as the Maginot Line. Such risks would be multiplied if a winter campaign took the place of a spring offensive. It was still routine procedure in the German General Staff to weigh a potential gain against probable losses. Hitler placed little value on human lives and cared nothing for the heavy sacrifices the people would have to make: "The campaign in the west will cost me a million men—but it would cost the enemy that too, and the enemy cannot stand it."

During this winter and the spring of 1940, the date for the attack was postponed 29 times, last but not least in order to occupy Denmark and Norway before the British could move in. In view of Germany's weak naval forces, the operation in Norway was very dangerous, and could only succeed by surprise. And, indeed, the secret was so well kept that a surprise attack on April 9, 1940, went off without a hitch. The occupation of Norway assured Germany a reliable supply of Scandinavian iron ore.

The campaign in the west opened on May 10. Hitler, true to fashion, violated the neutrality of Holland and Belgium without batting an eye. His plan differed from the strategy of 1914 in providing for a decisive thrust through the Ardennes forest where the French least expected it. General von Manstein made this suggestion, which proved so highly successful that the German offensive never faltered once. Paris was taken without a struggle a bare five weeks later.

Hitler made only one blunder which was to prove a future turning point of the war: he ordered the armored columns of General Guderian to halt a few miles south of Dunkirk, and thus allowed the British to evacuate 338,000 men of the British expeditionary forces and the French army from this last port of refuge. If they had been encircled and cut off, the British war potential would have been significantly weakened numerically and in morale.

But the French campaign as a whole brought Hitler overwhelming success. When he was handed the French plea for armistice on June 17, he danced with joy—the omnipresent photographers preserving the scene for posterity. The armistice was officially signed in the same *wagon lit,* in the Forest of Compiègne, in which the Germans had signed the armistice of 1918. Now it was Hitler who received the French delegation and, at this mo-

Hitler hears news of French capitulation, June 1940

ment, his career had reached its peak: "The one-time agitator, who had promised the masses in 1920 that he would not rest until he had torn up the Treaty of Versailles, . . . had kept his promise: the humiliation of 1918 was avenged."[17]

His success, however, was not due solely to military strategy, for, more importantly, the French people were not ready for war and were unwilling to defend themselves to the utmost. France had fancied herself all too secure behind the Maginot Line, and when this fortified zone was overrun, she accepted defeat as inevitable. The German generals also had expected considerably greater resistance on the part of the French; but Hitler's intuitive capacity for gauging the weaknesses of his enemy had been keener. He had bested his General Staff and was to boast dogmatically of this success on many future occasions.

After France had been beaten, Hitler expected England to come to terms. As so often in the past, he once again misjudged his enemy. Instructions were issued for the preparation of "Operation Sea Lion," a landing of German troops on the British coast, but in fact, the order was never given for the landing. No doubt, the difficulties of this operation were especially great, but Hitler had not been deterred by difficulties in similar situations. If he more than once postponed this decisive attack—in spite of all his "hate England" oratory—and if he finally abandoned it altogether, it was presumably due to his long-standing, healthy respect for the British Empire, and a vague but lingering dream of an eventual alliance with England.

Hitler may also have underestimated the tough fiber of the British, and actually believed that "the British were as good as beaten." In any event, these were the reasons he gave in July 1940, when he once more returned to an old political program: the German colonization of the east. He never considered the pact with Russia as more than a temporary tactical *détente,* and he felt no compunction whatever about ordering plans for an attack on Russia.

Furthermore, Hitler was increasingly concerned with Russia's advances in Europe, for the Soviet Union had squeezed the last ounce out of the "rights" granted her by the Secret Additional Protocol of the German-Soviet Non-Aggression Pact. A German-

Soviet Boundary and Friendship Treaty, made on September 28, 1939, confirmed the division of Poland and provided for the re-settlement of the Baltic Germans. Lithuania, too, was added to the Soviet sphere of influence.

A short time later, Estonia, Latvia, and Lithuania were forced to provide bases for the Red Army. When Finland failed to accede to Russian demands, Stalin ordered Russian troops to attack that small country in November 1939. They met with bitter resistance. In the peace treaty of March 1940, Finland was obliged to cede to the Soviet Union the Karelian Isthmus, parts of Eastern Karelia, and some islands.

Finally, during the German campaign in France, the Soviet Union forcibly annexed Estonia, Latvia, and Lithuania. Rumania was forced to cede Bessarabia and the Bucovina, thus bringing Soviet frontiers closer to the Rumanian oil-fields which were essential for Germany's war potential.

Although preparations for the attack on Russia had begun in August 1940, Hitler does not appear to have made the final decision to attack that early. In this, he followed a suggestion of Field Marshal Keitel, the Chief of the Supreme Command of the Armed Forces, who advised against starting operations in the fall of 1940. Moreover, just then his ally Mussolini diverted Hitler's attention to other theaters of war.

Hitler's success in France had decided Mussolini to rush into the war in order to share in the division of the spoils. But Italy's entry into the war also made it necessary to deploy German troops for the defense of Italy's colonial empire in North Africa.

In the fall of 1940, operations were focused even more strongly in the Mediterranean, because Mussolini—without consulting Hitler—extended the war to the Balkans. Mussolini had occupied Albania as early as April 1939, and had incorporated it into Italy. Now troops jumped off from there and invaded Greece in order to "round out" the Italian empire. This action was to be his answer to Hitler, who had secured military bases in Rumania—also without any prior consultation with his Italian ally—after the pro-Hitler General Antonescu had been appointed Prime Minister in Rumania.

Within a short time, the entire Balkan area was aflame. Ger-

German Stukas before an attack *Ullstein*

many, Italy, and Japan had concluded the Tripartite Pact on September 27, 1940, which was to outline the "new order" in Europe and East Asia. By March 1941, Hungary, Rumania, Slovakia, and Bulgaria had also joined the pact. The attempt to bring the Soviet Union into the pact as well failed because Hitler refused to recognize Soviet aspirations for further expansion of its share of influence (to Bulgaria, the Bosporus, and the Dardanelles).

On March 25, 1941, Yugoslavia declared its adherence to the Tripartite Pact. A few days later, this decision led to a military *Putsch* in Belgrade. Young King Peter II replaced Prince Regent Paul as chief of state, and on April 5, 1941, Yugoslavia concluded a Treaty of Friendship and Non-Aggression with the Soviet Union.

Following the military *Putsch* in Belgrade, Hitler decided to attack Yugoslavia and Greece simultaneously, since Mussolini's Greek campaign had ground to a miserable halt. Belgrade was bombarded from the air, and surrendered to German troops on April 6, 1941; Greece was forced to sue for an armistice on April

20. It had taken less than a fortnight to crush Yugoslavia and conquer continental Greece. Once again, Hitler had won two blitzkriegs. To be sure these proud mountain peoples did not lay down their arms according to schedule, and the beginning of partisan war, which to an even larger degree was controlled by Communists, created considerable difficulties for the victors.

A sizable part of the German armed forces was thus pinned down in widely separated theaters of war, and since February 1941 German troops under General Rommel were fighting as far afield as North Africa. Not for a moment, however, did Hitler lose sight of his goal to attack Russia. In vain, Admiral Raeder tried to explain to Hitler that the Mediterranean theater would allow him decisive action against England. As Bullock writes:

> Even a quarter of the forces then concentrated for an attack on Russia could, if diverted to the Mediterranean theater of war in time, have dealt a fatal blow to British control of the Middle East. But Hitler refused to see his opportunity; his intuition failed him. With his mind wholly set upon the invasion of Russia, he declined to look at the Mediterranean as anything more than a sideshow which could be left to the Italians with stiffening of German troops. . . . It was to prove one of the supreme blunders of his strategy.

Hitler threw to the winds the warning that England had to be defeated first before Russia could be attacked, and took the reverse tack, arguing that Russia had to be crushed so that England, which hoped for Russian and American intervention, could be beaten. He further claimed that he had to forestall a Russian attack—not a scrap of evidence for this has been unearthed to this day. Thus Bullock concludes: "Hitler invaded Russia for the simple but sufficient reason that he had always meant to establish the foundations of his thousand-year *Reich* by the annexation of the territory lying between the Vistula and the Urals."[18]

His previous campaigns had convinced Hitler that the Soviets, too, could be overrun in a short campaign of, at most, two or three months. He let slip most contemptuous remarks about the Russian army, and expected that Stalin would be toppled by his own people following the first defeats: "We only need to push the door open, and the whole rotten building will crash down."

While he had been right in the case of France, Hitler and the German people were to pay dearly for his low estimate of Russia. Now he drove England, Russia, and America into the very alliance he allegedly had wished to prevent. This, however, anticipates later events.

The first weeks after the attack of June 22, 1941, appeared to bear out Hitler's rash predictions. German troops penetrated deeply into Russian territory and reached points within 190 miles of Moscow. The number of Russian prisoners of war amounted to hundreds of thousands, but the tremendous manpower reserves of the Soviet Union could not be depleted by a few battles of encirclement. Hitler further made the strategic blunder of not concentrating his forces at one point. Generals Brauchitsch and Halder had proposed attacking Moscow as the most important strategic goal, but Hitler wanted at the same time to press on to Leningrad, and also fight a great battle of encirclement in the Ukraine. This battle was a great German victory, but it was followed by the Russian winter, with its rain and mud, and the moment for the attack on Moscow passed. Decisive action was taken out of their hands. Hitler had "fallen into the trap against which he had warned his generals before the invasion, that of allowing the Russians to retreat and draw the Germans farther and farther into the illimitable depths of their hinterland. When the dreaded winter engulfed the German armies, despite their victories and advances, they had still not captured Leningrad and Moscow, nor destroyed the Russian capacity to continue the war."[19]

Hitler, arrogantly sure of victory, refused to equip his troops for a winter campaign. The man who had repeated in his speeches *ad nauseam* "I have considered everything," bears the responsibility for the many German soldiers who perished as a result of exposure to the bitter cold. The victories of the first period turned into near catastrophe when the Russians, on December 6, 1941, began to mount their counter-offensive and threw 100 fresh divisions into battle for the relief of Moscow. Now retreat could have turned quickly into headlong flight. Napoleon's shadow loomed over the horizon.

Hitler realized this full well, and succeeded, against great odds, in mastering the crisis. Alan Bullock called this his greatest

During the winter campaign in Russia, 1942

achievement as a war leader. His method was as simple as it was brutal. He ordered the troops to stand and fight regardless of losses, and refused to authorize any retreats. Generals who, despite this, withdrew their troops in some sectors were relieved of their commands.

After the crisis Hitler was less willing than before to heed the advice of his generals. His confidence in experts had diminished. Field Marshal von Brauchitsch took the consequences and offered his resignation. Hitler accepted it but appointed no other general in his place. Instead, he added the rank of Supreme Commander of the Army to his other offices.

Since December 11, 1941, Germany had also been at war with the United States of America. The immediate cause was the Japanese attack on the American navy at Pearl Harbor on December 7.

Once more it became apparent that Hitler could not rely entirely on his allies. Ribbentrop had suggested that the Japanese should attack the British base at Singapore, or invade Russia from the rear. An attack on the United States had never been contemplated. Ribbentrop further pointed out to Hitler that the Tripartite Pact called for German support of Japan only in the event that Japan was "attacked by a power, at present not involved in the European war, or in the Chinese-Japanese conflict." The pact was obviously designed for possible U.S. intervention in the Asiatic or European conflict.

Probably thinking "the more, the merrier," Hitler declared war on the United States without a moment of hesitation. It is clear that he had no possible conception of the economic and military potential of the United States.

Against this background of events, the spring of 1942 arrived. This time, Hitler limited his operations to southern Russia. Yet, once again he reached out for two objectives simultaneously, the Volga at Stalingrad, and the oil-fields in the Caucasus. Again, he dissipated his forces and reached neither objective.

Even before the battle of Stalingrad reached its full fury, English and American forces landed in Morocco and Algiers on November 8, 1942, and, after a few days, pushed through to the Tunisian border. The war in Africa had entered its critical phase.

But a large number of Germans saw the handwriting on the wall only when Hitler abandoned the 330,000 soldiers of the Sixth Army at Stalingrad. Twenty-two German divisions had been cut off in this far-advanced sector of the front on November 19 and 20. An attempt to relieve them from the outside failed. Thereupon their supreme commander, General Paulus, asked for permission to break the stranglehold from within, and to pull his troops back. Hitler, however, held firm to the tactics which had proved successful during the previous winter: he forbade any retreat. Since no military supplies, not even food or medical stores, could reach the troops by air or by land, Hitler thus condemned 330,000 German soldiers to die for his prestige. He wanted to be able to claim that the German army, rather than capitulate, sacrificed itself out of loyalty to the Fuehrer. Hitler compared the Sixth Army to the three hundred Greeks at Thermopylae. When General Paulus reported at the end of January that the troops' suffering with cold, hunger, and epidemics could no longer be endured, and that to continue fighting was beyond human strength, Hitler was unmoved. He sent the order: "Capitulation is out of the question!"

Nazi prisoners before Stalingrad, November 1942 *UP*

A few days later, a Russian war communiqué announced the capture of the Sixth Army. It could no longer be hidden how senseless the order had been to "fight to the end." Questions began to be asked in Germany whether the sacrifice of an army still had anything to do with the art of war. For the first time, one felt that cold-blooded obstinacy which was to control the fate of Germany to the bitter end. The catastrophe of Stalingrad established the pattern for the debacle of 1945.

A good war leader needs a basic and solid knowledge of military strategy and technology. Most people, therefore, consider it very hard for an amateur to possess or acquire such knowledge. Considering that Hitler never attended military college or a similar school, it remains astonishing that he taught himself enough to judge military plans and to sway the experts, not merely through his superior political position but by his knowledge. Books on military subjects were among his favorite reading matter. He also had an excellent memory for details, which he liked to display by punctuating his monologues with columns of statistics on troop strength, armaments, equipment, etc.

In spite of this, his expert knowledge was not thorough enough for him to dispense with the advice of his General Staff. He would have been an incomparably greater war leader if he had known how to use the expertise and experience of his staff; but he never overcame his distrust for experts of any kind. He never felt at ease with them and preferred to rely on his own unsystematic reading. He did not really listen to arguments and would tolerate no opposition. These unfortunate attitudes made learning by experience impossible for him, since, like all opinionated people, he was able to experience only what fitted his preconceived notions. After the campaign in France had proved him right and not his generals, he was more firmly convinced than ever that he did not need their advice but could rely on his intuition.

In addition to military expertise, a good war leader also needs such qualities as determination, daring, the ability to assess and utilize the enemy's weaknesses, and a solid dose of self-confidence and strong nerves. Hitler undeniably possessed these qualities to such an extent that he was better fitted for military than for political leadership. Yet, these qualities were developed to such an excess in him that they ceased to be an advantage and became disadvantages. His determination turned into obstinacy, his daring into criminal pride, his sense for weaknesses became a continued underestimation of the enemy, his self-confidence megalomania.

Hitler's early successes had an especially disastrous effect on his supercharged self-confidence. After mastering the crisis of the winter campaign of 1941-42, he said in a speech commemorating his "seizure of power" that he was filled "with unbounded confidence, confidence in myself, so that nothing, whatever it may be, can throw me out of the saddle, so that nothing can shake me." He considered himself invulnerable, like the Achilles and Siegfrieds of the old tales. Unfortunately, his entourage studiedly confirmed this belief in his own infallibility. This is typified by an entry in Goebbels's diary (January 30, 1942): "As long as [the Fuehrer] lives and is among us in good health, as long as he can give us the strength of his spirit, no evil can touch us."

This deluded image of his own grandeur caused Hitler to live increasingly in a world of his own wishful dreams: "This was the reverse side of the strength which he derived from his own belief in himself—and it was the weakness which was to destroy him, for in the end it destroyed all power of self-criticism and cut him off from all contact with reality."[20]

It was, indeed, the decisive reason for Hitler's failure. He lacked a quality without which no warlord, politician, or business tycoon can be considered great: unswerving realism, and the courage to learn from mistakes. His successes lasted only as long as reality, by luck or chance, coincided with his wishful thinking. As soon as he met an enemy who was tougher or harder than he pleased to imagine, he proved incapable of adjusting his strategy and tactics to realities.

This can be illustrated by a single telling example reported by General Halder. It is closely connected with the catastrophe at Stalingrad.

German prisoners of war in Russia *Ullstein*

Once, when a quite objective report was read to him, showing that even in 1942 Stalin would be able to muster from one to one and a half million fresh troops in the region north of Stalingrad and west of the Volga, not to mention half a million men in the Caucasus, and with additional proof that the Russian output of front-line tanks amounted to at least 1,200 a month, Hitler flew at the man who was reading with clenched fists and foam at the corners of his mouth, and forbade him to read any more of such idiotic twaddle.

The last years of his rule showed ever more clearly that Hitler, irrational and obsessed, believed that his "unbending will" could change reality and turn defeat into victory. Just as he was prepared to send an army to its doom at Stalingrad, so he wanted to pull the whole nation down to annihilation with him.

10: The Fate of Our Jewish Fellow-Citizens

Nothing that must be reported about the Third *Reich* is so hard to grasp as the fact that nearly six million Jews were "exterminated according to plan" during this period. This figure is so monstrous that reason refuses to accept it, for the heart cannot fathom its horror. But as we must face this truth we are pursued by the nagging question as to how these monstrous deeds could have been possible. How could innocent people be treated in this fashion? How can one understand a hatred which had such terrifying consequences? A brief historical resumé will provide the answer.

Ever since the overthrow of the Southern Kingdom of Judah and the deportation of a large number of Jews to the capital of Babylonia, Jewish communities existed not only in Canaan but also, at first, in Babylonia, then at the Persian court, in Asia Minor, in Egypt, and in Greece. Jerusalem formed the spiritual center of all these communities. But with the destruction of the temple by the Romans in 70 A.D. the Jews lost their spiritual center. Wherever in the dispersion (Greek: *diaspora*) Jewish communities existed from then on, life revolved around the synagogue and around its most precious possession, the Torah or the Law of Moses. The Jews kept the Sabbath holy and observed the dietary laws and their festivals and ordinances wherever they went.

Loyal to their faith, the Jews did not intermingle or integrate with the people whom they lived among, even if mutual relations were otherwise fairly friendly and peaceful. This was the case for centuries in Europe. True, the Jews were considered strangers and placed under special legislation, but they also frequently enjoyed the special protection of the emperors of the Middle Ages. This, at the time, was not uncommon. As yet, the principle that all men have equal rights was unknown, and different families, estates, or occupations each enjoyed a carefully gradated legal position. The oldest German law code, for example, the *Sachsenspiegel,* excluded clerics, women, and Jews from the rules of feudal warfare.

It is true that some of these special laws were discriminatory, as, for example, the rules governing the taking of an oath for Jews (they had to stand barefoot, clothed in sack, upon a blood-smeared pigskin!). More important was the economic discrimination: in many places Jews were forbidden to own or cultivate land, and were excluded from Christian guilds. As a result, they turned to occupations which were not controlled by guild regulations. These included medicine, for example, to which Jews made significant contributions. Initially they also included trading, especially money dealing. Soon the Jews became an indispensable factor in the development of modern economic institutions: they were able to lend money at interest which was forbidden from 1215 on in Christian medieval church laws against usury. They rendered valuable services to economic life but had the frequent experience that debtors would try to cancel their obligations by instigating massacres of Jews. Later on, the laws against usury were relaxed, and the German Christian banking families, such as the Fuggers or the Welsers, also entered the loan business.

The first violent persecution on German soil occurred at the time of the Crusades. A wave of religious excitement whose ultimate causes remain unknown was sweeping Europe. Bands of crusaders and adventurers marched through the lands to wrest Christ's grave from the hands of infidels. Nothing was easier than to arouse these masses to violent acts against the Jews. "Who had nailed Christ to the Cross, and to this day deny his divine character?" Entire Jewish communities perished, as in Worms and Mainz. The Jews could have escaped persecution through baptism, but they usually scorned this escape. They preferred to die by their own hands, together with their wives and children. Such steadfast faith speaks for itself.

Once hatred begins, it resembles a fire which keeps smoldering unless completely extinguished. From then on, the small Jewish minority was always imperiled when famine occurred somewhere, or when epidemics or wars made people afraid. For the superstitious mind of the time, the Jew was cursed, in alliance with the devil. Jews again and again became the scapegoats: they were accused of poisoning the wells, or of defiling the host. In addition, the ghastly lie was spread that the Jews used the blood of a Christian child to celebrate Passover. Still, the Jews were by no means the only victims of medieval religious fanaticism and superstition. Heretics were persecuted and witches burned for the same reasons.

This changed only with the Enlightenment. It directed the light of reason into the dark recesses of popular superstitions, and so ended belief in witchcraft. It demanded religious toleration and an end to the use of force in matters of faith. For this reason, the relationship of the Christian to the Jew also had to be given a new meaning. Lessing's drama *Nathan the Wise* expressed the new spirit in the most beautiful and humane form.

With the Enlightenment there also arose a new sense of justice. All mankind was to enjoy equal rights, the privileged were to blend with the underprivileged. The more these ideas were accepted among broad groups, the more it was felt undignified that Jews were forced to dwell in segregated quarters (or ghettoes), that they were excluded from certain occupations, that they had to pay "duty" (the so-called *Leibzoll,* a head tax) when crossing a frontier as if they were things. The ghettoes were dissolved, and the Jews "emancipated," which meant they were given equal rights with the other citizens. This development occurred in Germany between 1797 and 1812.

This, however, did not yet solve all the problems. Now people began to take offense because centuries of segregation had left their mark on Jewish customs, language, and gestures. For example, Jews had become accustomed to lacing their German with Hebrew words, Hebrew being the language of the synagogue. Precisely because Jews now had "equal rights" they were felt to be "different"; and since people everywhere tend to look askance at minorities, people were not at all ready to abandon the old religious hatreds.

This hostile attitude was reinforced by the fact that the Jews were emancipated at the same time as the old, relatively secure guild economy gave way to a new competitive economy. Now people no longer produced in answer to a fixed demand but for an uncertain market. The word was now: "To each according to his ability! Only accomplishments count!" In the new, tougher climate many were yearning for the past. But among those favored by the new economic freedom were also many Jews. They successfully took up many occupations from which they had previously been excluded. Centuries of experience had prepared them for the new world of the market and of business. Thus, craftsmen and petty traders frequently came to believe that their livelihoods were endangered by Jewish competition, while, in reality, they suffered under the new competitive system. Once more, Jews were to serve as scapegoats.

Meanwhile, genuine emancipation continued, as one or two generations erased the imprint which the ghetto had left on the Jew. Many Jews were baptized. Services in Reform synagogues followed the pattern of the Protestant service. Most Jews did not adhere any more strictly to their traditions than Catholics or Protestants did to their Christian faith, for there had been a general loosening of all religious ties. For the most part, they also ceased to consider themselves as a people, or a nation. In Germany, they felt German, in France French, in England English. Everywhere in Germany they took a leading part in intellectual life, helped to preserve traditions, or to sponsor modern developments. They were conservative, liberal, or socialist, but they were Germans, and wanted to be nothing else. Thus, at last, conditions existed under which the medieval hatred of the Jews could have disappeared, just as the medieval fear of witchcraft had disappeared.

Then, however, the unexpected happened. It appeared as if people in Europe could not free themselves from old, deeply rooted hatreds. Since the old religious rationalizations were no more modern or progressive, they searched for new ones, and found them in the "race doctrine." This doctrine had originated with the

The Jewish quarter in Frankfurt in the nineteenth century

natural sciences that had brought about the great technological progress of the nineteenth century. But instead of working with reliable scientific methods, it brought forth arbitrary evaluations, and, from the very start, turned into a pseudo-science. Charles Darwin derived the origin of animal species from the "struggle for existence," in which the stronger or better adapted species survives while the weak or poorly adapted species perishes.

On this basis, people were now being subdivided into various sub-species, called "races," a concept previously used only in animal husbandry. In the absence of precise taxonomic standards each scientist had the field for himself. Some distributed people among three, others among five, twenty, or more races and sub-races.

If these scientists had limited themselves to categorizing physical characteristics, their doctrines would have been innocuous. They claimed, however, that physical characteristics were correlated with certain intellectual and psychological characteristics. Thus the French Count Gobineau declared those people grouped together as "Aryans" by philologists on the basis of language similarities, to be a separate race. He claimed that this race alone was creative, intelligent, and dynamic. Negroes, however, he considered as cowardly, insensitive, easily excitable, and of mediocre intelligence.

Such "scientific" results, of course, flattered the pride of the European, who just at that time was preparing to extend his rule over the entire globe. Scientifically, their evidence was zero. Not one scrap of conclusive evidence has ever been put forward to prove that millions of members of one particular race are endowed with like intellectual and psychological characteristics. Any unprejudiced observer can see that all groups include intelligent and stupid people, lazy and diligent ones, courageous and cowardly men, the brilliant and the dull. Such differences appear even in small families whose members probably resemble each other physically.

Since the delineation of races depended entirely on each scientist's whim, it was more than easy to declare the Jews a "race" too. This step was taken by Houston Stewart Chamberlain, an Englishman by birth, in a book *The Foundations of the XXth Century*. He described Teutonic or Nordic man as a noble and privileged creature while assigning primarily negative characteristics to the Jews. To meet the possible argument that Jesus, after all, was Jewish too, he simply changed his line and claimed that Jesus could not possible have been a "Jew by race" (*Rassenjude*).

A perusal of antisemitic literature (the word was first used in 1880) shocks the reader into recognizing that here the old religious hatred re-appears in a modern guise. Characteristically, it deals not with "the Jews" in the plural but speaks of "the Jew"

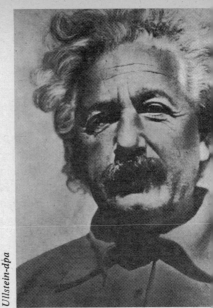

Ullstein-dpa

Two leading Jewish intellectuals who fled after 1933:
Bruno Walter and Albert Einstein

as if he were a demon or a devil. To this demon it ascribes super-natural powers: a Jew decomposes the "host nation" like a bacillus; he dilutes the nation with his alien spirit (even in cases where the Jews represent only 0.5 per cent of the population); he aims to rule the world. Antisemitic caricatures used to portray the Jew with all the features of the medieval devil.

Antisemitism served the double purpose of arousing primeval instincts—the fear of demons and a mania for persecution—and of allowing people to think that they were in step with "advanced natural science *Weltanschauung.*" With the same "scientific methods" it could have been proven just as easily that the misfortunes of the world stemmed from people with red hair.

This transformation of the medieval hatred of the Jew into racial antisemitism was to have disastrous consequences. In the Middle Ages, Jews could escape the alleged "curse of God" through baptism. The claim that they were "an inferior race" made them objects of persecution without allowing them either to stand up to their tormentors or to escape from them. As long as they were faced with traditional hatred, Jews could fall back on their proud and ancient faith. Their general defamation as a race left no defense. It hit all Jews as a group, or the fantasy image of *the* Jew. Whatever the individual Jew accomplished, whether he made great inventions, contributed to cultural life, fought bravely in wars, or donated his possessions to charity, made no difference to the antisemite. He either considered it an individual exception, or Jewish virtues and accomplishments were considered a mere camouflage for the hidden inner depravity of the Jew. In the face of antisemitism, each Jew suffered torment without a chance of escaping, like an innocent man cast out from society, torment as Jacob Wassermann has described it in moving words:

> In vain you hide away. They say: that coward, he crawls away, his bad conscience drives him to it. In vain you mingle with them and offer them your hand. They say: how does he dare, the Jew, to intrude? In vain you keep faith with them, as a comrade in arms, or as a fellow citizen. . . . In vain you live with them, or die with them. They say: he is a Jew. . . .[21]

Thus antisemitism violated the basic moral law that each man must be judged only by his deeds and thoughts. After 1945, we Germans rejected the accusation that we were collectively guilty for the crimes of the Nazis—and these crimes were, in truth, committed also "in the name of our people," while accusations which antisemites hurled against the Jews rested on nothing else but evil lies. In this way we can fathom the depth of the injustice which the antisemites, with impunity, were allowed to spread for decades.

But why was such an unjust doctrine of hatred accepted by all social strata, by educated as well as by ignorant people? A number of reasons can be propounded, none of which, of course, should be used to excuse the immorality of antisemitism. The nineteenth century ushered in fundamental economic and social changes, during the course of which the individual frequently lost his way in a maze of social relations he dimly understood. For any aggravation and any pain, antisemitism offered a simple, crude remedy: the Jews were to blame for it all. As the citizens took a greater part in determining their own lives, each individual was asked to accept

Cartoon by Eric Godal (1934):
"You admit you are guilty of being Jewish."

more responsibility for the government, and to determine his life by his own efforts. This burden became too great, and it was decidedly simpler to fight "Judah" than to improve conditions. In addition, class differences began to disappear as society progressed. Work and income increasingly became the only determinants of social status and replaced occupation or descent. In this situation, even mediocrities could easily fancy themselves as members of an elite: "The very moment one treats the Jew as an inferior and harmful creature, then he immediately feels he is a member of an elite."[22]

To nationalists, antisemitism was a useful weapon, since nationalism could be as easily stimulated attacking an "internal enemy" as by fighting against an "external" one. From its inception, antisemitism was thus closely allied with nationalism, while liberalism and socialism generally gave it a wide berth. Before the First World War, antisemitism was, for this reason, generally confined to the radical right, e.g. the Pan-Germans, and to those middle-class groups who suffered under social pressures, and had to protect themselves, on the one hand, against the competition of big business and, on the other, from the danger of "sinking into" the proletariat. As a result, they settled on the Jew as their sole enemy, responsible for capitalism and socialism alike. A few right-radical associations and student corporations also excluded Jews from membership. Violence was rare. The Jews did not really feel threatened by this antisemitism; they considered it as an ugly mental aberration, which, as yet, affected only a few of their fellow-citizens.

For various reasons, the situation of the Jews in Germany deteriorated after the First World War: national pride had been deeply hurt and humiliated by the war-guilt clause and other articles of the Treaty of Versailles. As nationalism spread, antisemitic propaganda followed in its wake. With the adoption of parliamentary democracy, the citizen, burdened with greater responsibilities, felt insecure and searched for easy solutions and remedies for all his difficulties. Finally, increasing attention was centered on the Jews when a large number of so-called "eastern Jews" emigrated from what were once Austrian and Russian areas in Poland.

The economic dislocation of inflation and the subsequent depression combined with nationalistic passions, monarchist dreams, and anti-democratic sentiments to form the unholy alliance which was to destroy the Weimar Republic. What role did antisemitism play in this? Did Hitler grow strong because he preached the most outspoken and vulgar type of antisemitism? Was "Death to the Jews!" the slogan which sent the majority of the German people marching under his banner?

The answer to these questions is probably "No." Surely the struggle against Versailles, against the "parliamentary talking shop," and the adoption of a vague socialism played a greater role in winning masses of voters. Still, the sobering doubt remains of why the slogan "Death to the Jews!" which screamed out from many Nazi posters, and was spread by many newspapers, did not frighten more people by its undisguised brutality.

Nazi propaganda was never soft, but it reached its peak of crudeness, falsehood, and vulgarity in its attacks on the Jews. The majority of the German people did not read such party papers as

Crowds listening to Hitler in the Berlin Sports Palace, beneath antisemitic slogans and banners proclaiming "Ladies, the Jews are your undoing."

Photo AP

the "Angriff," or the "Völkischer Beobachter," before Hitler "seized power," but with the advent of "co-ordination" (*Gleichschaltung*) the "nauseating, hideous brew"[23] of antisemitic propaganda became daily fare in all newspapers. Even the minds of children were poisoned by books picturing the "hellish features" of the Jew. So-called "scientific" works flooded the market in which sick and evil minds poured out their hatred without restraint. Since antisemitism had now become the official *Weltanschauung* of the state, one must wonder why violence against the Jews was still sporadic. The fact was that the German people were being indoctrinated but had not yet been conditioned to violence against individuals. Many Germans continued to buy in Jewish stores and went to Jewish physicians, and ultimately Hitler had to resort to laws and government measures to carry through his anti-Jewish policies.

On March 28, 1933, the Nazi party bosses organized a boycott of Jewish stores. Uniformed S.A. men daubed Jewish stars on the shop windows of Jewish stores, and picketed them with outsized signs demanding: "Don't buy from Jews!" Jewish merchants were intimidated and suffered damages, but their customers were not so easily driven away.

Paragraph 3 of a Decree for the Restoration of the Professional Civil Service [sic] provided the basis for dismissing "non-Aryan" officials (April 1933). Typically in this early period Hitler was still restrained by Hindenburg, who protested against the clause in this decree which permitted the removal from office of Jewish war veterans.

Hitler did not dare take the next large step until the *Reich* Party Congress in Nuremberg in 1935, when the Nuremberg Laws reduced Jews to the category of second-class citizens. Marriages and extra-marital relations between Jews and "citizens of German blood" were forbidden. Racial crime (*Rassenschande*) became a favorite theme of Streicher's hate sheet "Der Stürmer." Although the Nuremberg Laws did not touch already existing marriages be-

Boycotting a Jewish store in Berlin, 1 April 1933   *Ullstein*

The Oppeln synagogue on fire, November 1938

tween Aryans and non-Aryans, increased pressure was subsequently brought to bear on the Aryan partner to sue for divorce. These race laws drove many people to suicide, including the poet Jochen Klepper and the actor Joachim Gottschalk, to mention the most famous cases. Both men had Jewish wives and killed not only themselves but their wives and children as well.

Another discriminatory measure introduced in August 1938 made it obligatory for Jews to use only Jewish first names, and to add the names Israel or Sara if they had any forbidden first names. This measure was to help in identifying Jews more easily, but, ironically, it implicitly admitted that Jews did not really differ physically or intellectually from the rest of the populace.

A string of similar antisemitic decrees followed upon the assassination of Ernst vom Rath, a councillor at the German legation in Paris, by Herschel Grynszpan, a Polish Jew, on November 9, 1938. It started with the burning down of synagogues in Germany by S.A. troops, acting under orders. Altogether 267 synagogues went up in flames that night; in addition, 815 stores were destroyed, 20,000 Jews arrested, and 36 killed. In his press, Goebbels had the nerve to pass off these acts of arson which he had organized and directed in person as "a spontaneous reaction of the German people." It would, however, be truer to say that many people reacted with spontaneous indignation as the scales fell from their eyes about the true character of the Nazi regime. But they were not indignant enough to resist openly.

The cue was now provided for the party leaders to put their sick fantasies into practice. By a horrible perversion of justice, the victims, the aggrieved, the despoiled—the Jews—were ordered to "atone for their crimes" with a fine of one billion marks. Another decree stated:

> Paragraph 1: All the damage caused by the indignation of the people about the propaganda attacks of international Jewry against Nazi Germany in Jewish business premises and dwelling units on November 8, 9, and 10, 1938, is to be repaired at once by the Jewish owner, or the Jew who did business on the premises.
> Paragraph 2: The expense of the repair is to be borne by the owners of the Jewish business premises and dwelling units concerned. Insurance claims by Jews of German nationality are confiscated in favor of the *Reich*.

Other orders followed in close succession. First came the Exclusion of Jews from German Economic Life, and then Jews were forbidden to engage in business or crafts and could no longer be employed in an executive capacity. The Minister of Education ordered the removal of Jewish pupils from German schools. Many cities established a so-called "Jew ban," which meant Jews were forbidden to enter certain residential sections, or to visit movie houses, museums, and theaters.

At this time, many Jewish families decided to emigrate if they possibly could. They escaped the worse fate which, after the outbreak of the war, awaited those who would not or could not leave.

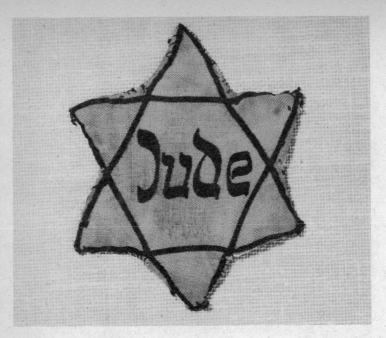

The yellow Star of David

This systematic and calculated chicanery was stepped up even more after the outbreak of the war. Beginning in 1940, Jews in many places could do their shopping only at fixed hours. Later, Jews were restricted to only a few designated stores. In September 1941, the Jewish Star Decree followed, according to which Jews 6 years and over had to wear in public "a hexagonal star, the size of a palm, bordered in black, made of yellow material, bearing the inscription 'Jew' in black letters, affixed to the left side of their garments at the height of the breast." The use of the star of David, a religious symbol, as a stigma was especially vindictive.

In countries occupied by German troops, where people had not lost their normal sensitivity through eight years of Nazi propaganda, the introduction of the decree led to many demonstrations of solidarity: on the streets people greeted Jews wearing the star with demonstrative cordiality, and non-Jews pinned yellow flowers or Jewish stars made of paper on their clothes. King Christian of Denmark announced in a message that all Danes were equally close to his heart, that he himself would be the first to wear the Jewish star, and that he expected all loyal subjects to follow suit, whereupon the Nazis withdrew their decree in Denmark. A decree on forced labor followed in October 1941. As far as possible, Jews had already been "forced to serve" as factory workers under a law proclaiming a universal obligation to work. Now the government-determined wage scales were declared inapplicable for them, and they were not permitted any bonuses, maternity benefits, or family allowances. Even the rules governing safety at work were dropped for Jewish workers!

It is embarrassing to enumerate the many petty humiliations to which the law was bent. In 1942 the *Reich* Law Gazette was filled with such decrees: all Jewish dwellings were to be marked by the star of David; Jews were not permitted to keep pets; Jews were forbidden to have their hair cut by Aryan barbers; Jews were not allowed to own electric appliances, record players, typewriters, bicycles; Jews were not allowed to visit heated public shelters, etc.

But these systematic, calculated annoyances had long since been overshadowed by an incomparably more terrifying threat. In November 1941, a decree Concerning the Deportation of Jews was announced. It read:

> Jews who do not hold jobs essential for the economy will be deported to a city in the east in the course of the next few months. The property of the Jews to be deported will be confiscated for the German *Reich*. Each Jew may keep 100 Reichsmarks and 110 pounds (50 kg) of luggage.

Beginning as early as the spring of 1940, the S.S. had re-established ghettoes in such Polish cities as Lublin, Lodz, Cracow, and Warsaw. The Jews were herded into designated parts of the towns, and the entire area was surrounded with fences and cordoned off with signs which warned: "No trespassing, Jewish quarter." At that time, Poland had 2.9 million Jews. These unfortunate people had been unable to emigrate, for they were mostly small farmers, tradesmen, and craftsmen and could not possible obtain the money for the voyage. They fell prey as helpless victims to the S.S.

On the pattern of these Polish ghettoes, an entire ghetto-city

Wobbelin concentration camp after its liberation, 1945 *Ullstein*

was established in 1941 in Terezin (Theresienstadt in Bohemia).
It was to serve as a forced residence for German Jews, primarily
for leading Jewish functionaries. In Germany, the rumor was
spread that this camp was "especially humane," that the Jews
were permitted to develop their own culture and put on plays and
concerts. The only purpose of this legend was, in the last analysis,
to soothe people's conscience. Those who heard that their Jewish
acquaintances were transported to Theresienstadt late at night or
early in the morning could perhaps rest content that after all conditions there were not too bad. In reality, this camp, like all other
camps, was a well-organized hell where man's mind withered under the narrow compulsions of collective life before his body died
of hunger. For many, however, Theresienstadt was only a station
on the way to the extermination camps established for the "final
solution of the Jewish question."

On July 31, 1941, Göring issued instructions to Heydrich, the S.D. chief, to submit a comprehensive draft for the carrying out of the "final solution of the Jewish question." It is difficult to determine Göring's precise intentions. The letter speaks only of emigration and evacuation. But where could the Jews have been evacuated to at that time? Hitler had attacked Russia on June 22, 1941. Not only were the Polish Jews in his net but also their coreligionists in Holland, France, Czechoslovakia, the Balkan countries, and western Russia. What was to happen to them? Among the S.S., plans were circulated for the deportation of all Jews to the island of Madagascar, off the African coast.

Since such plans were impractical, the doctrinaires around Himmler decided to "exterminate" the Jews. The minutes of a meeting held at the Grosse Wannsee to plan the "final solution" (known as the Wannsee Protocol) read as follows:

> As a further possibility of solving the question, the evacuation of the Jews to the east can now be substituted for emigration, after obtaining permission from the Fuehrer to that effect. However, these actions are merely to be considered as alternative possibilities, even though they will permit us to make all those practical experiences which are of great importance for the future final solution of the Jewish question.
>
> The Jews should in the course of the Final Solution be taken in a suitable manner to the east for use as labor. In big labor gangs, separated by sex, the Jews capable of work will be brought to these areas for road building, in which task undoubtedly a large number will fall through natural diminuition. The remnant that is finally able to survive all this—since this is undoubtedly the part with the strongest resistance—must be treated accordingly, since these people, representing a natural selection, are to be regarded as the germ cell of a new Jewish development, in case they should succeed and go free (as history has proved). In the course of the execution of the Final Solution, Europe will be combed from west to east.

Nowhere is the bureaucratic make-believe language of the S.S., the language of inhumanity, revealed more horribly than in this document. Following this blueprint, the S.S. began to call its subsequent mass murder "special treatment." Faced with tremendous numbers of absolutely helpless human beings, the executioners of the Third *Reich* were seized with a frenzy of extermination.

At first, "special treatment" consisted in mass shootings. The Jews were dragged out of their ghettoes and ordered to dig ditches in remote places. Next, every man, woman, child, and aged person had to strip naked, and carefully place his clothing and his shoes on piles. Then, five to ten people at a time had to step up together to the edge of the ditch, and were mowed down with a tommy gun. After the mass graves had filled with 500 to 1000 bodies, they were covered with lime and earth. It is reported that Himmler was so nauseated when he witnessed this "method," that he recommended from then on, as a "more humane means," the use of poison gas (to be released in vans or specially constructed chambers camouflaged as shower rooms). Suitable facilities for this form of mass extermination were constructed in the large extermination camps of Auschwitz, Maidanek, and Treblinka. Huge crematoria were built, and the bodies were burned around the clock.

To top this absolutely infernal system the Jews themselves were ordered to operate the entire machinery of murder. They had to remove the piled-up bodies from the gas chambers and to operate the crematoria. The only hope remaining to these workers in their ghastly work was, perhaps, to escape death.

Today, some people refuse to face up to these appalling facts. But can we be so cowardly as to evade even in our imaginations the suffering that real people, people such as you and I, had to bear in harsh reality?

When those Jews who were still free learned about the ultimate destinations of their deported co-religionists, they sought, by any available means, to go underground and live "illegally." Help was offered in Holland, where a large segment of the population proved its mettle, and there were similar cases in Germany, though not nearly enough.

The dangers were very great, indeed. Those underground had no more ration cards, the only means of obtaining food during the war years. They had to share the scanty rations of their protectors, and lived in constant danger of discovery. The "illegal" people also suffered many dreadful hours during air raids on German cities, where they had the alternative of staying unprotected in

Jews being herded out of the Warsaw ghetto   *Ullstein*

their apartments, or risking discovery by going to a public air-raid
shelter.

For the many who found this escape barred, the end was always
the same: first, work to exhaustion in factories "essential for the
war," each day filled with fear that relatives incapable of work had
received orders for deportation to the east. . . . This would come
for everyone some day. . . . In the last moment, many chose to
die by their own hands. . . . At collection points, the deportees
were robbed of their last belongings. Then, for days, the trip in
overcrowded cattle-cars. If Theresienstadt was the destination, it
could mean a small respite. If it was one of the notorious exter-

Jews waiting beside the railroad tracks at Auschwitz
concentration camp, separated into two groups

mination camps, incoming transports were led to "selection." Men
were separated from women, children torn away from parents.
The sick, the aged, the weak, and the children were sent to the left
at "selection": their destiny was death. Those still considered capable of work were sent into the barracks and had to work as slaves
for their miserable food until they died of hunger or epidemics, or
were themselves selected for extermination. The threat of death
hung ever present over all; the smell of the crematoria lay like a
cloud over the camps.

Nor was this all. The S.S. guards held daily roll-calls in these
camps, too, and forced the emaciated prisoners, in their garb of
rags, to stand in rain, snow, sun, or wind until all inmates had been
counted. Woe to any of these human beings who lost his pre-
carious hold on life and died unnoticed in a barrack on a heap of

232

rags! Then the prisoners were counted and re-counted and 24, even 48, hours might pass before the prisoners were allowed to disband. Those who fell down were kicked or beaten.

This lust for extermination was revealed to its full extent in the copious records where all murders were listed with bureaucratic pedantry. An S.S. Economic and Administrative Main Office was founded exclusively for such purposes as collecting and packaging all the possessions of the murdered, from tons of clothing to eye glasses, artificial teeth, gold teeth, and women's hair, and "utilizing" them. Man was not only exterminated as if he were vermin, he was also made into matter and exploited as a "source of raw material" for the war economy.

This was the result of the Final Solution:

COUNTRY	JEWISH POPULATION, SEPTEMBER 1939	JEWISH LOSSES	PERCENTAGE OF JEWISH LOSSES
1. Poland	3,300,000	2,800,000	85.0
2. USSR, occupied territory	2,100,000	1,500,000	71.4
3. Rumania	850,000	425,000	50.0
4. Hungary	404,000	200,000	49.5
5. Czechoslovakia	315,000	260,000	82.5
6. France	300,000	90,000	30.0
7. Germany	210,000	170,000	81.0
8. Lithuania	150,000	135,000	90.0
9. Netherlands	150,000	90,000	60.0
10. Latvia	95,000	85,000	89.5
11. Belgium	90,000	40,000	44.4
12. Greece	75,000	60,000	80.0
13. Yugoslavia	75,000	55,000	73.3
14. Austria	60,000	40,000	66.6
15. Italy	57,000	15,000	26.3
16. Bulgaria	50,000	7,000	14.0
17. Others	20,000	6,000	30.0
	8,301,000	5,978,000	72.0

Belsen concentration camp, 1945

Nobody will ever fully appreciate the suffering behind these figures: the humiliations, the shame, the agony. We cannot escape it by saying that we did not know about it and had never wanted it to happen. However true this may be, where were we when we should have opposed the beginnings? One of the most impressive short stories of Leo Tolstoy bears the title: "If you let the flame rise, you will never extinguish it!" We let the flame of hatred rise and did not extinguish it while there was still time. We allowed posters and songs to spread hatred and abuse while we were still at liberty to fight against them. This first sin of omission gave rise to all the later crimes.

To the injustice committed in our name we must not add the injustice of forgetting. While relatives still mourn their dead, can we forget because the shadows of the past are painful to us? There is no restitution for such enormous suffering. But by preserving the memory of the victims, we can perform a sacred duty imposed upon us by the guilt we bear toward our Jewish fellow-citizens.

11: The Right To Resist—Did It Exist?

In view of the monstrous crimes of the Nazi regime, the heading of this section should be rephrased: "Was there a duty to resist?" Was there no obligation to stop these criminals? Young people who never experienced terror themselves sometimes ask: "Why did you not kill Hitler in time?" They cannot understand why resistance did not spread widely and why it did not have more success. Others, however, say to this day that no resistance should have been offered while the war lasted, and that Hitler should have been made to account for his crimes afterwards. Both views misrepresent the actual situation. But they reveal also a central problem affecting German resistance.

Today, in the security of a state based on law (*Rechtsstaat*), it is simple to postulate a duty to resist. No doubt, it did exist as long as everybody was still free to defend himself—during the period of the Weimar Republic. It existed also to a large extent during the first few months following the "seizure of power," when Hitler was still feeling his way to see how far he could go. There is no doubt, too, that the first attacks on the institutions of the state based on law should have been more vigorously opposed (see p. 121). Once terror, with all its brutality, had been incorporated in the law, both open and clandestine resistance jeopardized life and limb to such an extent that it took extraordinary courage to risk the consequences. This is all the more true for relatives of resistance fighters, who were also endangered by such action. It would therefore be too harsh to claim that during that period there was a legal duty to resist; but the moral obligation is always valid. Everybody had to decide according to his own conscience how much he was prepared to tolerate, and at what point he felt obliged to make his stand. An incessant barrage of propaganda had blunted the consciences of many, and others who had retained a moral standard kept their distance from the NSDAP as much as possible and suffered injustices which they were too weak to oppose. Still others chose the way of martyrs and heroes. This is their story.

Members of the French resistance with two captured Nazis   *UP*

Their course was considerably more difficult than that of resistance fighters in areas occupied by Germany. In Holland and Belgium, in France and Yugoslavia, members of the Resistance fought against a foreign oppressor. Secure in the sympathy of their countrymen, they were motivated largely by a desire to liberate their nations. German resistance fighters had no such support. On the contrary, the regime they opposed was created and supported by a sizable section of their own people. In addition, they had to face the strong belief from most of their countrymen that their actions constituted high treason and a disgraceful disloyalty toward their own nation in wartime. This often sharpened conflicts of conscience until they became well-nigh unbearable.

Yet another difficulty to be overcome by German resistance fighters was the fact that Germany had almost no tradition of revolutionary action, of the moral freedom of the individual to oppose those in power, which has occurred on numerous occasions in British and French history. One of the German resistance fighters,

Pfarrer Dietrich Bonhoeffer

a pastor named Dietrich Bonhoeffer, has expressed this with unsurpassed clarity:

> Who would deny that the German, again and again, has done his utmost in bravery, and has risked his life while obeying orders, following his calling, or doing his work. . . . But, in doing so, he has not understood the world; he had not anticipated that his willingness to subordinate his ego, and to risk his life for his calling can be abused for evil. . . . Thus, the German never grasped a decisive and fundamental idea: the necessity to act freely and responsibly even if it impaired his work and his calling.

It was no accident that open resistance occurred principally where the commands of the state clashed with a higher command, where the question was raised whether one owed greater allegiance to God or man. First the clergy, then all those who took their Christian faith seriously, were faced with this question.

With the exception of the German Christians (see p. 167), the Protestant as well as the Catholic Church remained faithful to

237

their calling. The messages of the Synod of the Confessing Church, official declarations, pastoral letters, and many sermons were strong and clear, mincing no words about the Nazi substitute religion. One example is provided by the following quotations from an official declaration of March 1935. It was read in Protestant churches and led to the arrest of 700 pastors:

> The first commandment says: "I am the Lord Thy God. Thou shalt have no other gods besides Me." We obey this commandment in the sole belief in our Lord Jesus Christ who was crucified and rose again for us. The new religion is a rebellion against the First Commandment.
> 1. It turns the racial and *völkische Weltanschauung* into a myth. Blood and race, *Volk,* honor, and freedom become its idols.
> 2. The belief in "eternal Germany" demanded by this new religion replaces the belief in the eternal kingdom of Jesus Christ, our Lord and Savior.
> 3. This deluded faith creates God in the image and essence of man. In it man honors, justifies, and saves himself. Such idolatry has no truck with positive Christianity. It is anti-Christianity.

Elsewhere, the declaration demands emphatically that the Church shall not withdraw from the public and the world into a corner of private piety where it would, in its isolation, become untrue to its calling.

Soon, all Germany knew the names of some members of the resisting churches. Everybody had heard of Pastor Niemöller who, having been acquitted by a court, had been arrested by the Gestapo and taken to a concentration camp as "a personal prisoner of the Fuehrer," from where he was not liberated until 1945. Copies of sermons delivered by Bishop Clemens August, Count von Galen, passed from hand to hand. The fate of others was known only to their congregations; for example, the unspeakable tortures which Pastor Schneider of Diekenscheid had to endure in Buchenwald, or the sentence imposed upon Provost Bernhard Lichtenberg of the Berlin Cathedral. He earned himself a two-year sentence by including a prayer for the Jews and the poor inmates of concentration camps in his evening services.

Lichtenberg had also protested against the killing of the insane in a letter to the *Reich* Physicians' Leader. Such killings, dubbed "the destruction of life unworthy of living," had been ordered by

Hitler in an informal decree issued immediately after the outbreak of the war. The sick, destined for "mercy killing," were transferred to certain selected institutions (Grafeneck, Brandenburg, Hadamar, etc.) on some pretext, and gassed there. Their relatives were misinformed about the cause of their deaths.

In spite of all efforts to keep them secret, these planned murders became known. In this one area, the churches protested with success. The director of the Beth-El institutions, Pastor von Bodelschwingh, refused to release one single patient. Bishop von Galen asked for the prosecution of the murderers. Such protests, and the obvious indignation of the people, forced Hitler in 1941 to stop the program for the time being. A similar indignant outcry about the "evacuation of the Jews" might, perhaps, have led to similar results.

In general it is true that "Church opposition was the only opposition which achieved some visible successes."[24]

After the fall of the Nazi regime in 1945, many Germans tried to prove that they, too, had offered resistance. It is therefore essential to distinguish between real resistance and "silent opposition." There were different ways by which "co-ordination" could be avoided. Some stiff-necked people refused to give the Hitler-salute. Some professors would not be deterred from quoting Jewish scientists with respect. But resistance could be said to exist only where people knew that they risked their lives, and acted in full awareness of this risk.

Some figures testify to the extent of the resistance. The number of *German* concentration camp inmates has been estimated at 500,000 or 600,000, and the number of executions carried out for political crimes at about 12,000. One must remember, of course, that some arrests were made in pursuit of personal vendettas, and that people were sentenced to death merely for re-telling a political joke! Still, these figures give a general idea of the extent of the various resistance organizations deserving of the name. Motives for such action were diverse.

One large group was the Communists, who were driven into resistance from the first days of Hitler's rule. Belonging to an international party which traditionally engaged in illegal activities, they were, so to speak, predestined for planned resistance. Those who did not immediately vanish into concentration camps naturally took to building up illegal cells and cadres on Lenin's pre-scriptions.

This Communist resistance, however, cannot be grouped with other resistance efforts, because it was directed from Moscow and did not aim at democratic freedom but, instead, at replacing one dictatorship with another. Despite this, however, it must not be forgotten that some of these Communist resistance groups acted independently, as for example the well-known Red Chapel group which included such outstanding minds as Harro Schulze-Boysen and Arvid and Mildred Harnack, a married couple. There were also some attractive and brave women, two of whom were executed after giving birth to children.

Above all, we must never forget the Communist resistance in the concentration camps, which had to be carried on under absolutely unprecedented conditions. Many of these inmates had been arrested in 1933 or the next few years; some never regained their freedom, others were released for a short time but soon found themselves back in the concentration camp. These people were better acquainted with the appalling conditions of life in the camps than other groups of inmates. They served as office helpers or hospital orderlies, and made great efforts to strengthen the other prisoners' will to resist. They also shed some of their anti-religious prejudices, since they could not help paying their respect to the steadfastness of priests and monks and to the adamant faith of the Jehovah's Witnesses. Never before or since did Christians and Communists come as close to each other as under the terror of the S.S.

In Kurt Grossmann's phrase,[25] another group may be identified as the "unsung heroes." Risking their own lives, they saved their Jewish fellow-citizens from persecution and extermination by providing them with illegal passports and forged identification papers, or by sheltering them in their own homes. Such aid also included the employment of Jews in their businesses. Oskar Schindler can be cited for his impressive example of an employer who saved more than 1100 people from extermination by using Jewish labor in his enamel works in Cracow. He also placed on his payroll relatives of his workers, who were aged or incapable of work, and provided them with food and hid them every time the S.S. inspected his plant. When evacuations were about to start, he kept

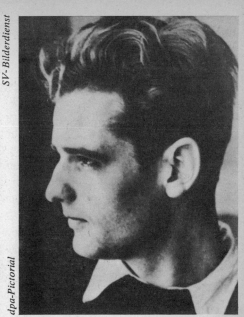

Sophie and Hans Scholl

the entire night shift working on some pretext to save them from S.S. raids. As a last resort, he often used bribes to pry one of his charges from the grip of the Gestapo. Almost his entire fortune was spent on such acts of mercy.

In this context, one must remember, too, those students in Munich who "fought against the giant conflagration with their bare hands and their faith and opposed the all-powerful state with their tiny mimeographing machine."[26] Their self-selected password, "White Rose," symbolizes their pure spirits. They were young, believing Christians, who loved everything noble and beautiful and were often exuberant and in high spirits; but they became increasingly conscious and tortured by the disgrace of what they called the "dictatorship of evil" in Germany. They were convinced that they had no right to keep silent. They knew that it was nearly impossible to "knock down an iron wall of fear and terror." But, nevertheless, they were ready to try. The leaflets they wrote, mimeographed, and distributed under constant dangers are imperishable monuments to their high-mindedness. A sentence in the last leaflet, which Hans and Sophie Scholl dropped from the top bal-

241

cony of the inner court of Munich University and which led to their arrest, reads: "Germany's name will remain disgraced forever unless German youth finally rises up at once, takes revenge and atones, smashes its torturers, and builds a new, spiritual Europe."

They may have believed, for a time, that they would succeed in carrying the torch of revolt from university to university, but they had never seriously calculated the dangers and risks against the chances of success. After their arrest they had no other thought but to incriminate themselves in order to protect their friends. They realized immediately that their lives were forfeit. Sentenced in a quick trial, all six of them mounted the scaffold with matchless courage. The only married man among them, Christl Probst, who left three small children behind, had once explained the meaning of this sacrifice to his friends: "We must show by our poise and our dedication that man is still free. Humanity, if once upheld, will prevail some day." Thus, these young people had refused to take success as the measure of their actions, and had realized the same ideal which eighteen months later was to guide the agony of hundreds of men and women of the larger German resistance movement: the meaning of the sacrifice lies in the sacrifice itself.

The resistance movement among German Socialists consisted of several smaller circles who only gradually came in contact with each other, to merge finally in the common action of July 20, 1944. Like the Communists, the Socialists were pushed to resisting by the treatment meted out by Hitler. Treating them as "November criminals," he had many of their leaders arrested and tried in 1933. Others were sent to concentration camps or managed to emigrate, and many lost their jobs and had no source of income. In spite of these difficult circumstances, they were unwilling to look on passively. They soon realized that the totalitarian state could not be undermined by the old revolutionary means of a strike and a riot, and by fighting at the barricades. Only those forces that disposed of means to exercise violence would be able to end the rule of absolute violence. The outbreak of the war made this insight even more cogent. Leading Socialists accordingly established contacts with resistance groups in the armed forces at an

242

Julius Leber at the People's Court   *Mitchell*

early date, for they considered as their main task the broadening
of the political basis for future action. They wanted to create conditions under which trusted representatives of the workers would
be available to make a coup d'état palatable to the masses after it
had succeeded.

Since all these men were intimately acquainted with Hitler's
prisons and concentration camps, their steadfastness and determination deserve the greatest admiration. Julius Leber, for example, former editor of the "Lübecker Volksbote" and a former
member of parliament, had been kept in a windowless cell for one
year, and "was refused everything: a bed, a chair, a table, work,
a daily walk, and warm food. At zero temperatures he lay on the
bare floor at night, without blanket, straw, or coat." Leber thus
described this period of his life in his letters: "Here the naked
heart lies in the balance. One can hide behind nothing, nothing. . ."

None of these men was narrowly dogmatic. There were ingen-
ious and imaginative persons among them, like Carlo Mierendorff,

243

Father Alfred Delp on trial, with Helmut Count von Moltke, paper in hand
Leber

philosophical minds like Theodor Haubach, precise and indefatigable negotiators like Wilhelm Leuschner, cosmopolitan educators like Adolf Reichwein, and disciplined fighters like Julius Leber. They were not concerned with economic or political doctrines but with the freedom of man, and they were thus prepared to ally themselves with like-minded "bourgeois" forces of the resistance.

Among these, there was first the "Kreisau Circle," led by Helmut James Count von Moltke, a great-great-nephew of the Field Marshal. Moltke was an attorney in international law in Berlin and served as an expert for international law with the Supreme Command of the Armed Forces during the war. He often used his position to help prisoners of war or persecuted Jews. Although he owned an estate at Kreisau in Silesia, he was anything but a typical country *Junker*. He divided a large portion of his estate into smaller peasant lots, thus carrying out a land reform scheme on his own. On this estate, various discussion groups were held with the aim of working out the fundamental political and social organization for a future and better Germany. Those who took part in these discussions became known as the Kreisau Circle. They included a Jesuit priest, Alfred Delp, who was a harsh critic of the middle class in search of security; the diplomat Adam von Trott zu Solz, who had friends all over the world, and was fond of far-reaching theoretical schemes; Peter Count Yorck zu Wartenburg, sober and unobtrusively efficient, and Eugen Gerstenmaier, later a President of the Federal Diet. The Socialists Haubach and Reichwein also belonged to the Kreisau Circle. These men made a common effort to "analyze the decadence of man and of the human community which had made Hitler's rise possible, and to identify those elements of strength which might endure in the midst of turmoil."[27] They felt that the violence and destruction which Germany had let loose over the world made a simple return to the Weimar Republic impossible. They knew that they had to dig deeper to reach the roots of the evil. How could man be freed from his subservience to technology? Where could he find new spiritual ties? How could he be prepared for his responsibilities? Such views were to guide the shaping of the educational system, the social order, and the entire state of the future. The Kreisau Circle was especially emphatic in denouncing the rape of justice; they stressed the validity of divine and natural law as opposed to mere statutes.

The Kreisau Circle was, above all, concerned with clarifying ideas. For a long time, these men rejected the use of violence to remove Hitler, but from 1943 on they realized that a military debacle was inevitable and made their plans accordingly. More than half the members paid with their lives for their thoughts. Moltke himself was imprisoned early in 1944. He felt that the spirit had triumphed when, in his trial before the People's Court, it was established clearly that he could not be accused of having advocated the actual use of violence, or of establishing an organization hostile to the state, but, rather, that he was on trial for his life for conversations about the ethical postulates of Christianity. This, however, does not imply that Moltke, had he remained free, would have opposed the attempt on Hitler's life. As it was, the members of his circle, after much soul-searching, dropped their reservations because they saw no other possibility "of saving Germany's dignity before the court of world history," in Eugen Gerstenmaier's words.

Different in thought and action was the circle that assembled

Carl Goerdeler   *Mitchell*

around the former Lord Mayor of Leipzig, Carl Goerdeler. Goerdeler had far-reaching connections with business leaders, officials, and diplomats, and used his almost inexhaustible supply of energy to "drive the moral conscience to revolt." He planned for immediate, practical needs: he drafted a new constitution; he drew up a list of ministers for the prospective government; he outlined proclamations for X-Day, and wrote speeches which would explain the events of the conspiracy to the public. Goerdeler was convinced from the very start that Hitler could only be removed from office by the armed forces, and he spared no efforts to arouse the generals to their moral responsibilities despite the grave risks. Among his friends these efforts found their symbolic expression in his cover name "itinerant preacher." He was an easygoing man, given to minimizing difficulties and obstacles, but this same easygoing nature led him to neglect the precautions necessary for the success of a conspiracy. He has been compared to an engine racing at top speed and making too much noise, and, yet, it was these very characteristics which made him the greatest source of strength for the German resistance movement, and which enabled him to convert more people to the cause than any other resistance fighter.

The names of some men connected with Goerdeler may be taken as representative of the entire group: Ambassador Ulrich von Hassell, whose diary reflected the daily activities and dangers which beset the men and women of the resistance; professors Popitz and Jessen, outstanding scholars as well as daring fighters; and Albrecht Haushofer, better known for his "Moabit Sonnets" than his scientific works. All these resistance groups had very similar motives and attitudes, although they differed in their particular image of a future and better Germany. None was driven by ambition or selfishness. They were guided by their conscience, their sense of justice, their love for Germany. But they could not act

Ludwig Beck

Mitchell

247

alone; Hitler could only be removed by military force: "The civilians might offer ideas, political plans, contact with the masses. The soldiers had to do the shooting."[28]

The army alone was in a position either to imprison Hitler following a coup d'état, or remove him by assassination. This is so obvious that the other difficulties, special to the army, pale by comparison. First, there was its traditional abstention from politics, which allowed many fence-sitters to suppress their moral scruples: "The soldier must fight battles, not determine the war aims." Of greater importance, specially for the enlisted men and younger officers, was the oath of allegiance sworn to Hitler's person (see p. 130). Before Hitler had made himself Supreme Commander of the Armed Forces, a soldier used to swear loyalty to his nation and his fatherland. The new method of swearing unquestioning obedience to Hitler implied a fundamental change and made an attempt on Hitler's life inevitable, because only through Hitler's death could the armed forces be formally released from their oath.

Under the circumstances, only a small group of "intellectual soldiers," after much soul-searching, arrived at the conclusion that an oath of allegiance implied a mutual obligation and was to be kept only as long as the "liege lord" kept faith with it on his part. Ludwig Beck, then Chief of the General Staff of the German Army, had said as early as 1938:

> Ultimate decisions about the existence of the nation are at stake here. History will hold these leaders responsible for the blood they shed, unless they act according to their technical and political knowledge, and their consciences. The soldier must stop obeying if his knowledge, his conscience, and his responsibility forbid him to carry out orders. . . . A soldier in a position of command lacks greatness and misses his task if, at such times, he confines himself to the narrow duties of his military command, and if he fails to understand that his first responsibility lies with his entire nation. Extraordinary times demand extraordinary deeds.

After the collapse of Hitler's *Reich,* theologians, jurists, and soldiers unanimously confirmed Beck's stand. The oath of loyalty ceased to be binding when the Fuehrer to whom it was sworn was prepared to drag nation and fatherland down with him into destruction. To support this view, Hitler, in his own words, could have been quoted as state's evidence, for he had said in *Mein Kampf:* "If through the power of a government a people is led to its own destruction, each member of such a people has not only the right but the duty of rebelling." If one wants to evaluate the opposition within the army one must remember that for moral reasons many military men felt unable to break their oath, while others used this merely as an excuse.

Another difficulty lay in the fact that some mildly sympathetic generals wanted to wait for the right psychological moment, which would not come while Hitler was winning. They also wanted to make sure that the Allies would offer more favorable peace terms if they dealt with a new government. These were to be guaranteed by the civilians. For a long time, they also demanded that the Western powers agree to continue the war against Russia.

When Hitler's prestige had begun to wane among the people, that is, about the time of Stalingrad, the position of the Allies improved from month to month. This correspondingly diminished the value of a German peace offer. Not long afterwards the news spread that, at Casablanca, the Allies had decided to ask for Germany's unconditional surrender. Roosevelt explained the decision: "It means not the destruction of the populace but the destruction of a philosophy which is based on the conquest and subjugation of other people." Unconditional surrender was also demanded from Japan, but an exception was made with Italy in order to facilitate its political reconstruction.

Although the civilians in the resistance used every opportunity —rare as these were—to inform the Allies of the existence of a German resistance movement, the Allies were not prepared to give the German opposition the same chances they had given the Italian resistance. As a result, the decisions of Casablanca slowed down the deliberations and decisions of the opposition officers. Why embark on a dangerous course if its success or failure would have no influence on the armistice or the peace?

Thus the only men in the army willing to act were those who did not make their decision dependent on military success but who considered foremost justice and their conscience:

One asks, what it will lead to, the other, what is just?
This separates the free man from the slave. (*Theodor Storm*)

The opposition was centered in the army. The other two services, the air force and navy, had a very small share in the resistance. One reason could well have been that these branches of the service were mostly staffed with officers who had been trained by the Nazis, while the army had retained a surprising number of the old Prussian traditions. These services also had less opportunities for witnessing burnings and killings by the S.S. in enemy territory and were less frequently ordered to mistreat prisoners in violation of international law, such as had been the case, on Hitler's orders, in Poland and during the Russian campaign. It is established that many officers in the resistance joined the opposition under the impact of experiences of this kind.

For many years, Lieutenant-General Ludwig Beck was the intellectual leader of the military opposition. He had handed his resignation to Hitler following the Czech crisis of 1938. Then, his home in Berlin had turned into a meeting place for like-minded people while he, thanks to his straightforward personality and his great ability, became the "nerve center" of all efforts. Here is Hossbach's evaluation of his personality: "He had no preconceived notions about people and affairs, he valued honest advice, accepted different and contrary opinions, and was an intelligent listener *par excellence*. He always controlled and disciplined himself and was thus kept from hasty judgments and decisions."

Another important center of resistance formed around Admiral Canaris, the counter-espionage chief, and his colleague, Major-General Hans Oster. Canaris was reputed to have been cunning as Ulysses, but pure of heart, "wily as a snake, and gentle as a dove." A friend described Hans Oster as "a man such as God meant men to be." Their special assignments (defense against foreign espionage) did not permit them to take an active part in planning the revolt, but they rendered inestimable services by supplying information, preventing many injustices, and giving much personal aid.

The most farsighted and determined among the officers of the army was Henning von Tresckow, who served in Russia as Chief of Staff of the Army Group Center. He had an extraordinary gift for inspiring confidence and imparting his enthusiasm to others.

He was at the same time open and yet reserved. Tresckow believed as early as 1942 that Hitler had to be removed in order to release the army from its oath. Two of the most important attempts on Hitler's life were made by men of his circle.

After carefully testing for months British-made plastic explosives and noiseless chemical fuses (also of British origin), Tresckow had asked Hitler to inspect the Army Group Center. Hitler came according to plan, and before he boarded his plane for the return trip, one of his party was handed a parcel with "two bottles of cognac" (a "present" for one Colonel Stieff, at headquarters). The fuse had been set a short time previously, and the conspirators waited, breathless and tense. The plane was to explode in mid-air 30 minutes later. . . . After two hours, a message came through that the Fuehrer had landed at headquarters. The conspirators, with luck, succeeded in retrieving the fake bottles of cognac without being detected. For some reason the detonator had not fired.

A second opportunity soon came. Hitler was to attend the opening of an exhibition at the Berlin Armory: "Tresckow selected one Colonel von Gersdorff, explained to him why he must act for the sake of liberty, and asked him whether he would risk the attempt while accompanying Hitler on a tour of the exhibition. (Gersdorff was on duty as the counter-espionage officer of the Army Group.) Gersdorff volunteered. . . . But before the tour began, and before Gersdorff could start the fuse in his pocket, Hitler's adjutant, Schmundt, informed him that the 30 minutes originally set aside for the tour were to be cut to 8-10 minutes. . . . Gersdorff could do nothing—the fuse with the shortest action time in his possession needed 15 minutes at room temperature."[29]

Superficial observers of the German resistance don't understand why the resistance failed to remove Hitler; for instance, why no one "simply" shot him. But it was by no means a "simple" matter. During the last years of the war, only a very few people had direct access to Hitler, and these rarely included anyone from the inner circle of the resistance. Each gesture was carefully watched by Hitler's bodyguard. Even a move to the holster aroused suspicion. In order to lower the risk, seven officers of Tresckow's Army Group volunteered to shoot Hitler simultaneously with their revolvers. But no amount of wiles or efforts could persuade Hitler to visit this sector of the front a second time.

Hitler was reputed to have sensed personal danger with the instinct of a beast of prey. It remains an uncanny aspect of the history of these attempts that he often canceled or cut short visits after all preparations had been made. Accidents, too, played a role. Thus, at one point a young captain, Axel von dem Bussche, had volunteered to throw himself upon Hitler and detonate a bomb while modeling new uniforms. Bussche was among those who had witnessed the systematic extermination of human beings in Poland and Russia. But shortly before the allotted time, an air raid on Berlin destroyed the demonstration models. Before new ones could arrive, Bussche was re-assigned to front duty, where he was gravely wounded soon after.

The list of such attempts is long. There was no dearth of officers willing to risk their lives, but these examples will suffice. All such attempts had the limited but very important purpose of releasing the army from its oath. That the opposition within the army engaged in arbitrary and pointless sabotage is a malevolent legend. Engineer Oderbruch, in Carl Zuckmayer's drama *The Devil's General,* who sabotaged planes and sent their crews to death, is a playwright's invention. Neither he nor anyone like him existed in the German armed forces. The small and embattled opposition in the army was concerned with weightier matters than preventing shipments of gasoline, or misdirecting matériel. Those who repeat these accusations are ignorant of the overall situation at the time. The procurement difficulties occurring during the last months of the war were certainly not caused by arbitrary acts of sabotage.

By the summer of 1944 the situation had become so acute that only Count von Stauffenberg was able to gain access to Hitler. This made it necessary for the intellectual leader of the conspiracy to execute the deed, and the dual role he took contributed greatly to the failure of July 20, 1944.

Claus Count Schenk von Stauffenberg was born in 1907. He was raised in Stuttgart, saw active duty with the Bamberg Cavalry Regiment, and in the fall of 1943 was posted to the General Staff. Already at the War Academy he was considered a brilliant scion of the great German general staff officers (he was a descendant of Gneisenau's on his mother's side). His colleagues have testified that Stauffenberg thought as early as 1938-39 that a revolt against Hitler had to be prepared, much as Gneisenau had risen against

Claus Count Schenk von Stauffenberg

Napoleon in his time. He joined the resistance movement as late as 1943, but soon held a central position. At the beginning of that year, he had been seriously wounded in Africa, had lost his left eye, his right hand, and two fingers of his left hand. After months of critical illness, he left his bed "with a totally new conviction, and a greater energy than ever," according to his friends and colleagues.[30] An almost casual remark he dropped to his wife at this period reveals his pre-occupations: "I have the feeling that I must do something to save Germany. We general staff officers bear our share of the responsibility."

After a few months, all the threads of the conspiracy converged in his hand. Being extraordinarily effective with people, he gained the allegiance of all those around him. His strong will inspired others. One of those who met him at the time summarized his impressions: "He served in a complex and difficult position, while simultaneously advancing the immense plans he had conceived. He always felt his way with the other groups, drew up military plans, exposed himself to the dangers and tensions of this double life—and still had to search his soul, his mind, his actions over and over again. With all the superhuman demands made on him, he spoke with every caller coolly and collectedly about his cause, and made clear and final decisions within minutes. . . ."[31]

Stauffenberg's basic conception of the uprising coincided to a large extent with plans already elaborated by Henning von Tresckow. "Operation Valkyrie" (this was its code name) was perfected, in General Staff fashion, by the most capable intellects. They secured the connections with the civilian forces. Outstanding men were prepared to move into every position in the prospective government. By October 1943, all that remained was to light the fuse: "With every day, the danger of discovery grew. Each delay increased fears that transfers, casualties, wounds received in battle, or leaves would tear apart the group which had been built up with so much effort. The participants could not stand this almost unbearable tension much longer."[32]

Thus began the series of attempts on Hitler's life described above. Every failure meant loss of time, and time did not work for the resistance fighters but against them. As the military situation deteriorated, many people, especially the still hesitant and passive generals, believed that each passing day made the action more meaningless. Every month, valuable and irreplaceable comrades-in-arms were arrested by the Gestapo. The fear was justified that the plan could not be kept secret much longer. When Canaris lost his position, Himmler dropped a hint that he was shadowing a conspiracy, and would act as soon as all its ramifications had been discovered. Even Reuters in England reported the existence of a resistance movement.

In June 1944, with the Allied landing in Normandy, the war entered a new and extremely critical phase. Fear grew among the conspirators that "the downhill trend could no longer be arrested. Anybody intervening now—whether successfully or unsuccessfully —would forever be cursed for causing Germany's defeat. Instead of teaching a sound lesson, he would be faced with another poisoned stab-in-the-back lie. The people would stone to death those who risked their lives for its welfare."[33]

These were telling arguments, but thanks to Stauffenberg's drive the crisis was overcome. He knew well what his duty demanded. Jacob Kaiser (later a minister of the Federal German Republic) has preserved the words with which Stauffenberg—a practicing Catholic—explained his decision: "We have examined ourselves before God and before our conscience. We must act; for this man is evil incarnate." At one meeting, Henning von Tresckow, whose thinking closely resembled Stauffenberg's, had stated the ultimate motives for the deed in these words:

> The assassination must be attempted at all cost. Even if it fails, the attempt to seize power in the capital must be undertaken. We must prove to the world and to future generations that the men of the German resistance movement dared to take the decisive step and to hazard their lives upon it. Compared with this objective, nothing else matters.

Stauffenberg decided early in July 1944 not only to direct the uprising in Berlin but also to carry out the attempt on Hitler's life, since none of the other conspirators had access to the Fuehrer. Even the colonel's closest friends, with some reservations, agreed to it as the only way left.

On July 11 and 15, Stauffenberg attended military conferences in Berchtesgaden and at Hitler's headquarters with a bomb hidden in his briefcase. On the first occasion he did not carry out the attempt because of the absence of Himmler, who was to be killed simultaneously. On the second occasion, Hitler had left the conference room shortly after the meeting had opened. On July 18, a report arrived that Julius Leber had been arrested, and that Field Marshal Rommel, who had joined the uprising, had been seriously wounded in France and could no longer be counted on. Stauffenberg, who had favored Leber for the future *Reich* chancellorship, passed word to Mrs. Leber: "We know our duty."

Stauffenberg was once more summoned to headquarters on July 20. The conference did not take place in a concrete bunker, as usual, but in a wooden hut. Stauffenberg, after lighting the fuse, placed his briefcase close to Hitler under the table, left the room on a pretext, and was a few hundred yards away from the first check-point when the explosion occurred. Had he waited only a short while longer he would not have been able to pass the three barriers, but, as it was, he managed to get through with great diffi-

Scene at headquarters after the assassination attempt.   *Ullstein*
The arrow indicates where Hitler was standing

culty. He entered a waiting plane convinced that the attempt had been successful, that Hitler had at least been seriously hurt by the large quantity of explosives.

On arrival in Berlin after a 2½ hour flight, Stauffenberg believed "Valkyrie" under way. Its success was decided during the first three hours while General Fellgiebel, at headquarters, was able to maintain the communications blackout he had ordered. General Olbricht, one of the top conspirators, had held up the orders because news began to filter through from headquarters that the attempt had miscarried. Thus, "Valkyrie" was set in motion only with Stauffenberg's arrival.

On the whole, it is quite useless to speculate whether proper timing might have proved more successful. The events of this black day proved the premise that the spell of Hitler's personality could only be broken by his death. As long as the conspirators in the Bendler Strasse (H.Q. Supreme Command of the Armed Forces) could successfully maintain the fiction that the Fuehrer was dead, "Valkyrie's" orders were obeyed by all. But there was no denying the fact that Hitler had suffered only minor injuries while four men of his entourage had been killed and others seriously wounded. Even Lieutenant-General Beck could not change this, in spite of the great determinaton and firmness with which he backed Stauffenberg: whatever the rumors, he said, whatever the truth, for him, Beck, Hitler had been killed.

Thus, in due time, the uprising collapsed in spite of all the *esprit,* the courage, and the devotion that had gone into it. We shall quickly complete the sad task of narrating the subsequent course of events. Three to four hours after the action, reports began to come in from everywhere that Hitler was alive. Among those who first knew it for sure was a Major Remer, who had been dispatched to arrest Goebbels. (He gained notoriety later on during a trial.) The Propaganda Minister put him on a direct telephone line which led from his apartment to Hitler, and Hitler ordered him to turn in the conspirators. In the Bendler Strasse, too, the counter-revolution began to get underway. Some younger officers procured tommy guns, freed Lieutenant-General Fromm from his office, where he was held for refusing to co-operate with "Valkyrie," and proceeded to summarily execute the main conspirators on Fromm's orders. Lieutenant-General Beck was allowed to die by his own hand. Colonel Stauffenberg, General Olbricht, Colonel Merz von Quirnheim, and Stauffenberg's personal adjutant, von Haeften, were shot in the courtyard of the Bendler Strasse building at about 11 o'clock. Stauffenberg died with the cry: "Long live holy Germany!"

Hitler's vengeance began that same night. Strong S.S. forces occupied the house in the Bendler Strasse and arrested all those suspected of complicity. By some unlucky accidents, the Gestapo found material which revealed contacts with the civilian resistance movement. A wave of arrests swept all over Germany. Using horse whips and third degree methods of torture—on the medieval model —Hitler's executioners attempted to tear the names of their accom-

Plötzensee prison, where many of the conspiracy were executed after 20 July 1944

plices in thought and deed from the lips of their victims. One who suffered these tortures and, by an act of providence, escaped capital punishment, Fabian von Schlabrendorff, writes:

> Those who suffered the tortures of the Gestapo learned that man can endure more than he considers possible. Those who had previously not known how, learned to pray, and found out that under such circumstances only prayers give comfort and superhuman strength.

Officers who had taken part in the conspiracy were expelled from the army and handed over to the People's Court for sentences. The trials were filmed; so we can still witness the brutal conduct of the trials by Freisler, the People's Judge, who hardly let any defendant speak, shouted them down, abused them in the most filthy manner, and humiliated them at every opportunity. The defendants had few opportunities to interrupt his poisoned tirades with courageous word of their own.

As to the executions, Hitler had ordered that "the condemned should be shown not even the slightest mercy; they were to hang like cattle; nobody should get the idea that the executed men were martyrs in the cause of freedom. He even had the first executions filmed, and demanded that the films be shown to him."[34]

Only a few succeeded in escaping these heinous forms of vengeance by taking their own lives. Henning von Tresckow, who could not be present at the Bendler Strasse because he was serving at the front, feigned a partisan attack and killed himself with a hand-grenade. Field Marshal Rommel's story is especially well known. He had not yet recovered from his serious wounds when two generals entered his house and informed him that the Fuehrer allowed him the choice of taking poison or facing the People's Court. Rommel chose poison. He drove off with the generals and, after half an hour, his body was brought to a hospital in Ulm. The cause of his death was given as embolism. In his desire to hide the fact that even Rommel had belonged to the conspirators, Hitler ordered a state funeral and had a eulogy read for this popular general!

The number of those killed as a direct result of July 20 is estimated at 180 to 200. That it stopped at that number is due to the unbelievable fortitude of all participants. After the attempt, Himmler formally decreed the "arrest of all kin" (*Sippenhaft*). At one time, eight of Goerdeler's and ten of Stauffenberg's relatives were held in concentration camps. Many of those sentenced to death by the People's Court were executed only a few hours before Hitler's regime disintegrated at a time when their liberation was already in sight.

History, it is said, remembers only the successful. The failures descend into the shadowy realm of anonymity. This is only partly true, because history must judge all human actions, using justice as its measure. Therefore, history always remembers the names of those, too, who failed in the service of a just cause. The tragic splendor which surrounds them touches our hearts more deeply than the glory of the successful who wore their laurels during their lives. It may well be that we are still too blinded today to understand the full meaning of this uprising against Hitler's tyranny. Later generations, however, will recognize that here deeds of heroism were performed as has rarely occurred in German history.

The men of July 20 did not stop to balance danger against success before taking their decisive step. Many of their own words testify to this:

> To hazard one's life for a good and just cause is a proper price to pay. We did what was in our power. It is not our guilt that all ended in this way, and not in another. (Julius Leber)
>
> It is a great mistake to presume that the psychological strength of the German people is exhausted; it has been systematically buried. Thus, to restore it one must remove the heavy top layer of secretiveness and terror, restore justice and decency, and set free, thereby, an immense psychological potential for growth. Let us not be deflected from our faith that the German people of past and future want justice, decency, and honesty. (Carl Goerdeler)
>
> God once promised Abraham that he would not destroy Sodom if ten righteous men be found within the city. Thus I hope that for our sake God shall not destroy Germany. None of us must deplore death. Whoever entered our circle puts on the shirt of Nessus. The moral value of a person begins only at the point where he is prepared to lay down his life for his convictions. (Henning von Tresckow)
>
> The attempt may well have failed—the odds always were 2 to 1 against its success—but it had to be risked. For this attempt was the last opportunity of risking the life blood of Germany for her liberation from evil tyranny. It was an attempt, too, of wresting millions of humiliated and wronged people from many nations of Europe from the dreadful power of the infamous killers of Buchenwald and Auschwitz, the very killers who had heaped shame on Germany's name. This attempt had to be made at all costs. (Eugen Gerstenmayer)

These men gave their lives to blot out the shame and erase the disgrace, while their brave wives, without complaints, endured sorrows and cares day after day, month after month, many of them year after year. Woe to the nation which considers such a revolt of the conscience merely as "sabotage by ambitious officers." It was Hitler who had invented this legend and, at the same time, gave it the lie by reaching into all strata of the population to satisfy his vengeance. Equally misguided was the view, at one point held abroad, that it was all done by reactionary nationalists. As early as 1946, Winston Churchill said in the House of Commons that there had been an opposition in Germany whose strength had been gradually sapped through its sacrifices and the degenerating international situation, but their achievements ranked among the most stirring and greatest deeds ever performed in the political history of any nation. These men, he continued, fought without any help whatsoever from inside and outside the country, spurred on solely by their restless consciences. As long as they lived, they remained unseen and unrecognized for they had had to disguise themselves. But, said Churchill, their resistance was revealed in their deaths. By dying they could not justify all that had happened in Germany; but their deeds and their sacrifice were the foundations for building anew.

How we think about the resistance against Nazi dictatorship will determine our future. We have been entrusted with a legacy. Our love for freedom and human dignity will be in doubt as long as we do not dedicate ourselves with all our hearts to the memory of those who laid down their lives in Germany's darkest hour.

12: Could Germany Have Won the War?

Whether Germany, in fact, could have won the war is a question which has not only military but also political implications. Talking about the First World War, we quoted Clausewitz's statement that war "has no sense or purpose" unless it serves rational political aims. What were Hitler's war aims?

Hitler, according to his own statements, wanted to expand the "German *Lebensraum*." This aim was a direct successor to the kind of colonial thinking prevalent among nearly all European nations in the nineteenth century. Meanwhile world history had moved on. People throughout the world now demanded the right to national self-determination proclaimed in 1919 and fought against outdated colonialism. For this reason alone, Hitler's ideas were anachronistic and inadequate. In addition, Hitler wanted to colonize territories which, for centuries, had been inhabited by nations shaped by European intellectual traditions, i.e. Eastern Europe. He did not understand them, since his racial doctrines made him believe that the east was settled by "racially inferior" people destined to be slaves to the "racially superior" Germans. Imperialists had been satisfied with conquering, ruling, and exploiting, but Hitler's drive for *Lebensraum* aimed at the physical annihilation of these Eastern peoples.

A German patrol combs the ruins of central Warsaw, 1944

Ullstein

The policies instituted in Poland after its defeat corresponded with these aims. Universities were shut down immediately. The intelligentsia was dragged off to concentration camps, where they were first stripped of all personal dignity and then exterminated. The population of the east was to be kept at the lowest cultural level. This is documented by a memorandum of Himmler's in May 1941:

> Fundamental in solving these problems is the question of education, including the question of how the young should be selected and tested. There must not be a more advanced education for the non-German population of the east than four years of primary school.
> This primary education has the following objective only: doing simple arithmetic up to 500, writing one's name, learning that it was God's command that the Germans must be obeyed, and that one had to be honest, diligent, and obedient. I don't consider reading skills necessary. Except for this school, no other kind of school must be allowed in the east. . . .
> The [remaining inferior] population will be at our call as a slave people without leaders, and each year will provide Germany with migrant workers and workers for special projects . . . and, while themselves lacking all culture, they will be called upon under the strict, purposeful, and just rule of the German nation to contribute to [Germany's] eternal cultural achievements and monuments. . . ."

This was to be the look of German "cultural activity" in the east—and, to a large extent, it was put into practice. After the campaign in Russia had begun, the superior race found the field wide open. The *Reich* Main Settlement Office elaborated colossal projects for the settlement and control of the eastern region. It assigned a major role to massive resettlement schemes of the kind that had been put into practice after the campaign in Poland (for Baltic Germans, Volhynian, and Bessarabian Germans). People were pushed around like pawns on a chess board. The language of these schemes defies all description: "racially valuable" population splinters were to be "Germanized" and "re-folked."* The question was raised whether "racially undesirable segments of the population could not be turned into scrap . . . through indus-

* Nazi neologisms. *Trl.*

trialization." The Nazi rulers were especially worried about the fertility of the "alien peoples" (*Fremdvölker*), especially the Russians. They were forced to acknowledge that "a liquidation was hardly possible and was also out of the question for political and economic reasons." Thus they recommended the "racial leaching of Russiandom" and the "destruction of their biological strength." This was to be achieved through a negative population policy, e.g. by prohibiting the use of methods which would lower the incidence of infant mortality.

Thus, the aim of the war in the east was the establishment of colonial rule of the most brutal kind. Had Hitler any better plans for the territories conquered in the west? It is important to answer this question, because a legend sprang up after the war that Hitler, in advance of the times, wanted to create a United Europe. Was this legend true?

It should be stressed first that there had been no overall strategic design at the beginning of the war. Characteristically, only partial plans had been worked out. As his appetite grew, Hitler grasped whatever favorable opportunities were offered him. At no point did he make a public statement or hold private discussions to decide the future of his conquests in northern and western Europe when at last peace was restored. Bismarck's theory that the defeated of today must be turned into the ally of tomorrow never made any impression on him.

Hitler's policies toward France reveal this with special clarity. After the failure of his negotiations with Franco, Hitler met with Marshal Pétain to talk the Vichy government into a joint campaign against England. They were anti-British at the time, because of the attack on the French fleet. This may have swayed Pétain toward acceptance of Hitler's proposals in principle, although, even then, he had little faith in Hitler's promises. When Pétain subsequently asked for a clarification of France's future status, he was informed that German leaders had no time to consider such problems. In this way, the opportunity of co-operating with France was lost; partly through over-transparent wooing and partly through supercilious rebuffs.

Occupied neutral countries received no assurances about their future, since Hitler had no intention of relinquishing any territory once his army had set foot on it. No enlisted man would ever understand such a policy, he claimed, drawing upon his own experience in the trenches of the First World War. Nor did he have any idea of giving any measure of freedom and self-administration to conquered countries. He could not conceive of loyal co-operation with members of other nations, and, in the final analysis, he even distrusted Himmler's policy of organizing S.S. units from "racially valuable elements" of conquered nations. Europe, according to Hitler's vision, would have been one gigantic terror-ridden state, absolutely controlled by the S.S. and members of the party. Hitler once said in his "secret conversations" that "a community can only be established and maintained by force." A policy based on such a fundamental error would never have led to a United Europe, for force always creates nothing but counter-force.

The line was changed only in the last stages of the Second World War. Nazi propagandists discovered the "European family of nations," which was to unite against Bolshevism; now European journalists were invited to congresses in order to talk about the culturally creative nations of Europe. But it was too late to indulge in this novel policy of sweetness and light, and nobody was deceived by this crude opportunism.

During the war, Hitler's speeches contained frequent references to "annihilation." "Wars end only with the annihilation of the enemy . . ." (November 23, 1939, to his supreme commanders). "We face a war of annihilation. If we don't understand this, we shall beat the enemy, but once again face the Communist foe in thirty years' time. We do not make war to conserve [sic] the enemy" (March 31, 1941, to the commanders of the armed forces). Nothing illustrates Hitler's limitless military aims more frighteningly or fittingly. The policy of annihilation extended from the denial of all rights to extermination. Aims like these, and policies based on them, were bound to fail, so it can be said without exaggeration that "the war was politically lost before the first shot was fired."[35]

As has been noted previously, Germany did not fare too well with her allies. One important reason for this was Hitler's inability to negotiate. Since he understood only force, negotiations with him forever resembled dictates. And even when he exuded charm, his

German advances during the Second World War

opponents sensed his shiftiness and the "ice-cold readiness to break any agreement at will," which he had emphasized so frequently.

Japan, one of Hitler's original allies, could hardly be expected to provide effective support, as she had been at war with China since 1937. But it was Japan's attack on the United States that caused Hitler to follow suit himself and declare war on the United States (see p. 207).

Italy had entered the war against France late in order to share in the spoils. She then did considerable harm to the overall war effort by declaring war independently against Greece. In any event, Mussolini did not want Germany and Italy to fight a joint war for control of the Mediterranean but was fighting for his own ends. Each was to fight his own battles. There were no common war aims, and military operations were very poorly co-ordinated. As the war progressed and Italy's weakness became more and more apparent, Mussolini was reduced to satellite status. As early as October 1941, German soldiers allegedly called him "our Italian *Gauleiter.*" This occasioned the following entry in Count Ciano's diary: "I merely remarked that such views explain easily why there is very little enthusiasm for the war in Italy."

Not so very different were the roles of Rumania, Hungary, and Bulgaria, which had joined the Berlin-Rome-Tokyo Axis at a later date and for practical purposes, influenced by their geographic location. Even Hitler realized that their "friendship" frequently rested exclusively on the government of a semi-fascist dictator, like Marshal Antonescu in Rumania. Hitler's attempt to add Franco and Spain to "the Axis" failed miserably.

After the collapse of France, England—in spite of the resources of her Commonwealth—was by no means in an enviable position. Appointed Prime Minister two days before Hitler was to begin his offensive, Winston Churchill wasted no time and told his people of the seriousness of the situation. He said, in his famous first address to the House of Commons (May 13, 1940):

> I would say to this House, as I have said to those who have joined this Government: "I have nothing to offer but blood, toil, tears and sweat." We have before us an ordeal of the most grievous kind. We have before us many, many long months of struggle and suffering. You ask, What is our

policy? I will say: "It is to wage war, by sea, land and air, with all our might and with the strength that God can give us: to wage war against a monstrous tyranny, never surpassed in the dark, lamentable catalogue of human crime. That is our policy."

The United States had not yet openly joined England at that time. Early in 1941, however, the Lend-Lease Act was passed which empowered the President to support any state with war material if he considered that this was necessary for the defense of the United States.

Unexpectedly, Churchill was helped by Hitler's illusions. In November 1940, Hitler, as Commander in Chief of the Armed Forces, appraised the situation as follows: "The war is won, it cannot be lost any more, it must merely be terminated. To this end, England, too, must be forced to realize that she has lost the war." From this appraisal Hitler concluded that the time had come to open a second front and attack Russia.

A year later, after Hitler had declared war on the United States, Germany faced three powers which between them controlled 75 per cent of the world's population, industrial production, and raw materials. A story current in Germany at the time illustrates this well.

> A boy asked his father whom Germany was fighting. The father fetched a globe and showed him first Germany, then the Soviet Union, the USA, Canada, Mexico, Brazil, England, India, Australia, and the rest of the British Commonwealth. Thereupon the son said with concern in his voice: "Dad, does Hitler know this?"

Germany's difficulties were further increased by the fact that all the occupied countries were basically hostile to Germany and on the side of the Allies. The occupation policies already described had had disastrous consequences.

After the invasion of Russia, a shrewd tactician might, perhaps, have exploited, to Germany's advantage, the Ukrainian desire for independence and the dissatisfaction with Stalin's systematic terror, and thus turned enemies into friends. Hitler, deluded by his racial pride, ordered Himmler and the S.S. to "pacify" the tremendous space he had conquered, and issued instructions that "anybody who as much as raised an eyebrow must be shot." The

Coventry Cathedral, England, the night after the city
was heavily bombed, November 1940

Central Press

German armed forces, too, received orders which violated all
accepted codes of war and all international law, orders like the
notorious Commissar Order, according to which political commissars of the Soviet Army "were, as a matter of policy, to be shot
immediately."

In occupied countries, the population was especially embittered
about the Night and Fog Decree. This stipulated that non-German
civilians who committed crimes against the German *Reich* or the
occupying power were to be executed without exception. Retalia-
tory measures such as the shooting of hostages and the wiping out
of whole villages (like Oradour in France, Lidice in Czechoslovakia, Kalavrita in Greece) laid a curse on the word "German" in
these countries. Thus, Hitler's *Reich* created its own implacable

269

enemies, stiffened the resistance of the partisans, and hastened its own defeat. An American study on World War II concludes that Germany's catastrophic occupation policies in Russia determined the outcome of the campaign.

After the defeat at Stalingrad, Goebbels delivered an address on total war in the Berlin Sports Palace. Millions of people listened on their radios to his spine-chilling performance, which was as somber and bleak as the situation itself, as the Minister of Propaganda asked ten questions and had a raving audience bellow their *Ja!* in return:

> I ask you: Are you, and is the German people, determined, if the Fuehrer so commands, to work, ten, twelve, if need be fourteen hours a day, and to give your utmost for victory? . . . I ask you: Do you want total war? If need be, do you want it more total and more radical than we can even imagine it today? . . . The nation is ready for anything. The Fuehrer has commanded, and we shall obey him. If we ever believed in victory faithfully and unshakably, it is in this hour of national reflection and re-dedication. We see it lie close at hand, we must merely reach out. . . .

German troops occupying the Warsaw ghetto, 1943, with (center) General Stroop   *Schoenberner*

The Big Three at the Yalta Conference, February 1945

The true motives for such "confidence in victory" Goebbels revealed in his diary a few days later:

> Göring knows perfectly well what will happen to us if we weaken in this war. He has no illusions about it. We are so committed, especially in the Jewish question, that we cannot escape. It is good this way. Experience teaches that a movement and a people that have burned their bridges fight with fewer holds barred than those who can still beat a retreat.

During the Nuremberg Trials, General Jodl, Hitler's closest military adviser, said that the "god of war" had left Germany in the spring of 1943 and "gone over to the enemy." Field Marshal von Rundstedt also believed that after the defeat of Stalingrad the war could no longer be won.

New disasters followed the first catastrophe in quick succession;

271

in April and May 1943, the German submarine war failed, even though more submarines than ever were being produced at that time. A new Allied invention, radar, caused heavy losses which could not be offset by the new and faster submarines under construction. They went into action in 1945, when it was already too late.

Blitzkriegs and victories were gone forever. Now talk turned to the defense of the "fortress Europe." In July 1943, Italy began to pick her way out of the fortress. Mussolini was arrested, and Marshal Badoglio formed a new government. Soon afterwards, he signed an armistice with the Allies. In the east, the Russians reconquered the Donets basin and cut off the German troops in the Crimea. At that time, about 3 million Germans were fighting 5.1 million Russians. The Russians had more than twice as much material and equipment, and they increased their lead ever more sharply with the passage of time.

Equally telling was the inferiority of the German air force from 1942 onwards. It was caused, primarily, by the limited 340-mile range of the German bombers and by the lack of defensive fighter planes. It became increasingly difficult to train new pilots. Even the great courage and endurance of the crews could not make up for the poor planning of the Supreme Command.

Today, no one can read what General Jodl jotted down in November 1943 in preparation for an address before the *Gauleiter* of the party without a sense of shock. Following an extensive and factual report on the military situation, Jodl ended with some words about "the basis of our confidence in final victory." All he could think of was his faith in Hitler as the man of destiny who was to lead Germany into a brighter future. He believed "that we shall win because we must win; otherwise world history would have lost its meaning." This was Hitler's direct influence. Propaganda, as well, followed this line from then on—we shall win because we must win; we shall win even without weapons through our fanatical faith alone.

Meanwhile, events had moved inexorably on. In the spring of 1944 the Allies dealt decisive blows to Germany's gasoline supply. They systematically bombed the Rumanian oil-fields, mined the waterways, and attacked synthetic gasoline plants from the air.

Even the unusual organizing abilities of an Albert Speer, who had been in charge of war production since 1942, could no longer make good these losses. Speer was the first one clearly to see this, and he tried to explain the seriousness of the situation to Hitler in a series of memoranda which have been preserved. Speer's reaction to his failure to persuade Hitler will be dealt with later.

Then, on June 6, 1944, came the Allied landing in Normandy. At several of his wartime conferences Hitler had equated a successful landing with Germany's final defeat, and now it had happened. Greatly outnumbered German troops fought heroically, as Field Marshal Rommel teletyped Hitler from his command post in the west. It was an unequal fight. Rommel implored the Fuehrer to accept at once the consequences of an untenable situation, by beginning negotiations for an armistice. Hitler stubbornly refused. He had burned his bridges, so his destructive urges now turned against his own people.

This was the situation in which the German resistance tried a last hazardous rescue operation (see p. 254). These men knew that the war was lost, and that Hitler wanted to prolong this senseless conflict in order to bring the German people down with him in annihilation. Yet, after 1945, these men had to be defended

U.S. troops going ashore in Normandy, on D-day, 6 June 1944

against the charge of having betrayed their country. In a rebuttal, the public prosecutor stated during the trial against Remer (see p. 257), held in Brunswick:

> By July 20, the war was definitely lost. By July 20, the German people had been totally betrayed, betrayed by their own government. One cannot commit treason against a totally betrayed people any more than one can stab to death a dead man.

Additional confirmation of this view appears in the testimony of Hitler's Minister for Armaments, Albert Speer. At the Nuremburg Trials Speer said that he had come to the same conclusions as the men of July 20, even though somewhat belatedly. He had realized that Hitler wanted to prolong the war without regard for his own people:

> I realized that, in losing the war, Hitler mistook the fate of the German people for his own fate, and that he identified his death with the death of the German people. . . . Every thinking person in his entourage must have realized that Hitler did not keep faith with the nation. Hitler had no right to gamble away the future of his people with his own future.

Long before that, in conversations with Rauschning, Hitler had expressed the views which Speer ascribed to him. Rauschning had asked what would happen if England, France, and Russia were to unite against Germany. Hitler had said: "Even though we cannot win, we shall go down and pull half the world down with us to destruction." In 1942 he had said in a "secret conversation": "As long as one man is left who holds the flag high nothing is lost. Here, too, I am as cold as ice: if the German people is not willing to stake its life on its self-preservation, it may die."

In the same spirit, Hitler issued his Scorched Earth Order on March 19, 1945: "All military transportation, communication, industrial and distribution facilities, as well as all objects of value found within the *Reich* territory, as far as the enemy would be able to use them immediately or in the foreseeable future for military purposes, must be destroyed." Speer tried in vain to change Hitler's mind but was summoned and told:

274

The last photo of Hitler—sending children into battle, 1945

> If we are going to lose the war, the nation, too, will perish.
> The outcome is inevitable. It is not necessary to worry
> about the minimum needs of the people and how they are
> to live later at subsistence level. On the contrary, it will be
> better for us to destroy these things ourselves. For this na-
> tion will have proved to be the weaker one. The future will
> belong exclusively to the stronger nations of the East.
> Those who survive the war are, in any event, the inferior
> ones, for the good ones have been killed.

On another occasion he said that it was obvious that the German
people were not worthy of him. What was really obvious was that
Hitler's life was dominated by one overriding motive: limitless
egotism.

Anyone with any intelligence must acknowledge that even the
bravest soldiers could not win a war against half the world. Anyone could learn, night after night, that even the strongest faith was
no shelter against Allied superiority in the air, in which the odds
were at that time 25 to 1. Still, as late as April 1945, there were

Emerging from a cellar after an Allied air raid, Mannheim, 1944

Germans who "believed in victory." They had become gullible victims of propagandists who kept insisting that the Fuehrer held in reserve "secret weapons" of such terrible effectiveness that he had postponed using them for "humanitarian reasons." The shabby truth was that German engineers had built a new submarine type (see p. 272), and that new rockets were used against England during the last months of the war. But these V-rockets were mere pin-pricks, and had no effect on British morale. There were rumors of a German atom bomb, but it was neither ready nor even half-ready. In fact, its production could not be considered at all, because Germany could not obtain the necessary raw materials.

For this reason, many people realized how appallingly Hitler had gambled with his own people only when the radio reported the Fuehrer's death, and when unconditional surrender was accepted on May 8, 1945.

How bitter was the path from July 1944 to those days! How many cities had still to be destroyed from the air: Duisburg, Essen, Cologne, Dresden, Würzburg, Darmstadt, to name just a few. From east and west, Allied troops irresistibly penetrated German territory: on February 8, an offensive was launched on the Lower Rhine; on February 23, another one near Cologne. On March 23, British troops crossed the Rhine, and on April 18, resistance in the encircled Ruhr area had to be broken off. On January 12, Soviet troops began their offensive in the east; on

German soldiers surrender to the Russians in Königsberg, 9 April 1945

American tanks take over war-torn Munich, April 1945   *Ullstein*

January 23, they reached the Oder in Lower Silesia; on February 26, they broke through Lower Pomerania and reached the Baltic Sea; on March 30, they took Danzig, on April 9, Königsberg capitulated, on April 16, a general offensive began on the Oder and Neisse rivers, and on April 24, Berlin was completely encircled. On April 25, American and Soviet troops linked up near Torgau on the Elbe.

The end of the Nazi regime had come. Since January, Hitler had been living in the bunker of the Chancellery in Berlin, where he had lost sight of the overall military situation. He had been urged several times to leave Berlin, but had decided to meet his death there. During these last weeks he spoke incessantly of the treason he suspected from every side.

To the very end, he continued his lifelong habit of looking for scapegoats in order to excuse his own failure. As one of his last acts, he expelled Göring from the party because the latter had radioed that he wished to be entrusted with the overall leadership of the *Reich*. Himmler likewise was expelled because he had begun to discuss terms of surrender with the help of the Swedish Count Bernadotte. Göring was arrested by the Americans later on and sentenced to death at Nuremberg; Himmler was recognized by the British near Bremervoerde, and took poison, which the S.S. had thoughtfully given to all top leaders for just such a contingency.

On April 29, Hitler dictated his political testament. Grand Admiral Dönitz was to succeed him as head of state, and Goebbels as Chancellor. He asked the German people to carry on his anti-semitism and his plans for the colonization of the east, and ascribed his failure to lead his nation to victory to "disloyalty and treason." He was already writing his own stab-in-the-back legend.

On April 30, he legally married Eva Braun, his mistress of many years, said goodbye to his entourage, and shot himself with a revolver. Eva Braun took poison. The bodies were carried into the Chancellery garden, soaked with gasoline, and burned. On May 1, Goebbels poisoned first his children, and then shot his wife and himself. The announcement of Hitler's death was delayed until the evening of that day.

Thus ended the life of a man who had written that only he could be a Fuehrer, who was prepared to bear full responsibility. When Japan surrendered three months later, the Japanese emperor threw himself at the mercy of the Allies but demanded that his people be spared.

On May 1, Dönitz succeeded Hitler. His sole task was to provide a central authority for carrying out the unavoidable surrender, and to avert further air attacks. On May 9, the surrender went into effect for all the armed forces. During this interval, 1½ million soldiers had managed to escape from the area occupied by Russian troops. Then Dönitz dissolved the NSDAP. On May 23, he and his entire government were arrested.

Hitler had boasted that the Third *Reich* would last a thousand years, but, in fact, it lasted only twelve years. The Third *Reich* was to provide the German people with the *Lebensraum* it allegedly lacked, but, in fact, it caused the division of Germany and the cession to Soviet Russia and Poland of areas which had been inhabited by Germans for centuries: Brandenburg, Pomerania, East Prussia, and Silesia.

When Hitler seized power, he spoke continually of the "field of ruins" he had to take over. When he left the stage, there was hardly a town in Germany whose debris, ashes, and ruins did not bear silent and impressive testimony to his megalomaniac policies.

Here are the losses as recorded in the last formal entry made in the diary of the Leadership Staff of the Armed Forces (January 31, 1945). Up to that day, the figures were:

Killed in action, Armed Forces (incl. *Waffen* S.S.)	1,891,361
Died of illness, accidents, suicide, executions	191,338
SUB-TOTAL	2,000,699
Missing	1,902,704
GRAND TOTAL	3,903,403

It was the equivalent of more than 120 armies in battle strength. The number of soldiers killed in action, taken prisoners, or miss-

Refugees from the east fleeing from the Red Armies

280

German lands under:

||||||| Soviet administration   ≡ Polish administration

The end of Hitler's war—Occupied Germany in 1945

ing after January 31, 1945, has not yet been determined, but it must have been considerable.

Add to this account the victims of aerial warfare (estimated at 500,000), those who perished in concentration camps, and the untold numbers who had fallen by the wayside or died of hunger in the snow and cold while fleeing from the east. To this we must add the appalling total of nearly six million murdered Jews, and the prisoners of war, and foreign slave laborers who were killed by starvation or air raids within Germany.

Among the war victims must also be counted the following: 12,300,000 people expelled from East Prussia, Silesia, Pomerania, and the Sudeten area. Germany further counted at the end of 1945:

> 1,600,000 wounded in action
> 1,200,000 war widows
> 1,400,000 children with one parent
> 60,000 orphans (under 21 years of age).

Like the German people, the other nations, friend and foe alike, had suffered heavy losses. Great Britain, France, and the United States had a combined loss of 1,200,000 dead, including 412,000 civilians. Russia's losses were estimated at 13,600,000 soldiers and 7,000,000 civilians. Japan had lost 1,500,000 people. Never before had death reaped such a harvest.

Never before in history had reckless arrogance led to such a fall. Never before had a nation experienced so painfully the abuse of uncontrolled power. Will it take this lesson to heart? Or will it merely pay lip-service to it while conditions are good? Will it make sacrifices for it and, when the hour of trial comes, stand united for justice and liberty?

Conclusion

Those who treat history as an inexorable series of events tend to explain that things had to happen the way they did, that Fate had imposed her eternal laws. They conclude thereby that nothing can be learned from history for the future conduct of affairs.

Yet everybody knows that his life is conditioned by many factors, such as physical constitution, intellectual gifts, the social status of his parents, or nationality, but that he has nevertheless been faced repeatedly with decisions which were to change the future course of his life. He would, perhaps, be saying in retrospect: "If you had listened to this or that advice, had had more confidence here, used more caution there, had been more persistent at one point, or less self-centered at another—your life would have taken a different turn!"

A nation is made up of individuals whose ideas—right or wrong—determine their actions, their decisions, and their common life, and for this reason a nation, too, can look back at its history and learn from it. As Germans, we should not find it too difficult to understand the meaning of the fourteen years of the Weimar Republic and the twelve years of the Hitler regime.

The ancient Greeks already knew and taught that no state can remain free without free citizens. If the citizens of a commonwealth are not prepared to make sacrifices for their liberty, to take matters into their own hands and participate in public affairs, they deliver themselves into the hands of a tyrant. They do not deserve anything but tyrannical rule: "A class which fails to make sacrifices for political affairs may not make demands on political life. It renounces its will to rule, and must therefore be ruled." These words of a German liberal about the educated class are valid for people everywhere.[36]

The Greeks called a man who abstained from politics "idiotēs." The Oxford English Dictionary translates this as "private person," "ignorant," "layman," or "not professionally learned." And what are we to call those who have learned nothing from our recent history but the foolish slogan "without me" (*Ohne mich*)? Are they not like fish who expect to improve their condition by jumping from the frying pan into the fire?

We have paid dearly once before for the folly of believing that democracy, being an ideal political arrangement, must function automatically while the citizens sit in their parlors berating it, or worrying about their money. Everybody must share in the responsibility and must be prepared to make sacrifices. He must also respect the opinions of others and must curb his hates, which are too blinding to be good guides for action. In addition, we need to be patient, we must have confidence in small advances and abandon the belief in political miracles and panaceas.

Only if the citizens are thoroughly imbued with democratic attitudes can we put into practice those principles of political life which were achieved through centuries of experience, and which we disregarded to our great sorrow. The first such principle is the need for a continuous and vigilant control of power. For this, we need not only a free and courageous press but also some mechanism for shaping a vital political opinion in associations, parties, and other organizations. Equally necessary are clearly drawn lines of political responsibility, and a strong and respected political opposition. Interest groups must not be diffused too widely but must aim at maximum cohesiveness. Present developments appear to indicate that we are deeply aware of at least this necessity.

More than anything else we must base our concept of law on the idea of justice. We have had the sad experience that the principle "the law is the law" does not suffice, if the laws are being abused to cover up for crimes and to wrap injustices in a tissue of legality. Our actions must once again be guided by that idea which is the basis of a just life: no man must be used as a means to an end.

This principle must also be applied to our relationships with other nations. Although, on the international scene, there is as yet no all-inclusive legal body that would have enough power to solve all conflicts peacefully, still there are legal norms in international affairs which are not at all the "sound and smoke" (Faust) Hitler had presumed them to be. In no other matter was he as divorced from reality as in his belief that it was shrewd to conclude treaties today and "to break them in cold blood tomorrow," and that he could undo 2000 years of legal evolution without having such action recoil upon him. He considered force the one and only means of politics, while, in reality, it had always been the worst. Hitler's so-called *Realpolitik* was terrifyingly unreal, and brought about a catastrophe which has undone the gains Bismarck had made through moderation. Bismarck gave Germany its unity. Hitler, goaded by his limitless drive for world power, divided Germany and destroyed the work of generations.

Thus we are now faced with the difficult task of regaining, by peaceful means, the German unity that Hitler has gambled away. We must strive for it tirelessly, even though it may take decades. At the same time, we must establish a new relationship, based on trust, with the peoples of Europe and the nations of the world. Our word must again be believed, our commitment to freedom and humanity again be trusted. Our name has been used too much for lies and treachery. We cannot simply stretch out our hands and hope that all will be forgotten.

These are the questions which should touch the younger generation most deeply: What position could and should we have among the nations? Can we restore honor to the German name? Can we shape a new and better future? Or shall we be burdened with the crimes of the Hitler regime for generations to come?

However contradictory the problem may look at first sight, there can be no shilly-shallying, but only a clear Yes to these questions. The past cannot be erased, but the future is free. It is not predetermined. We have the power to re-examine our decisions and mend our wrong ways; we can renounce force and place our trust in peaceful and gradual progress; we can reject racial pride. Instead of impressing the world with war and aggression, we can strive for world prestige through the peaceful solution of conflicts, as the Swiss and the Scandinavians have done for centuries to their national glory. For us, the choice is open to condemn Hitler's deluded destructiveness and to embrace Albert Schweitzer's message—respect for life.

If we are really serious about this new respect for life, it must also extend to the victims of the unspeakable policy of extermination. Ever since human beings have existed, respect for life has included respect for the dead. Everywhere it is the duty of the living to preserve the memory of the dead. Should we listen to insinuations that the time has come to forget crimes and victims because nobody must incriminate himself? Is it not, rather, cowardly, mean, and miserable to deny even now the dead the honor they deserve, and to forget them as quickly as possible?

We owe it to ourselves to examine our consciences sincerely and to face the naked truth, instead of minimizing it or glossing over it. This is also the only way we can regain respect in the world. Covering up or minimizing crimes will suggest that we secretly approve of them. Who will believe that we want to respect all that is human if we treat the death of nearly six million Jews as a "small error" to be forgotten after a few years?

The test of our change of heart should be not only the dead but the living. There are 30,000 Jewish fellow-citizens living among us. Many of them have returned only recently from emigration, overwhelmed with a desire for their old homeland. It is up to all of us to make sure that they live among us in peace and without being abused, that their new trust in us, won after much effort, is not destroyed by desecrated cemeteries, gutter slogans, or hate songs. Those who will never learn must not be allowed to take refuge in the freedom of opinion. A higher value is at stake here, the honor of the dead, and respect for the living. But it is not up to the public prosecutor to imbue our lives with new and more humane principles. This is everybody's business. It concerns us all! It will determine our future.

Translator's Note

The German people, Miss Vogt remarks in a discussion of the revolution of November 1918, "has had no liking for revolutions." Hitler and the parties on the right understood this national attitude and scored significant propaganda victories during the Weimar period by ascribing to the events of 1918 a revolutionary character which, in Miss Vogt's opinion, they did not have, since the social and economic institutions and the power structure of Imperial Germany had not really been changed by the upheaval (p. 36).

It is not the translator's task to discuss the merits or the sources of the various generalizations on which Miss Vogt has based her arguments about the events of 1918. Yet, the paragraph reveals clearly the classical dilemma of the translator because it shows that the German concept *Revolution* plays a role in German political culture and carries emotional overtones, which differ from the mainstream of American political culture. This makes a translation of major political concepts from one language into another an eternally frustrated search for perfect equivalents. The German language knows a number of similar concepts which, like the word *Revolution*, vibrate with memories of German history and the decisions of centuries past: *Staat, Volk, Rechtsstaat, Treueid, Sitte, legal*, and many similar words frequently used in this book originate in the German political climate, and denote different objects than their equivalent state, people, state based on law, loyalty oath, custom, and legal. The reader, like the translator, will have to remain aware of this dilemma.

But differences of this kind pale when compared to the situation created by the style and language of the Nazi period. Miss Vogt frequently quotes Nazi speeches and writings verbatim, and she has made no effort to hide the clipped barbarisms of their military minds, the cynical, camouflaged language of their murder squads, or the vague bombast of their political thought. Any attempt to smooth over the utter ugliness of Nazi style or thought would have defeated Miss Vogt's purpose to expose them, once again, in their true nature. It would have been wrong to aim for stylistic uniformity in translating the various parts of Miss Vogt's book. Hitler's literary style of 1925, the style of *Mein Kampf,* reveals too much of his petty bourgeois image of science, politics, and human nature, and of the derelict beer-hall irresponsibilities of the *Stammtisch* to be prettified in translation; his frequently noted ability to adapt his thought to any tactical situation or audience is too well mirrored in the different styles he used in his addresses, proclamations, conversations, orders, etc. to be ground down into standard phrases. Like other Nazi neologisms, the style revealed the men, and the translator has no business hiding them.

A further characteristic is the freedom of German writers to report on a speech or a document in a text without constantly reminding their readers by quotation marks that they are quoting the original words. Miss Vogt has made frequent use of this freedom, and the reader needs to be aware of this practice which it was thought unobjectionable to adopt in the translation, somewhat along the lines of reports on presidential news conferences.

Finally, the translator wishes to thank the editors of Oxford University Press, Miss Josephine Freedman, and, last but not least, his wife Lotte Strauss for aid and advice in a labor he came to love. The shortcomings of the translation remain, of course, his own.

New York June 1964

HERBERT A. STRAUSS

Notes

1. Erich Eyck, *Das persönliche Regiment Wilhelm II* (Zurich: E. Rentsch Verlag, 1948), p. 715.
2. Bernhard Schwertfeger, *Das Weltkriegsende* (Potsdam: Rütten und Loehning Verlag, 1937), p. 12.
3. Erich Eyck, *A History of the Weimar Republic*, vol. 1 (Cambridge, Mass.: Harvard University Press, 1962), p. 17.
4. Arthur Rosenberg, *The Birth of the German Republic, 1871-1918* (New York: Oxford University Press, 1931), p. 245.
5. M. J. Bonn, *So macht man Geschichte* (Munich: List Verlag, 1953), p. 192.
6. Max Weber, "Politics as a Vocation," in H. H. Gerth and C. Wright Mills, *From Max Weber: Essays in Sociology* (New York: Oxford University Press, 1946), pp. 77-108.
7. This is a critical appraisal by Hugo Preuss who was much concerned with the lack of understanding for the constitution.
8. F. A. Hermens, "Democracy or Anarchy? A Study of Proportional Representation," *The Review of Politics* (Notre Dame, Indiana: University of Notre Dame, 1941), pp. 214-300.
9. Rudolf von Ihering, *Der Kampf ums Recht* (Vienna: Manz Verlag, 1872).
10. Erich Eyck, *A History of the Weimar Republic*, vol. 1, p. 214.
11. Golo Mann, *Deutsche Geschichte 1919-1945* (Frankfurt: Büchergilde Gutenberg, 1958).
12. S. E. Morison and H. S. Commager, *The Growth of the American Republic*, vol. 2 (New York: Oxford University Press, 1950), p. 543.

13. Erich Eyck, *A History of the Weimar Republic*, vol. 2 (Cambridge, Mass.: Harvard University Press, 1963), pp. 387-8.
14. Erich Eyck, op. cit. p. 436.
15. Ernst Niekisch, *Das Reich der niederen Dämonen* (Hamburg: Rowohlt Verlag, 1953), p. 325.
16. Hans Herzfeld, *Die moderne Welt 1789-1945* (Braunschweig: Westermann Verlag, 1952), p. 325.
17. Alan Bullock, *Hitler. A Study in Tyranny* (New York: Bantam Books, 1961, revised ed.), p. 529.
18. Bullock, op. cit. pp. 575-87.
19. Bullock, op. cit. p. 590.
20. Bullock, op. cit. p. 602.
21. Jakob Wassermann, *Mein Weg als Deutscher und Jude* (Berlin: Fischer Verlag, 1921), p. 122.
22. J.-P. Sartre, *Anti-Semite and Jew* (New York: Schocken Books, 1948).
23. Franz Böhm, *Antisemitismus,* an address delivered on March 13, 1958. Private printing.
24. Hans Rothfels, *The German Opposition to Hitler* (Chicago: Regnery, 1962, new revised ed.), pp. 42-4. (The statement quoted in the text appears to have been omitted or changed in this edition of Rothfels's book. Trl.)
25. Kurt R. Grossmann, *Die unbesungenen Helden* (Berlin-Grunewald: Arani Verlag, 1957).
26. Mann, op. cit. p. 909.
27. Eberhard Zeller, *Geist der Freiheit* (Munich: Rinn Verlag, 1954), p. 97.
28. Mann, op. cit. p. 910.
29. Zeller, op. cit. p. 141.
30. Zeller, op. cit. p. 158.
31. Zeller, op. cit. p. 171.
32. Zeller, op. cit. p. 203.
33. Zeller, op. cit. p. 217.
34. Zeller, op. cit. p. 307.
35. Hans Adolf Jacobsen, *1939-1946. Der zweite Weltkrieg in Chronik und Dokumenten* (Darmstadt: Wehr und Wissen, 1959), p. 502.
36. Friedrich Naumann, "Die politische Mattigkeit der Gebildeten," in *Ausgewählte Schriften* (Frankfurt: Schauer Verlag, 1949), p. 190.

Biographical Index

(These biographies only deal with people not adequately treated in the text. Note: References to years, e.g. "1913," indicate the earliest date of an appointment, event, etc., and not its duration.)

Antonescu, Jon, 1882-1946. Chief of Staff in the Rumanian Army, 1933. Appointed chief of state by King Carol II, 1940. Antonescu forced the king to abdicate, introduced an authoritarian regime, and declared war against the Soviet Union, 1941. Arrested 1944, executed 1946.

Beck, Ludwig, 1880-1944. Chief of Staff of the Army, 1935. Determined but unsuccessful opponent of Hitler's war plans, resigned during the Sudeten crisis, 1938. Head of the military resistance movement during World War II. Committed suicide after the unsuccessful attempt on Hitler's life, July 20, 1944.

Beneš, Edward, 1884-1948. Fought for independent Czech state, 1915. Foreign minister, then chief of state of Czechoslovakia (fd. 1918), 1918-35. Resigned after Munich Pact, 1938, went abroad, became president of the Czech government-in-exile, was re-elected chief of state after end of German rule, 1945. Unable to stop Soviet takeover. Lost effective power through coup d'état, February 1948, and resigned.

Bernadotte, Count Folke, 1895-1948. President of the Swedish Red Cross, 1946. Himmler tried to use Bernadotte's service as an intermediary for his armistice efforts, 1945. Killed by a Jewish terrorist in Jerusalem while negotiating armistice between Arabs and Jews, 1948.

Bethmann-Hollweg, Theobald von, 1856-1921. *Reich* Chancellor, 1909, forced to resign, 1917.

Bismarck, Prince Otto von, 1815-98. Studied law. Took over family estate in Pomerania, 1845. Entered the Prussian civil service, 1851; became Prussian Prime Minister, 1862. After the Seven Weeks' War with Austria (1866) he favored a compromise peace which prepared the later alliance with Austria. Bismarck succeeded in unifying the German state during the Franco-Prussian War, 1870-71, and in having Wilhelm I proclaimed German Emperor in Versailles. Chancellor of the German *Reich* until 1890. His domestic policies were less successful than his diplomacy. He contributed to the consolidation of political Catholicism (Center Party) through the so-called *Kulturkampf* (State-Church controversy in Prussia during 1870s. *Trl.*). The anti-socialist laws (1878-90) favored by Bismarck were ineffective and embittered German workers. The social welfare legislation promoted by Bismarck failed to deflect the workers from the goal of sharing in government control. Bismarck was dismissed by Wilhelm II in a brusque manner, 1890.

Bonhoeffer, Dietrich, 1906-45. Protestant theologian, director of the preachers' seminary of the Confessing Church in Finkenwalde. Arrested 1945, and executed by the S.S. shortly before American troops liberated Flossenbürg concentration camp.

Braun, Otto, 1872-1955. Printer, then editor, Social Democratic member of the Prussian House of Representatives, 1913, member of the Weimar National Assembly and the *Reichstag,* 1919. Prussian Prime Minister (except for short interruptions), 1921-32. Removed from office through Papen's coup d'état, 1932, he emigrated to Switzerland, 1933.

Briand, Aristide, 1862-1932. Lawyer and journalist, deputy, 1902. Minister in various French governments, 1906 and later. Foreign Minister, 1925; major goals were Franco-German understanding and disarmament. Nobel Peace Prize, 1926.

Brüning, Heinrich, 1885-   . Executive Secretary of the Christian Trade Unions, 1920-30. Member of the German *Reichstag* (Center Party), 1924-33. Outstanding financial expert. Appointed *Reich* Chancellor, 1930, dismissed by Hindenburg, 1932. Chairman of Center Party, 1933, forced to dissolve the party, July 1933. Brüning avoided imminent arrest by emigrating to the USA, appointed professor at Harvard University. After his return to Germany in 1952, Brüning was appointed professor in Cologne.

Canaris, Wilhelm, 1887-1945. Director of Foreign Bureau (Counter Intelligence) in Armed Forces Supreme Command, 1938. Canaris organized resistance cell in co-operation with Lieutenant-General Beck, was dismissed, 1944, arrested after July 20, 1944, hanged in Flossenbürg concentration camp.

Chamberlain, Houston Stewart, 1855-1927. Writer, studied natural science. Chamberlain lived more in Germany and Austria than in England, and settled in Bayreuth after marrying Richard Wagner's daughter Eva. *The Foundations of the XIXth Century,* his major work, glorified the Germanic race while deprecating the Jews.

Chamberlain, Joseph, 1836-1914. British statesman. Colonial Secretary, 1895, aimed at close political co-operation with the USA and Germany. His efforts for an alliance with Germany failed.

Ciano, Count Galeazzo, 1903-44. Participated in the March on Rome. Married Mussolini's daughter Edda, 1930. Diplomat in various posts, appointed Foreign Minister by Mussolini, 1936. Ciano increasingly opposed Mussolini's policy from 1938 on. Sentenced to death by a special court set up by Mussolini, January 1944, and executed by firing squad.

Clemenceau, Georges, 1841-1929. French statesman. In several ministerial posts, 1906 and later. Prime Minister, 1917. Clemenceau directed the unified French war effort while virtually excluding parliament from authority. As one of the Big Four, Clemenceau was largely responsible for Versailles Treaty. He retired from political life, 1920.

Darré, Walter, 1895- . Studied agriculture, appointed Minister of Food and Agriculture by Hitler, 1933. Author of the "blood and soil" ideology. Darré was sentenced to seven years' imprisonment by an American court and released after 16 months.

Delp, Alfred, 1907-45. Converted to Catholicism, joined Jesuits, 1926. Delp became a member of the Kreisau Circle in 1942 and prepared a draft for a Christian social order. He was arrested at the end of July 1944, sentenced to death by the People's Court, and executed.

Dönitz, Karl, 1891- . Chief of submarines, 1936, Supreme Commander of the Navy, 1943. Hitler appointed him as his successor, and Dönitz, accordingly, formed a new *Reich* government in Schleswig-Holstein on May 2, 1945. Dönitz was sentenced by the International Military Tribunal in 1946 to 10 years' imprisonment which he served at Spandau Prison.

Dollfuss, Engelbert, 1892-1934. Executive Secretary of the Lower Austrian Peasant Association, Minister for Agriculture, 1931, Federal Chancellor and Foreign Minister of Austria, May 1932. Dollfuss governed without parliament or parties, 1933-34, and was murdered in the Federal Chancellery during an Austrian Nazi *Putsch.*

Ebert, Friedrich, 1871-1925. Upholsterer. Editor of a Social Democratic newspaper, 1893, Secretary of the Party Executive in Berlin, 1905. He succeeded August Bebel as elected Party Chairman in 1913, and was elected to the *Reichstag* in 1912. Ebert worked for the peaceful settlement of the Berlin munitions workers strike of January 1918, and was named *Reich* Chancellor by Prince Max von Baden, November 9, 1918, and elected *Reich* President (pro tem) by the National Assembly, January 1919. Ebert remained in office until his death.

Erzberger, Matthias, 1875-1921. Originally a school teacher, then editor and politician, Erzberger represented the Center Party in the *Reichstag* from 1903 on. As Secretary of State, he signed the Armistice, 1918. Finance Minister, 1919-20, was murdered by two officers, August 26, 1921.

Feder, Gottfried, 1883-   . Engineer, founded Combat Association for the Breaking of Interest Slavery, 1917. Author of 25-point program of the NSDAP.

Foerster, Friedrich Wilhelm, 1869-   . Educator. Professor in Munich, 1914-20. Foerster was converted (for moral reasons) to pacifism under the impact of World War I and wrote on education from a Christian viewpoint. Lives in New York.

Franco, Bahaminde Francisco, 1892-   . Spanish Chief of Staff since 1934. Franco suppressed a Communist Revolution (October 1934) in Asturia. He was exiled to the Canary Islands, 1936, prepared the revolt against Popular Front Government from there, started it in 1936, and inaugurated the Spanish Civil War. Chief of State in Spain (Caudillo), 1936. Franco established a national dictatorship in 1938 and was supported primarily by the Catholic Church in his domestic policies. Aided by Germany and Italy, he defeated his opponents (who also received foreign aid) only in the spring of 1939.

Frank, Hans, 1900-1946. Lawyer, Minister of Justice in Bavaria, 1933. *Reich* Minister and *Reich* Law Leader, 1934. Appointed Governor General of Poland by Hitler, October 1939. Frank wrote 38 volumes of diaries on his activities which were introduced as evidence at the Nuremberg Trial. Hanged in 1946.

Freisler, Roland, 1893-1945. Lawyer, member of the NSDAP, 1925. President of the People's Court, August 1942. Radical representative of Nazi criminal law and judicial terrorism, especially in persecuting resistance fighters. Freisler was killed during air raid, early January 1945.

Galen, Count Clemens August von, 1878-1946. Bishop of Münster, 1933. Famous for his protest against the anti-church and racial policies of the Third *Reich*. His episcopal letters were copied and passed from hand to hand. Cardinal, 1946.

Gerstenmaier, Eugen, 1906- . Chief church counsellor (*Oberkonsistorialrat*), active in the Office for External Affairs of the Protestant Church. Member of the Kreisau Circle. Gerstenmaier was arrested on July 20, 1944, and sentenced to hard labor. Liberated in 1945, he organized the Evangelical Aid Society. Member of the Federal Diet since 1949, its President following the death of Herman Ehlers.

Gneisenau, August Count von Neithardt, 1760-1831. Officer in the Prussian Army, 1786. He and Nettelbeck defended Kolberg fortress against the French. During the War of Liberation, Gneisenau was appointed Chief of the General Staff of the Silesian Army, and became a major military opponent of Napoleon's. He belonged to the circle of Prussian reformers (like Freiherr von Stein and Scharnhorst) and combined soldiering with liberal political views.

Gobineau, Arthur Comte de, 1816-82. French writer and diplomat. The race theory, developed in his "Essay on the inequality of the human races," was scientifically unsound but widely effective. Today, his novels are considered to be his main achievement, including the historical descriptions contained in *The Renaissance* which are very well known in Germany.

Goerdeler, Carl Friedrich, 1884-1945. Lord Mayor of Leipzig, 1930. *Reich* Commissioner for Prices, 1934-35. Goerdeler resigned in protest against the Nazi government in 1937 and became the leading intellectual in the civilian resistance movement in 1939. As a result of July 20, 1944, he was denounced, arrested, sentenced, and executed (in Plötzensee prison).

Hassell, Ulrich von, 1881-1944. Diplomat in the Foreign Service, 1919. Ambassador in Copenhagen, Belgrade, and Rome. Member of the resistance movement, 1938. His diaries ("The Other Germany") were published after his execution. They describe the difficulties and problems of the resistance fighters.

Haushofer, Albrecht, 1903-45. Professor of Political Geography, Berlin, 1940, connected with the Foreign Office until 1941. He was arrested for his contacts with resistance groups in 1944 and wrote the "Moabit Sonnets" in Moabit Prison (Berlin) which were preserved by accidental circumstances and published later. Haushofer was shot by the Gestapo while being transferred to another prison.

Henlein, Konrad, 1898-1945. Bank clerk. In charge of gymnastics (*Turnwart*) in the German Gymnastics Association of Czechoslovakia, 1931. Founder of the Sudeten-German Home Front, 1933. He was appointed *Gauleiter* of the NSDAP in the Sudeten area following the Munich Pact. Head of the Civil Administration in Czechoslovakia, 1939. Henlein committed suicide in an Allied internment camp, 1945.

Heuss, Theodor, 1884-1963. Editor-in-chief of "Die Hilfe," a periodical founded by Friedrich Naumann, 1905-12. Lecturer at the Academy (*Hochschule*) for Politics, Berlin, 1920-33. Member of the *Reichstag* for the Democratic Party. Following 1933, he wrote extensive biographies (of Naumann, Bosch, etc.), and, under an assumed name, contributed to the *Frankfurter Zeitung.* Minister of Culture in Württemberg-Baden, 1945-46. One of the founders of the Free Democratic Party in 1946, he represented this party in the Parliamentary Council (responsible for preparing the Constitution). Heuss was elected first President of the Federal Republic by the Federal Diet in 1949.

Heydrich, Reinhard, 1904-42. A naval officer, he was dismissed after a trial by a court of honor, 1931. Chief of the S.S. Security Service, 1932. As Himmler's right-hand man, 1934, Heydrich was put in charge of the Gestapo in 1936. Appointed *Reich* Vice-Protector for Bohemia and Moravia in March 1942, he was killed by Czech resistance fighters in Prague on June 4, 1942. The S.S. retaliated by murdering the inhabitants of Lidice and destroying their village.

Hindenburg, Paul von Beneckendorff und von, 1847-1934. Following a successful career as professional officer, Hindenburg retired from active service in 1911. Appointed as Commander-in-Chief of the Eighth Army in 1914, he defeated the Russians at Tannenberg. His victories on the eastern front made him the most popular army leader of World War I. With Ludendorff, took over the Supreme Army Command, 1916. In 1918, Hindenburg favored the abdication of Kaiser Wilhelm II. After 1919, he lived in retirement in Hanover. Elected *Reich* President, 1925.

Holstein, Friedrich von, 1837-1909. Privy Councillor in the Foreign Office, 1878, dismissed 1906. Holstein avoided any responsible position and acted as the "grey eminence" in the background, entangled in intrigues.

Huch, Ricarda, 1864-1947. Studied history in Zurich. Huch became known first through her poems and novels reflecting a passionate love for life and beauty. During her later years, she was predominantly concerned with historical and philosophical subjects. Wrote a history of the Thirty Years' War describing it in dynamic scenes and images. A three-volume history of Germany appeared in Switzerland in 1933. Huch resigned from the Prussian Academy of Fine Arts (1933) when it introduced "Aryanization."

Hugenberg, Alfred, 1865-1951. Following 10 years of service on Krupp's Board of Directors, Hugenberg built up his own concern by gaining control of newspapers, news agencies, and motion picture firms (Ufa). Co-founder of the Pan-German League, member of the *Reichstag,* 1919, chairman of the National German People's Party, 1928. A member of Hitler's first cabinet (Minister of Economics and Finance) in 1933, he was forced to resign as early as June 1933, and lost all influence on the developments he had inaugurated.

Jodl, Alfred, 1890-1946. General Staff officer, Chief of the Leadership Staff of the Armed Forces, 1939-45. Jodl advised Hitler on strategy. Sentenced to death by hanging by the International Military Tribunal at Nuremberg.

Kaiser, Jacob, 1888-1961. Bookbinder, executive of Christian Trade Unions, 1912. Kaiser co-operated with Wilhelm Leuschner in leading the trade-union sector of the resistance movement. Co-founder of the Christian Democratic Union in 1945. Federal Minister for All-German Affairs, 1949-57.

Keitel, Wilhelm, 1882-1946. Appointed Chief of the newly established Supreme Command of the Armed Forces in 1938, Keitel became Hitler's chief military adviser. An "obedient citizen," he accepted Hitler's decisions without offering any resistance. Sentenced to death by the International Military Tribunal for planning and leading a war of aggression, and for crimes against humanity. Executed by hanging.

Leber, Julius, 1891-1945. Editor-in-chief of the "Lübecker Volksbote," 1921. Social Democratic member of the *Reichstag.* Imprisoned, 1933-37, Leber joined the Kreisau Circle after his release, was imprisoned again prior to July 20, 1944, sentenced to death by the People's Court, and executed.

Leuschner, Wilhelm, 1890-1944. Sculptor. Trade-union leader. Social Democratic Minister of the Interior in [the state government of] Hesse, 1928-30. Then member of the Board of General German Trade Union Federation (ADGB). Leuschner was arrested following Hitler's seizure of power, 1933. Released, he organized the trade unions' resistance movement against Hitler, was sentenced to death after July 20, 1944, and executed.

Ley, Robert, 1890-1945. Chemist, *Gauleiter* of the NSDAP for the Rhineland. *Reich* Organization Leader of the party, 1934. Ley dissolved the trade unions and, on Hitler's orders, founded the German Labor Front. Ley became notorious as an eccentric platitudinarian. Committed suicide in his cell in Nuremberg to avoid being sentenced by the Military Tribunal.

Liebknecht, Karl, 1871-1919. Lawyer, Social Democratic member of the *Reichstag,* 1912. Liebknecht voted against the war credits in December 1914, and left the Social Democratic group in 1916. Following an anti-war rally, he was sentenced to four years of hard labor for high treason. Pardoned in 1918, he and Rosa Luxemburg headed the Spartacus League. He was shot by government troops in January 1919.

Lloyd George, David, 1863-1945. Liberal member of the House of Commons, 1890. Chancellor of the Exchequer, 1908. As Minister of Munitions, then Minister of War, he had a major influence on the conduct of World War I. He subsequently headed a coalition Cabinet and symbolized the British determination to win the war. Following the Armistice he favored a moderate peace. The election debacle suffered by the Liberal Party in 1928 removed him from politics. He was strongly criticized for sympathizing with Hitler later on.

Ludendorff, Erich, 1865-1937. Appointed with Hindenburg, as Chief of Staff of the Eighth Army in World War I, he was credited with important German victories on the eastern front. As Quartermaster General with the Supreme Army Command (1916), he was in charge of the overall direction of the war, and interfered in political decisions. He wrote his memoirs after World War I, participated in Hitler's 1923 *Putsch,* and, with his wife Mathilde, founded the antisemitic Tannenberg League as a "German-Teutonic religious community."

Luxemburg, Rosa, 1870-1919. Born into a well-to-do Jewish business family in Poland, she early became a Socialist, took part in the 1905 Russian Revolution, and subsequently taught in Germany at the Social Democratic Party School in Berlin. She wrote important works on social and economic problems, and, with Karl Liebknecht, founded the Spartacus League. She became famous through her sensitive letters from her prison cell. With Karl Liebknecht, she was shot without trial in 1919.

Mann, Thomas, 1875-1955. Scion of an old Lübeck patrician family, he first achieved world fame with his novel *Buddenbrooks* (1901) describing the history of a Lübeck family through three generations. He was the most universally known German writer of the twentieth century. Fled to Switzerland, 1934, to California, 1939, where he wrote *Dr. Faustus* (a novel reflecting the writer's personal concern with developments in Germany). Mann spoke out repeatedly against the evils of Nazism in some important addresses.

Manstein, Erich von, 1887-   . The Eleventh Army, under his command, conquered the Crimea and Sebastopol, 1941. In charge of an Army Group at the Eastern Front, 1942-44. Sentenced to 18-years' imprisonment by a British Military Tribunal. Released, May 1955.

Meissner, Otto, 1880-1953. Entered diplomatic service, 1918, joined the staff of the *Reich* President in 1919, and was Secretary of State under Ebert, Hindenburg, and Hitler. He was acquitted in the Wilhelmstrasse Trial [Trial of high German officials. *Trl.*] in 1949.

Mierendorff, Carlo, 1897-1943. Journalist, active in the trade-union movement, 1918. Social Democratic member of the *Reichstag,* 1930. Mierendorff was interned in a concentration camp, 1933-38, and subsequently joined the Kreisau Circle. He was killed during an air raid on Leipzig in 1943.

Mussolini, Benito, 1883-1945. Elementary school teacher, 1901. Subsequently Socialist Party functionary and journalist. Mussolini founded the first *Fascio di Combattimento* in 1919. He marched on Rome with the para-military Black Shirts in 1922, and was asked by King [Umberto] to form a government. He gradually usurped dictatorial powers and meanwhile gained prestige abroad. The Ethiopian war (1935-36) inaugurated a period of ever more uncontrolled power politics which increased Mussolini's dependence on Hitler. The Grand Fascist Council declared its lack of confidence in him in 1943, and he was arrested, then liberated by a special German commando group. He was apprehended and shot by Italian partisans shortly before the war ended.

Naumann, Friedrich, 1860-1919. Pastor, journalist, and politician. He founded the National Social Association as an independent liberal party primarily concerned with social problems (1896). Unable to succeed at the polls, he then joined the Progressive Association (*Freisinnige Vereinigung*) and became a *Reichstag* Deputy. Co-founder of the German Democratic Party, 1918. Founder of (what became later) the Academy (*Hochschule*) for Politics in Berlin, 1917. Founder and editor for many years of "Die Hilfe," a periodical. A gifted speaker with a strong personality, he influenced an entire generation far beyond the limits of his own party.

Niemöller, Martin, 1892-   . A submarine commander during World War I, Niemöller subsequently studied theology and became a pastor in Berlin-Dahlem in 1931. Founded the Pastors' Emergency League of the Confessing Church in 1933. Niemöller was imprisoned in a concentration camp as "personal prisoner of Hitler's" for resistance against the Nazi regime, 1937-45, after being acquitted by the courts. President of the Protestant Churches in Hesse and Nassau since 1947.

Noske, Gustav, 1868-1946. Lumberjack. Social Democratic editor, 1897, member of the *Reichstag,* 1906. Member of the Council of People's Representatives, December 1918. The Spartacus revolt was suppressed on his orders. Appointed Minister for the Armed Forces (1919-20), he laid the basis for the development of the *Reichswehr.* Was provincial governor of Hanover province, 1920-33.

Ossietzky, Carl von, 1889-1938. Editor of "Die Weltbühne," a periodical, 1927. Pacifist and secretary of the German Peace Society. Sentenced to prison for treason (for criticism of the Armed Forces) in 1931, he was pardoned in 1932. Ossietzky was interned in a concentration camp in 1933. Granted the 1935 Nobel Peace Prize, he was forbidden to accept it by the Nazi government.

Papen, Franz von, 1879- . Officer. Member of the Prussian Diet (Center Party), 1923-32. Succeeded Brüning, June 1932. Papen had a major share in smoothing the way for Hitler's cabinet, early in 1933, and was Vice-Chancellor in Hitler's first cabinet. During the Röhm *Putsch,* two of his closest collaborators were assassinated and Papen left his cabinet post. Ambassador in Vienna, 1934, in Turkey 1939-44. Acquitted at the Nuremberg Trials.

Pétain, Philippe, 1856-1951. General in command of the defense of Verdun, 1916, Commander in Chief of the French Army, 1917. Minister of War, 1934. Following the French defeat of 1940, he became Premier and concluded the armistice with Germany. The Vichy National Assembly gave him far-reaching powers as chief of state in unoccupied France. In April 1946, Pétain voluntarily surrendered to the French Supreme Court, and was sentenced to death for collaboration. He was pardoned by de Gaulle and deported to the Isle of Yeu where he died and was buried in 1951.

Poincaré, Raymond, 1860-1920. Lawyer. Deputy, 1887. Minister in several cabinets, 1893, and later, President of the French Republic, 1913-20. As chairman of the Reparations Commission from 1920 on, he demanded the complete fulfillment of the terms of the Versailles Treaty.

Popitz, Johannes, 1884-1945. Lawyer. Secretary of State in the *Reich* Finance Ministry, 1925-29, Professor at Berlin University, 1922. Considered one of the outstanding financial experts. A friend of Beck's, he took part in the resistance movement, was sentenced to death, and executed after July 20, 1944.

Rathenau, Walter, 1867-1922. Emil Rathenau, his father, founded the General Electric Company (AEG) in 1887. Walter Rathenau joined its board in 1899 and became chairman in 1915. Rathenau established controls to secure the German supply of raw materials at the outbreak of World War I. He was appointed adviser to several commissions by the German government, 1919. Foreign Minister, 1922. Concluded the Rapallo Treaty. Hated by antisemitic nationalists for his so-called "fulfillment policies" and for being Jewish, he was shot on his way to his office on June 24, 1922.

Rauschning, Hermann, 1877-   . Director of cultural activities for German ethnic groups in Poznan, 1918. Chairman of the Danzig Land League, 1932, President of the Senate of the Free City of Danzig following the Danzig elections of 1933. Rauschning soon clashed with the NSDAP, resigned in 1934 and fled abroad in 1936. There he wrote his sensational *Conversations with Hitler* which unequivocally documented Hitler's war-like intentions. Rauschning has lived in the USA since 1948 and is a farmer in Oregon.

Reichwein, Adolf, 1888-1944. An educator, Reichwein helped to organize the Pedagogical Academy of Halle where he held the rank of professor, 1930-33. After 1933 he taught school in the village of Tiefensee, near Berlin. He belonged to the resistance movement and was executed as a result of July 20, 1944.

Remarque, Erich Maria (pseud. for *Kramer*), 1898-   . Teacher, subsequently editor and writer. His novel *All Quiet on the Western Front* (1929) became a world success. Remarque went to Switzerland as early as 1932, then to New York; has lived in Switzerland since 1948. Published numerous novels.

Ribbentrop, Joachim von, 1893-1946. Businessman (champagne salesman). Active for the NSDAP in Germany and abroad, 1930. Ambassador to England, 1936, *Reich* Foreign Minister, 1938. Ribbentrop was sentenced to death at the Nuremberg Trials, 1946.

Röhm, Ernst, 1887-1934. Army officer. Röhm took a leading part in organizing the Storm Troopers (S.A.), 1925, and became S.A. Chief of Staff, 1931. After seizure of power by Hitler, became *Reich* Minister. His attempt to gain greater influence over the armed forces was frustrated by Hitler. He was arrested by Hitler in person, June 30, 1934, and shot soon after, after having been given a gun with which to commit suicide.

Rommel, Erwin, 1891-1944. One of the most popular generals of World War II. Commander of the German Africa Corps, 1941, and of an Army Group in Northern France, 1943. Rommel joined the resistance movement and was forced to commit suicide (by poison). He received a state funeral in order to cover up for his hostility against Hitler and the circumstances surrounding his death.

Rosenberg, Alfred, 1893-1946. Originally from the Baltic area,

Rosenberg became editor-in-chief of the "Völkischer Beobachter" in 1921. The Christian churches strongly rejected his *The Myth of the Twentieth Century*, based on the race doctrine and antisemitism. *Reich* Minister for the Eastern Occupied Area, November 1941. Rosenberg was sentenced to death in Nuremberg as "originator of race hatred," 1946.

Rosenstock-Huessy, Eugen, 1888-   . Expert in the history of law and sociology. Professor in Breslau, 1923-34. Helped to found work-camps for workers, peasants, and students, 1926. Since his emigration, Rosenstock-Huessy has taught at American universities.

Schacht, Hjalmar, 1877-   . Banking expert. Director of the National Bank, 1916. Schacht stabilized the currency as *Reich* Currency Commissioner, 1923. President of the *Reichsbank*, 1924-29. Schacht favored the Harzburg Front, 1930-32, and thus aided Hitler's seizure of power. Re-appointed President of the *Reichsbank*, 1933-34, Schacht was credited with the efficient financing of the work creation program. After unemployment had been reduced, Schacht opposed further inflationary measures and was removed from office. He was imprisoned in a concentration camp for his ideas, 1944-45. Acquitted at the Nuremberg Trials.

Scheidemann, Philipp, 1865-1939. Printer, Social Democratic writer, 1890, member of the *Reichstag*, 1903, member of his party's executive committee, 1911. In October 1918, he was appointed Secretary of State in the cabinet of Prince Max von Baden. Scheidemann proclaimed the Republic on November 9, 1918, and headed the first parliamentary cabinet (Prime Minister), February 1919. *Reichstag* deputy, 1920, fled abroad, 1933.

Schleicher, Kurt von, 1882-1934. General Staff Officer, 1913, Director of a department of the Armed Forces Ministry, 1926. Schleicher used his position to gain political influence. He was the last Chancellor before Hitler, December 1932-January 1933. He and his wife were shot in their apartment during the Röhm Revolt.

Scholl, Hans and *Sophie*, born 1918 and 1921, died 1943. They studied in Munich where they met Theodor Haecker and Kurt Huber and, with other students, formed a resistance group, "The White Rose." Arrested, while distributing leaflets at the university, they were sentenced to death on February 22, 1943, and executed on the same day.

Schuschnigg, Kurt von, 1897-   . Lawyer. Christian Social Party deputy in the Austrian *Nationalrat*, 1927. Minister of Justice, 1932. Federal Chancellor following the assassination of Dollfuss, 1934. Schuschnigg tried to maintain Austrian independence through an authoritarian constitution and an estate system. He was imprisoned in a concentration camp from the *Anschluss* (1938) until 1945, and subsequently emigrated to the USA.

Severing, Carl, 1875-1952. Trade-union official, then journalist. Member of the *Reichstag,* 1907-33, Minister of the Interior in Prussia, 1920-26, *Reich* Minister of the Interior, 1928-29, then once again Prussian Minister of the Interior until removed by Papen.

Seyss-Inquart, Arthur, 1892-1946. Lawyer. Seyss-Inquart was appointed to the Council of State by Schuschnigg in 1937 as representative of the "national opposition" in Austria. As Federal Chancellor following Schuschnigg's fall from power, Seyss-Inquart engineered Austria's *Anschluss* with the German *Reich* in 1938. *Reich* Commissioner for the Occupied Netherlands, 1940-45. Sentenced to death by the International Military Tribunal at Nuremberg.

Speer, Albert, 1905-   . Architect. Inspector General for Construction, 1937. Speer succeeded Todt as Minister for Armaments and Munitions and Inspector General of Highways. He opposed Hitler's senseless "scorched earth" orders of 1944. Sentenced to 20 years' imprisonment at the Nuremberg Trials.

Strasser, Gregor, 1892-1934. Apothecary. Strasser took part in the Hitler *Putsch* of 1923 and was chairman of the party during Hitler's prison term. Hitler opposed Strasser's anti-capitalistic "national Bolshevist" ideas. Strasser left the NSDAP in 1932 and was murdered during the Röhm Revolt of 1934.

Streicher, Julius, 1885-1946. Teacher. Founded the antisemitic hate sheet "Der Stürmer," 1923. *Gauleiter* of Franconia, 1924-40. Sentenced to death and executed in Nuremberg for crimes against humanity, 1946.

Stresemann, Gustav, 1878-1929. Managing director of the Association of Saxon Industrialists. Member of the *Reichstag* (National Liberal Party), 1914. Stresemann was identified with the Pan-German program during World War I. Founder of German People's Party (DVP), December 1918. Stresemann led his party from opposition to constructive co-operation with the Republic. He received the Nobel Peace Prize (together with Briand) for his policy of Franco-German rapprochement and European co-operation.

Thälmann, Ernst, 1886-1944. Transport worker, member of Social Democratic Party, 1903. Member of the Communist Party, 1919. Member, Hamburg city council, 1919, *Reichstag* Deputy, 1924; chairman of Communist Party of Germany, 1925. Thälmann was responsible for bringing the party into line with Moscow's directives.

Arrested in 1933, he remained in concentration camps until he was shot without trial in Buchenwald in 1944.

Todt, Fritz, 1901-42. Todt was appointed Inspector General of German Highways by Hitler in 1933 and directed the construction of the *Reichsautobahn* and the fortifications on the western frontier (*Westwall*, 1938). Minister for Armaments and Munitions, 1940. Todt was killed in a plane accident, 1942.

Trott zu Solz, Adam von, 1909-44. After studying law, Trott zu Solz became *Legationsrat* in the Foreign Office, 1939. He aided the resistance movement through his wide personal contacts in Great Britain and the USA but failed to change the Allied policy of unconditional surrender in spite of strong efforts. He was sentenced to death in 1944 and executed in Plötzensee prison.

Weber, Max, 1864-1920. One of the outstanding German sociologists, and professor in Berlin, 1893, then Freiburg, Heidelberg, Munich. Famous for works on sociology of economic and religious institutions. In politics Weber fought passionately for a democratization of the German constitution.

Weizsäcker, Ernst Freiherr von, 1882-1951. After serving as a naval officer, Weizsäcker entered the diplomatic service in 1920. As Secretary of State in the Foreign Office, 1938-42, he worked for the preservation of peace under difficult circumstances. Ambassador at the Holy See, 1943-45. Sentenced to 7 years' imprisonment in the so-called Wilhelmstrasse Trial in Nuremberg. After his term was reduced, he received amnesty in 1950.

Wels, Otto, 1873-1939. Upholsterer, member of the executive of the Social Democratic Party, 1913, *Reichstag* Deputy, 1920-33. Wels was the only German party chief to address the *Reichstag* on March 23, 1933, with an extensive explanation of his party's rejection of the Enabling Act. He emigrated soon afterwards and died in Paris in 1939.

Wessel, Horst, 1907-30. Student. Member of the NSDAP, 1926. Wessel wrote the so-called Horst Wessel Song ("Hold high the flag, and close ranks firmly") which was adopted as the national anthem besides the *Deutschlandlied*. Wessel was killed in a street brawl and played up as a martyr in Nazi propaganda.

Acknowledgments

We are most grateful to the following for giving us permission to reprint their photographs:

Archiv für Kunst und Geschichte, Berlin
Associated Press G.m.b.H.
Leo Baeck Institute, Inc.
The Bettmann Archive
Brown Brothers
Central Press Photos, Ltd.
Copress, Munich
European Picture Service
Giangiacomo Feltrinelli Editore, Milan
Historia-Photo, Bad Sachsa
Historisches Bildarchiv Handke, Bad Berneck
Historisches Museum, Frankfurt am Main
The Imperial War Museum, London
Keystone, Munich
Verlag Annedore Leber, Berlin
Pictorial Parade, Inc.
Paul Popper, Ltd.
Radio Times Hulton Picture Library
Gerhard Schoenberner, Berlin
Statni Zidovske Museum, Prague
Süddeutscher Verlag, Munich
Public Information Division, U.S. Coast Guard
Ullstein Verlag, Berlin
United Press International, Inc.
Vallentine, Mitchell & Co., Ltd., London

The maps have been redrawn for this edition by Frank Romano.

Index

Latvia, 28, 196, 203, 233

Lausanne Conference of 1932, 105n.

Law. *See* Nazi Party, Weimar Republic.

League of German Maidens (*Bund Deutscher Mädel*), 163-6

League of Nations, 40, 43, 47, 86, 87, 105, 178, 181, 183

Leber, Julius, 243, 244, 255, 260, 297

Lenard, Philipp, 161

Lend-Lease Act, 268

Lenin, Vladimir Ilich, 26, 27, 163

Lessing, Gotthold Ephraim, 214

Leuschner, Wilhelm, 244, 297

Ley, Robert, 140, 297

Lichtenberg, Bernhard, 238

Liebknecht, Karl, 34n., 38, 54, 298

Lithuania, 28, 42, 190, 192, 203, 233

Lloyd George, David, 3, 23, 40-41, 298

Locarno Pact, 84, 85-6, 179

London *Daily Mail,* 178

London *Daily Telegraph,* 5

Lubbe, Marinus van der, 120, 122

"Lübecker Volksbote," 243

Ludendorff, Erich, 18, 20, 21, 22, 23, 26, 28, 29, 33, 34, 72, 77, 78, 83, 84, 298
   see also German General Staff

Luxemburg, Rosa, 34n., 38, 54, 298

M

Madagascar, 229

Maginot Line, 200, 202

Mann, Heinrich, 79

Mann, Thomas, 79, 162, 298

Manstein, Erich von, 201, 299

Marx, Karl, 158

Marx, Wilhelm, 83, 84

Mein Kampf, 47-8, 57-8, 110, 135, 163, 180, 184, 249

Meissner, Otto, 106, 299

Memel, 42, 190, 192

Michaelis, Georg, 23, 26

Mierendorff, Carlo, 244, 299

Mit brennender Sorge (Papal Encyclical), 168-9

Mohl, Robert von, 60n.

Moltke, Helmut James Count von, 244-5

Moltke, Helmut Johannes Ludwig von, 13

Morocco, 10

Munich Pact (1938), 188-90

Munich *Putsch* (1924), 77-8, 141

Mussolini, Benito, 117, 180, 181, 182, 185, 189, 193, 196, 203, 267, 272, 299

Myth of the Twentieth Century, 143

N

Nathan the Wise, 214

National Socialist Factory Cell Organization, 153

National Socialist People's Welfare, 156

National Socialist Teachers' League, 162

Nationalism. *See* German nationalism.

Naujocks, Alfred Helmut, 196-7

Naumann, Friedrich, 64, 299

Nazi Party (National Socialist German Workers' Party; NSDAP)
   Accession to power, 98-110, 118
   Antisemitic programs, 115, 137, 139, 158-60, 161-2, 220, 222-8, 238, 239, 244
   Brutal methods, 114, 122-3, 126, 129, 171, 172-5, 228-34, 238, 239, 240, 243, 250, 258-9, 263-4, 268, 269

Russo-Finnish War, 203

Y

Z